European Union and its Neighbours in a Globalized World

Volume 5

The series "The European Union and its Neighbours in a Globalized World" will publish monographs and edited volumes in the field of European and International Law and Policy. A special focus will be put on the European Neighbourhood Policy, current problems in European and International Law and Policy as well as the role of the European Union as a global actor. The series will support the cross-border publishing and distribution of research results of cross-border research consortia. Besides renowned scientists the series will also be open for publication projects of young academics. The series will emphasize the interplay of the European Union and its neighbouring countries as well as the important role of the European Union as a key player in the international context of law, economics and politics.

Unique Selling Points:

• Deals with a wide range of topics in regard of European and International Law but is also open to topics which are connected to economic or political science

• Brings together authors from the European Union as well as from accession candidate or neighbouring countries who examine current problems from different perspectives

• Draws on a broad network of excellent scholars in Europe promoted by the SEE | EU Cluster of Excellence, the Europa-Institut of Saarland University as well as in the South East European Law School Network

More information about this series at https://link.springer.com/bookseries/16257

Neven Andjelic

Covid-19, State-Power and Society in Europe

Focus on Western Balkans

Springer

Neven Andjelic
London, UK

ISSN 2524-8928 ISSN 2524-8936 (electronic)
European Union and its Neighbours in a Globalized World
ISBN 978-3-030-91072-3 ISBN 978-3-030-91073-0 (eBook)
https://doi.org/10.1007/978-3-030-91073-0

This Springer imprint is published by the registered company Springer Nature Switzerland AG.
The registered company address is: Gewerbestrasse 11, 6330 Cham, Switzerland

In loving memory of my father, Milenko Anđelić, who taught me that it was possible to be dedicated and loyal to the idea but critical and aware of its shortcomings at the same time, to be honest above all. To my mother, Milica.
To the most supportive son and wife, Oskar and Davorka.

Preface

I have been conducting and broadening my research in the field of comparative political regimes with particular attention to the failings of liberal democracies. When I started developing the idea of a possible manuscript, the publications were few, but numerous authors have offered their excellent contributions since. At the time when I was thinking of abandoning the idea, the COVID-19 pandemic changed our lives. A busy, lively and generally free working life was transformed to the existence of restricted movement, social distancing, fake news and suppressed rights. Corrupt performances by some politicians that saw the pandemic as a business opportunity were not restricted to illiberal, hybrid or authoritarian regimes. Technological developments enabled governments to trace our movements, contacts and communications. The "Big Brother" society was genuinely possible and developed in some forms in some countries. Governments sought to increase their power while civic space came under immense pressure. Society was resisting rising state powers, but the new era had undoubtedly begun. Life, as we knew it, was interrupted. Stopped.

This gave me the idea that it might allow me to try and find out the state of play across 45 European states at the same time—on the eve of the pandemic, at the end of an era or at the interruption of the era. Instead of providing opinionated views based on lengthy and thorough research, I decided to focus on indices that many organisations are periodically publishing in fields of political regimes, personal, economic and media freedoms, corruption, the rule of law and human rights. The idea was that empirical findings of others would enable me to study society and state-power objectively. The 20 indices consulted invite for interpretation of their findings. They use different methodologies and are conducted at different periods. Academic vigorousness would probably say, perhaps, they should not be combined. However, I found that I am personally very interested in measuring the performances of the state. A look at the media confirms many people share this interest. This made me more determined to the idea of compiling the indices. After all, the lockdown restricted our possible activities to books and television. The project offered an alternative that might have helped me keep my sanity. It is not certain that it was successfully preserved, but, more importantly, the result of this attempt is before you to inform yourself, think of it critically and make your judgement.

Therefore, I decided to do the "unthinkable" and create an index based on 20 indices. The state-power and society index represents 20 specific measurements looking into the elements of this relationship that came under specific scrutiny during the pandemic. The issue has been around before. This is an experimental attempt to discover the specifics of relations between the state and the society and offer further empirical support to arguments about specific countries. The resulting categories have been developed by me and are based on different categories in the consulted indices. They range from the "open society" to the "closed society". The three categories between the extremes are "fairly open", "opening" and "suppressed" society. I hesitated from arguing that one type of society is better than the other. However, the general question is whether you would prefer to live in Ireland or Switzerland, the two most open societies, or in Azerbaijan or Belarus, the two most closed societies.

I have been testing my students at Regent's University London for generations by asking them to choose a leader they would like to live in the imaginary state. They were offered a choice between Donald Trump, Vladimir Putin, Angela Merkel, Xi Jinping and Prince Mohammed bin Salman. Angela Merkel was always the most popular choice by far. Vladimir Putin usually came a distant second while the other leaders would receive a vote only incidentally.

Restricted movements and social interaction indeed increased our email correspondence with friends and colleagues. The intellectual exchange with Mareike Fröhlich proved crucial in sticking to the original idea of producing the index. Together with Anja Trautman and Manuela Schwietzer at Springer, her opinion and advice provided me with the agility and determination to continue with the project and, eventually, finish it. I am immensely grateful to Mareike, Anja and Manuela. Abdus Salam Mazumder helped me with a technically complex process of submitting the manuscript. Shikha Chopra edited the text. I am grateful to Shikha and a colleague of mine, Kenneth Morrison, who put me in touch with her and with whom I had many lengthy conversations.

James Gow was one of the examiners of my doctoral thesis over 20 years ago. I am lucky that we have stayed in touch, and his ideas, intellectual challenges and advice always helped me to further develop some of the arguments, ideas and thoughts. Friends of mine, Mladen Sančanin and Zoran Stevanović offered not only a friendship but were tortured by drafts of some chapters when I needed critical responses and was afraid to show it to anyone but confidentially to a few friends. Many conversations with Cornelia Sorabji inspired my further thoughts on state and society. Tihomir Loza's expertise in media was often an excellent direction on where to look for further knowledge and information.

My research in the recent past resulted in academic articles published by the *Journal of Regional Security* in Belgrade, Forum za sigurnosne studije (Forum for Security Studies) in Zagreb, and Friedrich Ebert Stiftung in Sarajevo. Initially, I planned to use large sections of these articles in this book. However, I ended up with a few ideas and sentences, a paragraph on occasion already published there. My colleagues and editors of these publications provided me with a critical overview and editing that indirectly helped sharpen my arguments here. Hence my gratitude to Filip Ejdus, Ružica Jakešević, Nermin Kujović and Alfredo Sasso. Marko Kmezić helped me access some works published by him and his colleagues that mainly gravitate towards the University of Graz and the Balkans in Europe Policy Advisory Group. Duško Zavišić and Dunja Latinović helped access some documents and articles.

My regular correspondence with Vildana Selimbegović, editor of the Sarajevo daily Oslobođenje, provided me with additional insight into the societies of Western Balkans. At the beginning of the lockdown, I published one article in this newspaper that was received well and helped me to develop my thoughts presented in the introductory chapter of this book.

The book is based on 20 indices. Permissions to use them were sought and provided by those authors and organisations who required them. Otherwise, they are referenced throughout this work. Of course, I am grateful to all the authors and contributors to those twenty indices:

- Article 19 (2020) The Global Expression Report
- Cato Institute (2019) Human Freedom Index
- Center for Systemic Peace (2017) Global Report 2017
- Civicus Monitor (2020) National Civic Space Ratings
- Economist Intelligence Unit (2019) Democracy Index 2019
- Fraser Institute (2017) Economic Freedom Index
- Freedom House (2019) Freedom and the Media 2019
- Freedom House (2020) Freedom in the World 2020
- Friedrich Neumann Stiftung (2019) Freedom Barometer Index
- Friedrich Neumann Stiftung (2020) Human Rights Index
- Foundation for the Advancement of Liberty (2019) World Electoral Freedom Index
- The Heritage Foundation (2020) Index of Economic Freedom
- Reporters Without Borders (2020) World Press Freedom Index 2020
- Transparency International (2019) Corruption Perceptions Index
- V-Dem Institute (2020) University of Gothenburg. Annual Democracy Report 2020
- V-Dem Institute (2019) University of Gothenburg. Freedom of Expression Index 2019
- V-Dem Institute. (2019) University of Gothenburg. Political Corruption 2019
- The World Bank. (2018) Index of Economic Freedom Score
- World Economic Forum (2020) Social Mobility Index 2020
- World Justice Project. (2020) Rule of Law Index

Some of these organisations continued to observe developments during the pandemic and offer new findings. Many independent researchers, international organisations, governmental and non-governmental and think tanks produced valuable documents resulting from their research. Many works have been consulted. It is worth noting the project by the Oxford University's Blavatnik School of Government that follows stringency measures by governments of the world.

It all comes back to the idea of an open society. Are we happier in the society developed within a state where we do not necessarily know the name of its president and are left to individual existence, or are we more inclined towards the society that glorifies the president of the state, sing songs to honour the leader and enjoys in the imaginary collective mission? The alienation might be unpleasant, even unhealthy, in the open society. However, the dictatorship of the majority in the closed society might be even less pleasant and ultimately dangerous for free minds.

London, UK
October 2021

Neven Andjelic

Contents

1 Instead of the Introduction 1
- 1.1 The Shift Away from Liberal Democracy 1
- 1.2 The Rise of Inequality 3
- 1.3 Challenges to the International System 10
- References 13

2 Diversity of European Societies: Regimes, Freedoms, Rights, and the Rule of Law 15
- 2.1 Method of Analysis 15
- 2.2 State of Play on the Eve of the Pandemic 20
- 2.3 Democracy Under Threat 22
- References 33

3 Western Balkans Regimes Between European Democracy and Autocracy 37
- 3.1 Findings on European Democracy 37
- 3.2 Failings of Democratic Development in the Western Balkans 43
- References 55

4 Personal Freedoms 59
- 4.1 Consideration of the Category and the Term 59
- 4.2 The Findings 61
- 4.3 The Western Balkans 67
- 4.4 Struggle for New Liberties and Equality in Western Balkans 70
- References 73

5 Dissonant Findings of Economic Freedoms and Social Mobility 75
- 5.1 Diversity of Economic Freedoms in European Countries 75
- 5.2 Economic Freedoms in the Western Balkans 80
- 5.3 Western Balkans and "Malign Influences" 87
- References 91

6 Insufficient Human Rights, the Rule of Law, and Superfluity of Corruption . . . 93
6.1 The Complexity of the Category . . . 93
6.2 A Pan-European View . . . 96
6.3 A Surplus of Corruption and Shortages of the Rule of Law and Human Rights in the Western Balkans . . . 100
6.4 The Rule of Law . . . 105
6.5 Human Rights in the Western Balkans . . . 108
References . . . 114

7 Freedom of Expression and Media Freedoms on the Eve of the Pandemic . . . 117
7.1 State of Mind, State of Freedom, and the State of the State . . . 117
7.2 The Democratisation of Media and the State . . . 120
7.3 Media in Public Service or the Service of Government . . . 123
7.4 Findings by the Evaluators . . . 125
7.5 Media Freedoms in the Western Balkans . . . 129
References . . . 134

8 Democracy, Liberties and Rights Under the Threat of State Fighting the Pandemic . . . 137
8.1 Societies Under Pressure from State Measures . . . 137
8.2 Messages from the Indices on Stringency . . . 141
8.3 Western Balkans in the Time of Pandemic . . . 146
8.4 News, Fake News and Anti-Government Propaganda in the Western Balkans . . . 151
8.5 Covid Diplomacy and the State in the Western Balkans . . . 157
References . . . 160

9 Instead of the Conclusion . . . 165
9.1 Divisions in Europe Confirmed . . . 165
9.2 Civic Space Endangered . . . 167
9.3 Callous Cunning Shysters . . . 171
9.4 Democracy, Sovereignty or Globalisation, That Is the Question . . . 174
9.5 Mapping the Division . . . 176
References . . . 179

Index . . . 181

List of Abbreviations

AKEL	*Anorthotiko Komma Ergazomenou Laou* (The Progressive Party of Working People)
BBC	British Broadcasting Corporation
B & H	Bosnia-Herzegovina
BiH	Bosna i Hercegovina (Bosnia-Herzegovina)
BIRN	Balkan Investigative Reporting Network
CEDAW	Committee on the Elimination of Discrimination Against Women
CEE	Central and Eastern Europe
CEO	Chief Executive Officer
CNN	Cable News Network
CPI	Corruption Perceptions Index
DNA	Deoxyribonucleic acid
DPS	Demokratska partija socijalista (Democratic Party of Socialists)
DW	Deutsche Welle
ECNL	European Center for Not-For-Profit Law
EC	European Commission
EIU	Economist Intelligence Unit
EU	European Union
FTSE	Financial Times Stock Exchange
HDZ	Hrvatska demokratska zajednica (Croatian Democratic Community)
HRW	Human Rights Watch
IDEA	Institute for Democracy and Electoral Assistance
ILO	International Labour Organisation
LGBTI	Lesbian, Gay, Bisexual, Transgender, Intersex
LGBTI+	Lesbian, Gay, Bisexual, Transgender, Intersex and other sexual minorities
LGBTQ+	Lesbian, Gay, Bisexual, Transgender, Queer or Questioning, and other sexual minorities
LSE	London School of Economics
M5S	*Movimento 5 Stelle* (Five Star Movement)
NATO	North Atlantic Treaty Organization

NGO	Nongovernmental Organisation
OCCRP	Organised Crime and Corruption Reporting Project
OSCE	Organisation for Security and Cooperation in Europe
OSCEPA	Organisation for Security and Cooperation in Europe Parliamentary Assembly
RAE	Roma, Ashkali and Egyptians
RFE	Radio Free Europe
RT	Formerly stood for Russia Today
SDA	Stranka demokratske akcije (Party of Democratic Action)
SNSD	Savez nezavisnih socijaldemokrata (Alliance of Independent Social Democrats)
SOE	State Owned Enterprise
TRT	Turkish Radio Television
UK	United Kingdom
UN	United Nations
US	United States
U.S.	United States
V-Dem	Varieties of Democracies
V4NA	Visegrád Four News Agency
VOA	Voice of America
WB	Western Balkans
WB6	Western Balkans Six
WWII	World War Two

List of Tables

Table 2.1	State-power and society	18
Table 2.2	Stringency index according to the Oxford University's Blavatnik School of Government	24
Table 2.3	Parallel tables	26
Table 2.4	Pandemic violations of democratic standards index	28
Table 2.5	Pandemic backsliding index	30
Table 2.6	Democracy during the pandemic: parallel tables	32
Table 3.1	Regime type	38
Table 3.2	Regime type index	40
Table 3.3	The EIU Democracy Index 2006–2019: Western Balkans Six	45
Table 3.4	Unemployment rates	52
Table 3.5	Average monthly earnings of the employed	53
Table 3.6	Number of legal arrivals from Western Balkans to the EU in 2018	53
Table 4.1	Personal freedom	64
Table 4.2	Personal Freedom Index	65
Table 4.3	Personal Freedoms in the Western Balkans Index	68
Table 5.1	Economic freedoms and social mobility indexing	79
Table 5.2	Economic freedoms and Social Mobility Index	81
Table 5.3	Western Balkans only: Economic Freedoms and Social Mobility Index	84
Table 6.1	The Rule of Law, Human Rights and Corruption Indexing	97
Table 6.2	The Rule of Law, Human Rights and Corruption Index	98
Table 6.3	Western Balkans: The Rule of Law, Human Rights, Corruption Index	101
Table 6.4	The Rule of Law Index in the Western Balkans	106
Table 6.5	Personal Safety Sub Index	110
Table 6.6	Access to Education Sub Index	110
Table 6.7	Tolerance & Inclusion Sub Index	111
Table 6.8	Personal Rights Sub Index	112
Table 6.9	Human Rights Index	112

Table 7.1 Expression and Media Freedoms Index 127
Table 7.2 Media Sustainability Index 131
Table 7.3 Expression & Media Freedoms in the Western Balkans 132
Table 8.1 Stringency Index According to the Oxford University's Blavatnik School of Government 142
Table 8.2 Countries that violated Human Rights according to HRW report 143
Table 8.3 Stringency on 31 December 2020 145

List of Maps

Map 9.1 EU member states: cultural-political division on LGBTQ+ discrimination 167
Map 9.2 State-power and society in Europe 177

Chapter 1
Instead of the Introduction

1.1 The Shift Away from Liberal Democracy

"COVID-19 has been likened to an x-ray, revealing fractures in the fragile skeleton of the societies we have built,"[1] the UN Secretary-General, António Guterres, described the global situation in 2020. When the EU's Brexit negotiator, Michel Barnier, conferred to a group of ambassadors in Brussels that "a British government effort to distract from domestic criticism over the handling of the coronavirus crisis may have contributed to London's decision to backtrack on the Brexit deal,"[2] it was yet another example of how the pandemic has shifted politics. When the government in a long-established liberal democracy contemplates breaking international law and its own commitments they have agreed to, it is a clear sign that a crisis of this political model has been accelerated by the spread of COVID-19 or has been used by the political elite to justify their abandoning of some of the essential values of liberal democratic regimes.

The pandemic did not change politics and society. It rather accelerated and strengthened tendencies and trends that were already present and developing before the virus spread. Like in the past, major incidents initiated significant changes that would happen regardless, albeit at a slower speed. In 1666, the Great Fire of London forced construction changes and relying on fireproof material like bricks. Cholera in the nineteenth century and a plague, several times in history, changed characters of European cities by shifting values of professions. With fewer surviving city dwellers, works of skilled manufacturers came in greater demand and became more valued. Major rivers running through the cities were not used as sewage canals any more. At the turn of the nineteenth to twentieth centuries, the invention of cars cleaned streets of horse dung and dirt. Another illness, tuberculosis, urged city planners to plan more open spaces and parks. Pollution and smog forced the shift

---

[1]Guterres (18 July 2020).

[2]Politico (15 September 2020b).

N. Andjelic, *Covid-19, State-Power and Society in Europe*, European Union and its Neighbours in a Globalized World 5, https://doi.org/10.1007/978-3-030-91073-0_1

from coal to gas in the mid-twentieth century. COVID-19 is following the suit. It is revolutionising the way people work, communicate and commute.

Politics and society have already been changed by 2020, or, at least, vital signs were there that significant changes might occur. COVID-19 might be seen as a catalyst for a change that might have been wished for by many in society, but in effect, it is merely an accelerator of the inevitable changes. After all, Trump, Brexiters, Xi, Putin, Bolsonaro, Obrador, Duterte, Modi, Orbán, Erdoğan, Borisov, Rama, Vučić, Đukanović, Izetbegović, Dodik, and Čović have already been in power and doing their best to change societies. Le Pen, Salvini, and Wilders were pushing for changes from the opposition benches. COVID-19 might be their ally in attempts to change politics in Europe.

The state of liberal democracy had been endangered before the pandemic by the growing influence of populist political parties across Europe and the increasing number of regimes that could not be described as liberal. Jan Zielonka even named it a "Counter-Revolution."[3] Political forces on the rise are often described as nationalists. However, they prefer different terms when describing their policies like "patriots,' "sovereigntists," "statists," or, by those willing to show off their education, "*étatists*." The diversity of populist political forces is not reflected only in how they describe themselves. It is primarily a politics' tool that galvanises popular support in reaction to the established elites' policies. Some authors noted that "liberal democracies are increasingly dominated by highly educated and liberal elites whose backgrounds and outlook differ fundamentally from those of the average citizen."[4] The global financial crisis negatively affected the masses and significantly increased support for what is often perceived as anti-elitist forces. They have already existed in society, but the political margins were their supposed destination under the usual circumstances.

Mudde and Kaltwasser remind "that the ultimate source of political power in a democracy derives from a collective body, which, if not taken into account, may lead to mobilisation and revolt."[5] Mounk argues about the nature of populism that "we must recognise that it is both democratic and illiberal – that it both seeks to express the frustrations of the people and to undermine liberal institutions."[6] The change in voting habits of working-class citizens in European democracies "allowed those parties, which have been tainted by their links to European authoritarianism, to claim the mantle of democracy."[7] "Since the start of the century," Edward Luce writes, "the West has forfeited much of its prestige.... As Western democracy has come into question, so too has its global power."[8]

[3]Zielonka (2018), p. 2.

[4]Eatwell and Goodwin (2018), p. 85.

[5]Mudde and Kaltwasser (2017), p. 10.

[6]Mounk (2018), p. 35.

[7]Judis (2016), p. 108.

[8]Luce (2017), p. 104.

To understand the Western Balkans, one needs, in addition to the knowledge of the local politics and society, to accept the global changes and put them into the context of the rule in the Western Balkans. Lack of developed liberal democracy in this region has produced charismatic populist leaders who tend to exercise an authoritarian form of governance. Some European democracies seem to have moved in this direction. This was the context just before the COVID-19 pandemic.

States have reacted to the virus's spread by taking the increased powers and concentrating them internally while initially applying isolationist policies externally. Although these actions have been caused by emergency measures and have generally attracted popular support, there is a question of whether all the states will return to the "status quo *ante bellum*."

1.2 The Rise of Inequality

The support for the concentrated powers might have come out of necessity. However, pre-COVID electoral results in several countries usually associated with a highly developed liberal form of democracy, like Germany, France, Spain, Italy, have been showing a rise of populist parties, many of whom have an authoritarian agenda. A form of neoliberal capitalism, supported by the deregulation at a national level and the unprecedented strength of globalisation processes, has created an economic model that, when powered with the developed liberal-democratic political model and economic forms of neoliberal capitalism, increased profits exponentially. During the pandemic, the state's behaviour seems to have been contrary to its role in the pre-COVID times. Strong powers and isolationist policies have succeeded policies of deregulation and globalisation. The change was potentially welcome by parts of the society who felt left aside by the global liberal order processes.

The economic model of neoliberal capitalism has been accepted in its various forms almost universally. One of the significant results is increasing economic inequality. It is reflected in the increased economic inequality between states. Besides, the inequalities within states have risen. The population is becoming polarised as a consequence. The created inequality has developed the potential for a political power to be gained by a yet to be created new illiberal elite. Another significance to the process has been manifested in the spread of populist movements during the early twenty-first century. Realising that the polarisation further increases inequality and discrimination, regardless of whether it is imaginary or real, the masses turned away from traditional political parties and leaders. They were attracted towards the alternative, most notably presented in the form of the rising populist leaders. However, the privileged elites have managed to establish global domination but are being challenged at a national level. The populist movements are not global but national, which is where the major challenge to the status quo arises.

Eatwell and Goodwin name it "national populism".[9] "Capitalism," says Branko Milanović, "has thus become too powerful, and in regions such as Europe, it is in collision with strongly held beliefs."[10]

On another occasion, Milanović said that "in every political system, even a democracy, the rich tend to hold more political power. The danger is that this political power will be used to promote policies that further cement the economic power of the rich."[11] In the case of the extension of the COVID-inspired current state of affairs, a new economic order is possible. This will inevitably be reflected in political changes, or if political changes occur first, then economic change might be forced in the longer run. Historical precedents have usually been marked by upheavals like the black death in the fourteenth century that decimated the population in Europe and created demand for certain professions. Prolonged undisturbed periods without interruptions like wars, pandemics or economic upheavals had a stabilising factor for societies and provided opportunities for increasing inequality in society. It was only following the upheavals that more equalising economies have emerged for shorter periods. Since the end of the Second World War, this period has been the longest in European history without major conflicts and has eventually produced a rise in inequality in society.

One should bear in mind that current inequality levels are lesser compared to the periods before the First World War but are on the rise compared to the 1980s or 1990s. The major shock for economies came with the global financial crisis in 2007 and 2008. The bailouts by national governments or international organisations saved over 30 European banks, as they have been named in Reuters' investigative report.[12] Ordinary people have not been saved from redundancies, while national and European budgets, filled in by taxpayers' money, have saved banks that have created the crisis in the first place. Political elites can be checked in democracies at the elections, but economic elites are out of reach of voters, i.e., ordinary people. Of course, there were exceptions, like in Iceland where "the currency crashed, unemployment soared and the stock market was more or less wiped out," but the government "let its three major banks – Kaupthing, Glitnir and Landsbankinn – fail and went after reckless bankers. Many senior executives have been jailed."[13] It would be difficult to draw from this a general conclusion, but Iceland was ranked in the World Happiness Index in the fourth place in 2019, and it was second in 2015.[14] It is impossible to establish a direct correlation between the government policy towards bankers in Iceland and the nation's happiness, but it is worth considering.

In the system of checks and balances, something is wrong because it is economic elites, as it has been shown, that have accumulated unprecedented powers during the

[9]Eatwell and Goodwin (2018), pp. 67–80.

[10]Milanović (27 November 2019).

[11]Milanović (2 May 2017).

[12]Reuters (21 August 2015).

[13]BBC (10 February 2016).

[14]World Happiness Index (2019).

rise of the neoliberal form of capitalism. Another element of the state elite is being made up of professionals employed by the state, civil servants who are professional executioners of the political will of the elected political elites. This group of professionals incorporates cultural elites running major institutions, and media elites that dominate information platforms whose appointments rely on political decisions but are responsible only to a political elite or shareholders. Thus, those in power, whether as part of the political or economic elite, dominate yet another sector that voters cannot directly influence. Like bankers and generally economic elite, this professional elite of civil servants and leading professionals in public service are safe in their position and out of reach of voters and the system of checks and balances as one of the essential values of liberal democratic regimes.

Thus, two out of three layers of the elites, perceived or actual, are out of popular reach and with restricted instruments of accountability in voters' hands. Furthermore, the global financial crisis has shown that they altogether sometimes behave irresponsibly. The economic elite caused the crisis, and the political elite chose to save the economic elite by sacrificing ordinary workers while the state bureaucratic elite has put the processes in place and executed political will. The resulting loss of jobs, homes and general hardship for the public had to be blamed on someone. The only ones within the potential reach of voters are the political elite. Therefore, the rise of populist politicians critical of some liberal democratic values has been stepped up following the crisis. Beppe Grillo led his Five Star Movement to a dominant position in Italian politics by naming the "'three destroyers' – journalists, industrialists and politicians."[15]

This is where the talk of the crisis of liberal democracy comes in place. However, the potential for considering the crisis of capitalism, as it is established at present, has also been developed. Some of those affected by policies dictated by elites want a change, both economic and political. The support for traditional parties in many European countries has shifted towards newly developed movements or opportunist politicians who argue against the status quo and attract the masses' increasing attention if not the voters' overwhelming support.

The state is controlled by an elite which is perceived by some of its citizens as corrupt. According to the same understanding, the people are good but misled by the elite, bringing in the core of the definition of populism as antagonistic positioning of bad elites and good people. The dominating elites are or have been largely liberal and global. Therefore, the opposition to them logically comes from nationalist, often illiberal, forces usually led by a charismatic leader. Who can resist globalisation and liberal order that benefits most international elites but the national and strong state? While liberal world order did not provide for a strong state and undermined many of the state's mechanisms to provide for free movement of goods, labour, services and capital, the challenge comes from the opposition to such an order and attempts to control movement across national borders. The Brexit motto of "take back control" or a "trumpist" slogan "make America great again" reflect the desire and apparent

---

[15] Judis (2016), p. 88.

popular support for the return of the sovereign state of the past. Replacing America with any other state in Trump's slogan, it is possible to see universality of the rise of nationalism and its popular potential.

Thus, the spread of populist methods has brought to power authoritarian leaders in some states, providing them with a possibility of strengthening the state-mechanisms, which helps create an image, and often a reality, of the charismatic and strong national leader. The very same state has not been stronger since the end of the Cold War. Whether populist leaders and parties are in power or not, the fact is that popular support for a stronger nation-state has risen and that integrative processes are endangered. A less controlling state is synonymous with internationalism, integration, and ultimately liberal order. The examples of rising powers of the state, like in Hungary, Turkey, Russia, Poland, Serbia, and Montenegro, show an alternative that attracts significant, even if orchestrated, popular support. The real problem is that all these examples are characterised by strong individual leadership and authoritarian rule. While democratic choice, albeit heavily controlled, is present and allowed, dissent in these kinds of regimes is often suppressed and dealt with. The next stage, if it comes to it, can only be tyranny.

Haaretz reported that "Turkey has arrested 410 people for making 'provocative' posts on social media about the coronavirus outbreak."[16] Financial Times reported more conservative figures "for investigating more than 300 people for 'provocative' social media posts about the illness, with at least 64 arrests."[17] Turkey is just one of many states where illiberal regimes have used alleged fake news to silence their liberal critics. A journalist in Serbia spent a night under arrest in Serbia because of her post on social media.

Regimes created by increased state-power, intolerance towards criticism and rising control over society could, at best, be called hybrid. Democracy seems to have been suspended. The Croatian parliament restricted its sessions to two deputies per political party during the COVID-caused lockdown. French President Emmanuel Macron announced that "we are at war,"[18] while British Prime Minister Boris Johnson was not to be outdone, claiming a day later, "we are engaged in a war against the virus."[19] Numerous politicians have introduced "frontline" into the rhetoric about the virus. German Chancellor, however, Angela Merkel avoided such metaphors.[20] She spoke of "this situation," "a historical task," a "real test" in "serious times." A "great challenge" in her speeches evolved into a "gigantic challenge" as the "dramatic crisis" progressed.[21] Merkel spoke to the nation for the first time "other than in her annual New Year's address" when she stressed the time frame saying, "since German reunification, actually, since World War Two,

[16] Haaretz (25 March 2020).

[17] Financial Times (31 March 2020b).

[18] Politico (16 March 2020a).

[19] The Guardian (17 March 2020).

[20] The Conversation (22 May 2020).

[21] The Conversation (22 May 2020).

there has never been a challenge for our country in which acting in solidarity was so very crucial."[22]

Like in Hungary or the United Kingdom, legislative branches of power have surrendered their authority to the executives during the first wave of the pandemic. In other countries parliaments, authorities were largely restricted and transferred to the executive branch. The imaginary life of parliament was preserved in some form of online sessions or limited numbers of parliamentarians allowed to attend sessions that were often meaningless. Judiciary was widely suspended across the continent.

"Across Europe," it was reported in March 2020, "governments have shut down their court systems altogether."[23] Bloomberg reported that "the legal systems in much of western Europe are shutting down," specifying "National French courts all but shut down" and "the Italian court system was shut."[24] Courts in Ireland and Italy "have been closed, under government decrees."[25] "The European Court of Human Rights has cancelled all hearings" except for "those where a suspension would cause "irreparable damage," and "The European Court of Justice is suspended for the next two weeks at least,"[26] it was reported in March 2020.

In France, the courts were closed for all but "essential litigation." When it comes to patent courts, "operation of the courts were not completely stopped, [but] oral hearings were widely suspended" in Germany. "The French civil (patent) courts have been largely put on hold, except for urgent matters." Italian courts have been forced to postpone all hearings between 9 March 2020 and 11 May 2020, and put on hold most proceedings, except for urgent matters."[27]

Serbian executive was under complete control of the president while the legislation was under the control of his party, which is also following his orders. The first parliamentary elections in COVID-19 Europe took place in Serbia and returned total control of the parliament to the president's party. The Hungarian Parliament has approved the decree ruling. The British Parliament provided Prime Minister Boris Johnson with broad powers during the crisis. It became the executive branch's decision whether to keep borders open. Legal restrictions on the length of police detention have also been suspended in many places. State security agencies follow and monitor citizens' behaviour during the crisis and provide the state apparatus with unprecedented powers in democratic societies. The result is the concentration of powers in one person's hands or a very restricted group of people. It raises the question of whether such a regime could be called liberal democracy. What kind of state is being developed?

George Soros warned in 2019 about what could happen when advanced artificial intelligence is put in the service of an authoritarian regime and a single-party state

[22] Reuters (18 March 2020b).

[23] Prospect (18 March 2020).

[24] Bloomberg (16 March 2020).

[25] Prospect (18 March 2020).

[26] Prospect (18 March 2020).

[27] Lexology (18 May 2020).

like China.[28] Citizens come under even greater control while it is algorithms that are in charge of overseeing citizens. Face recognition technology means that every movement is registered. This process is put under normal circumstances in the service or the regime preservation, as Soros warned, but it also determines individual citizens' careers and lives under such a regime. People attending specific events are registered by artificial intelligence. Every movement, every action is potentially monitored, and the information stored by artificial intelligence. This kind of information potentially determines the future. Of course, it is the regime that programmes and determines ideological pattern that decides positive from hostile citizens, but the execution is by artificial intelligence. The new monitoring technology and artificial intelligence have enabled China to put the epidemic, i.e., a pandemic in their own territory, under control in 2020. Some other countries followed suit.

The overall control over society was not established by the Soviet regime and its satellite countries during the Cold War. They lacked technology for this, if not the will. Technologies developed since the end of the Cold War, and the pandemic in 2020 has created conditions for developing this model of control by the state over the society and not exclusively in totalitarian systems.

It has already been shown that some former liberal democracies have stepped back and suspended some of the democratic forms of governance. Thus, a new system might be expected to be tested, but its structure is unknown. However, this means "the end of history" theory is defeated in its normative form. "The higher the inequality," Milanović argues, "the more likely we are to move away from democracy toward plutocracy."[29] Once functioning democracy is abandoned and basic principles of humane society degraded, even plutocrats are at risk. Russian oligarch Mikhail Khodorkovsky ended up in prison despite his personal wealth. "China executed 14 people with assets of at least a 1 billion yuan ($155 million) during the past eight years," Bloomberg reported in 2011, "as the government expanded its fight against corruption."[30]

The economic elite is not under such pressure in liberal democracies. "Bosses of FTSE 100 companies only need to work until 5 pm on Monday 6 January.," Daily Telegraph reported, "to earn as much as the average worker does in a year. . ."[31] The Financial Times reported similarly that "FTSE 100 chief executives were paid 117 times more than the average worker in the UK in 2018."[32] In the United States, this gap is even bigger. The Economic Policy Institute found that "the 2017 CEO-to-worker compensation ratio of 312-to-1 was far greater than the 20-to-1 ratio in 1965 and more than five times greater than the 58-to-1 ratio in 1989."[33] "The ratio between the pay of US CEOs and that of the average production worker increased

[28] Soros (24 January 2019).

[29] Birrell (1 November 2012).

[30] Bloomberg News (23 July 2011).

[31] The Telegraph (6 January 2020).

[32] The Financial Times (6 January 2020a).

[33] Mishel and Schieder (16 August 2018).

from 20 times in 1965 to 231 times in 2011, after peaking at 383.4 times in 2000."[34] Pargendler also draws attention to alternative findings by Paul Krugman, "noting that while the annual compensation of the top 100 CEOs was on average 39 greater than that of the average worker in 1970, the difference had soared to 1,000 times more by 1999."[35] The ratio uncovered by Chrystia Freeland's book on Plutocrats was quoted by Ian Birrell in The Guardian: "Three decades ago the average American chief executive made 42 times as much as the average worker; today this ratio is an obscene 380."[36]"Inequality defines our time,"[37] said António Guterres in his Nelson Mandela Lecture.

Some of the findings might have slightly different numbers depending on the specific year or decade they began their survey, but the pattern is the same in all. The inequality gap between the average paid worker and the top executive has exponentially risen during the 1990s and twenty-first century. The figures quoted here reflect a growing demand for transparency in corporate governance. The results come as a confirmation of suspected trends for a long time. They offer yet another strong argument to those criticising the state of play and demanding changes and action. The dissenting people globally, the UN Secretary-General argues, "saw economic policies channelling resources upwards to the privileged few."[38]

Populist politicians thus have another field to step in with their rhetoric if not their action. Populism is being used by state nationalists urging for stronger powers to central authorities. Similar tools, however, could also be found among political authorities at a sub-national level. Although notionally still unitary like Spain, some complex states have used new opportunities to impose some measures during the pandemic crisis that have previously been devolved to the regional level. Catalan authorities' complaints showed a continuous struggle for power between the two levels of governance by different means under the changed circumstances. The preservation of the nation and its health is used as an excuse for usurping more powers. It only depends on whether the political group using the rhetoric is *etatist,* i.e., the state level nationalists, or separatist, i.e., nationalists or secessionists with authority at a local level only.

The Scottish government, like Northern Irish and Welsh authorities, exercised fully their devolved powers, which enabled them to create sets of different responses to the pandemic from the government in London. The irony is that Boris Johnson's government came in power on the wave of Brexit, and the alleged reinstatement of sovereignty is presiding over the period when regional authorities increasingly set up their own policies. Even usually powerful German leader Angela Merkel had to use all her skills to persuade regional governments to need a lockdown and restrictions of freedoms.

---

[34] Pargendler (2016), p. 390.

[35] Krugman (2002).

[36] Birrell (2012).

[37] Guterres (18 July 2020).

[38] Guterres (18 July 2020).

At the sub-national level, powerholders resisted some of the measures in many states while central authorities acted in the opposite direction of concentrating powers. Externally, several countries looked at ways to reconfirm or establish new alliances, some of which confirmed readiness for change of the international system. Medical workers from Albania came in aid of Italy, replacing the usual migration of less-skilled labour and refugees that traditionally marked the migrations between the two countries. Cuba sent a large contingent of their health workers to Italy, but geopolitically, Russia scored the main point in Italy by producing aid and using it as a soft-power tool in public diplomacy when the EU was not engaged.

1.3 Challenges to the International System

The opportunity for a change in the international system became apparent even more when the US received aid from Russia. President Trump said, "Russia sent us a very, very large planeload of things, medical equipment, which was very nice."[39] While this information made global headlines, the American return of favour 2 months later was less noticed. It is not only the major powers facing challenges, and some of them not reacting fast enough, but international organisations also came under public scrutiny as many of them needed some time to reorganise themselves.

The closure of national borders did not help them. The European Union and the Schengen Agreement were particularly challenged. A closer look uncovers that the four freedoms of movement, which are essential values upon which the integration processes have been based in the EU, have been challenged and, in some cases, suspended. "Germany has banned the export of medical protection gear to avoid supply shortages,"[40] Reuters reported. While other EU member states criticised Germany for the ban, the EU has made a similar policy by limiting medical equipment exports outside the union. Thus, egoistic behaviour at the national and international level has become a norm at the beginning of the pandemic. By moving to online work, both the EU and the Council of Europe were objectively forced to suspend some of their activities.

Nevertheless, reactions among member states and their citizens were not always showing understanding. This all contributed to the crisis of internationalisation policies at the pan-European level, which provided additional strength to nationalist arguments across Europe. The UN Security Council's meeting schedule for March 2020 shows their collective idleness and difficulty to adapt to changed circumstances. They had no meetings between 12th and 24th March.

What citizens felt the most was state-provided aid which was often based on internal and external borrowing. The mass deregulation that provided fundaments for neoliberal capitalism has been partially suspended under the new circumstances.

[39]Foreign Policy (1 April 2020).

[40]Reuters (4 March 2020a).

The closure of national borders also undermined globalisation. Labour force within the state, albeit under an unprecedented challenge and job safety endangered, might have seen the state doing their utmost to protect its position. The issue is whether the measures introduced by governments and other forces otherwise eager to deregulate and open markets and societies to globalisation will be enough to protect labour force at national level. The new situation and circumstances might even force governments to adopt some elements of "humanised" policies that would change the nature of capitalism. After attempts to develop "socialism with a human face" in the twentieth century, perhaps the consequences of the COVID-19 pandemic might bring about "capitalism with a human face" in the new millennium.

State interventionism is changing the character of neoliberal capitalism. The irony is that the pandemic forced libertarian politicians in power in many states to implement interventionist policies. Taxes will inevitably rise to cover state borrowing during the crisis. Questions will be raised as to how impoverished states without powerful patrons will find resources to deal with economic challenges and, in some cases, security challenges in forms of mass migrations, organised crime and secessionism. The reconfiguration of international alliances is increasingly likely as some states will struggle for self-survival.

A modified economic system might be needed to avoid aggressive and confrontational policies at international, national, and sub-national levels. Disturbances at any of these levels inevitably undermine global security. Changes to authorities' jurisdictions and powers at any level, economic redistribution, international alliances, and international organisations' work and their roles will have to be addressed to preserve relative security and peace. Weaker states are more vulnerable in such challenging times.

There are three zones in Europe where power-struggle between Western states and Western-dominated international organisations is challenged by the increasing influences and interests of Russia and some other ambitious powers like China, Turkey, Iran, and Saudi Arabia. None of these powers has developed a liberal democratic regime. Some democratic models have been developed in the contested zones, but the weak presence of international organisations created conditions for developing alternative political models and regimes that authoritarian leaders often lead. Two such regions are in the former Soviet space, the Caucasus and former Soviet republics in eastern Europe that used to form a "common neighbourhood" where both Russia and the EU's interests have been acknowledged.

The three republics in Caucasus, Armenia, Azerbaijan, and Georgia and the three former Soviet states in Eastern Europe, Belarus, Ukraine, and Moldova, have all struggled with democracy and territorial integrity. These states' attempts to increase the integration with the western world were frequently met with internal rebellion and covert or even open Russian intervention. The regimes in Belarus and Azerbaijan are not only authoritarian but autocratic. Georgia and Ukraine lost control over their regions after taking steps towards integrating themselves with the West. Moldova's integrity was challenged with Russian support even without the pro-western steps. After all, Armenia's control over the NagornoKarabakh was supported by Russia until the revolutionary changes in 2018 and the shift from authoritarianism in Yerevan towards the development of democratic institutions. The result is Azerbaijan's successful retake of the province with the support of another autocratic regime of Turkish president Erdoğan.

The one region in Europe outside the former Soviet space experiencing the geopolitical power-struggle of different political models is the Western Balkans. Russia's increasing ambition to establish presence and influence there brings this region into the spotlight. In addition to burgeoning internal authoritarianism, struggling democratic institutions and global geopolitics, the pandemic provided a new tool for cementing the power. While leading established liberal democracies showed apparent struggle for power between different centres and institutions, resulting in the suspension of some levels of freedom, regimes in emerging democracies have shown even more ambition to secure their powers.

The pandemic's spread requires greater state involvement that has been translated into centralising powers in fewer institutions or individual power-holders than it was imagined. States with strong institutions and a long tradition of democracy might struggle with this change but are more likely to return to the system of checks and balances and separation of powers. The states with weak or underdeveloped institutions, short democratic tradition, and history of all-powerful leaders, "fathers of their nations", are seemingly cementing the type of the regime that has already been described as "hybrid".[41] This might be an opportunity to stabilise this kind of regime on a long-term basis. Such regimes and leaders dominate the Western Balkans countries.

The longer the crisis, the greater the risk of moving the hybrid regimes further from liberal democracy. Suspension of instruments of control, weak institutions, and polarised electorates keep these societies within the domains of nationalist politics where challenges to populist leaders are weak. The state-power is increased, as elsewhere, but these regimes' power is personalised and not institutionalised. Some writers describe "the apparent licentiousness of the Balkans"[42] when attempting to analyse local politics and find the origins of the support for a strong-man rule.

Whilst showing a critical analysis of the hybrid type of regimes typically found in Western Balkans, this text, at the same time, acknowledges democratic deficits and some failures of developed liberal democratic systems. "A caustic comment" in a novel written by Serbian writer Borislav Pekić, "that democracy makes stupidity statistically identifiable with reason and, only if there is enough of them, allows idiots to rule the world"[43] might be strengthened by the results of democratic processes in some areas. Authoritarian leaders in the Western Balkans' hybrid regimes seemingly are well informed with this view and are putting in practice tactics of galvanising enough support to rule their fiefdoms.

[41] Bieber (2020), p. 141.

[42] Süddeutsche Zeitung (25 August 2020).

[43] Pekić (1999), p. 174.

References

BBC (10 February 2016) How did Iceland clean up its banks? https://www.bbc.co.uk/news/business-35485876. Accessed 6 Oct 2021

Bieber F, Prelec T, Jović D, Nechev Z (2020) The suspicious virus: conspiracies and COVID19 in the Balkans. Balkans in Europe Policy Advisory Group. https://biepag.eu/wp-content/uploads/2020/12/Conspiracies-and-COVID19-in-the-Balkan-English.pdf?fbclid=IwAR3qLIFRnCATCi2j8aSijDABkxg7gKFDdlCGI5kpyCI8G_fGv3GnG5iVqkE. Accessed 20 May 2021

Birrell I (1 November 2012) Plutocrats: the rise of the new global super rich by Chrystia Freeland – review. The Guardian. https://www.theguardian.com/books/2012/nov/01/plutocrats-super-rich-freeland-review. Accessed 6 Oct 2021

Bloomberg News (2011) China executes 14 billionaires in 8 years, Culture News Reports. (23 July 2011). https://www.bloomberg.com/news/articles/2011-07-23/china-executes-14-billionaires-in-8-years-culture-news-reports. Accessed 18 Feb 2021

Bloomberg News (2020) U.K. Courts Carry on While Virus Halts EU Cases, Lawsuits. (16 March 2020) https://www.bloomberg.com/news/articles/2020-03-16/virus-closes-european-courts-but-can-t-stop-u-k-tradition. Accessed 6 Oct 2021

Eatwell R, Goodwin M (2018) National populism: the revolt against liberal democracy. Pelican Books, London

Foreign Policy (2020) Russia Scores pandemic propaganda triumph with medical delivery to US. (1 April 2020). https://foreignpolicy.com/2020/04/01/russia-scores-pandemic-propaganda-triumph-with-medical-delivery-to-u-s-trump-disinformation-china-moscow-kremlin-coronavirus/. Accessed 6 Oct 2021

Guterres A (2020) Secretary-general's Nelson Mandela Lecture: "Tackling the inequality pandemic: a new social contract for a new era" [as delivered]. Video Message for the International Nelson Mandela Day, 18 July 2020. https://www.un.org/sg/en/content/sg/statement/2020-07-18/secretary-generals-nelson-mandela-lecture-%E2%80%9Ctackling-the-inequality-pandemic-new-social-contract-for-new-era%E2%80%9D-delivered. Accessed 6 Oct 2021

Haaretz (2020) Turkey arrests hundreds for 'Provocative' social media posts about coronavirus. (25 March 2020). https://www.haaretz.com/middle-east-news/turkey/turkey-arrests-hundreds-for-provocative-social-media-posts-about-coronavirus-1.8709336. Accessed 6 Oct 2021

Judis JB (2016) The populist explosion: how the great recession transformed American and European Politics. Columbia global reports, New York

Krugman P (2002, 20 Oct) For Richer. N.Y. TIMES. http://www.nytimes.com/2002/10/20/magazine/for-richer.html?pagewanted=all quoted by Pargendler M (2016) The corporate governance obsession. J Corp Law 42(2):390

Lexology (2020) COVID-19: pressure points: developments at patent courts in Europe in light of the health emergency (UK, Germany, France, Italy & the EPO). (18 May 2020) https://www.lexology.com/library/detail.aspx?g=5f36e085-ecb8-4d71-93f8-94e17baa8c06. Accessed 6 Oct 2021

Luce E (2017) The retreat of Western Liberalism. Abacus, London

Milanović B (2017) The higher the inequality, the more likely we are to move away from democracy. The Guardian (2 May 2017), https://www.theguardian.com/inequality/2017/may/02/higher-inequality-move-away-from-democracy-branko-milanovic-big-data. Accessed 6 Oct 2021

Milanović B (2019) The 'crisis of capitalism' is not the one Europeans think it is.The Guardian (27 November 2019) https://www.theguardian.com/commentisfree/2019/nov/27/crisis-of-capitalism-europeans-gig-economy. Accessed 6 Oct 2021

Mishel L, Schieder J (2018) CEO compensation surged in 2017. Economic Policy Institute, Washington, D.C. https://www.epi.org/publication/ceo-compensation-surged-in-2017/. Accessed 6 Oct 2021

Mounk Y (2018) The people vs. democracy: why our freedom is in danger and how to save it. Harvard University Press, Cambridge

Mudde C, Kaltwasser CR (2017) Populism: a very short introduction. Oxford University Press, Oxford

Pargendler M (2016) The corporate governance obsession. J Corp Law 42(2):359–402

Pekić B (1999) Besnilo. Tir Solaris, Novi Sad, Serbia

Politico (16 March 2020a) Emmanuel Macron on coronavirus: 'We're at war'. https://www.politico.eu/article/emmanuel-macron-on-coronavirus-were-at-war/. Accessed 6 Oct 2021

Politico (15 September 2020b) Michel Barnier: coronavirus failings may have played role in UK Brexit shift. https://www.politico.eu/article/barnier-covid-could-have-played-role-in-uk-brexit-strategy-shift/. Accessed 6 Oct 2021

Prospect (18 March 2020) How will the justice system withstand the coronavirus pandemic? https://www.prospectmagazine.co.uk/politics/how-will-the-justice-system-withstand-the-coronavirus-pandemic-covid-19-outbreak-courts-democracy-law. Accessed 6 Oct 2021

Reuters (2015) FACTBOX-What has happened to more than 30 bailed-out European banks. (21 August 2015), https://www.reuters.com/article/europe-banks-bailouts-idUKL5N10W0XJ20150821. Accessed 6 Oct 2021

Reuters (2020a) Germany bans export of medical protection gear due to coronavirus. (4 March 2020) https://www.reuters.com/article/health-coronavirus-germany-exports-idUSL8N2AX3D9. Accessed 6 Oct 2021

Reuters (2020b) Merkel tells Germans: Fighting virus demands war-time solidarity. (18 March 2020) https://www.reuters.com/article/us-health-coronavirus-germany-idUSKBN2153GX. Accessed 6 Oct 2021

Soros G (2019) Remarks delivered at the World Economic Forum. Davos, Switzerland, 24 February 2019. https://www.georgesoros.com/2019/01/24/remarks-delivered-at-the-world-economic-forum-2/. Accessed 6 Oct 2021

Süddeutsche Zeitung (2020) Balkan: So nah und doch so fern. (25 August 2020) https://www.sueddeutsche.de/kultur/corona-balkan-europa-1.5007391?reduced=true. Accessed 6 Oct 2021

The Conversation (2020) How politicians talk about coronavirus in Germany, where war metaphors are avoided. (22 May 2020) https://theconversation.com/how-politicians-talk-about-coronavirus-in-germany-where-war-metaphors-are-avoided-137427. Accessed 6 Oct 2021

The Financial Times (6 January 2020a) Top UK chiefs paid 117 times more than the average worker in 2018.https://www.ft.com/content/9d971c48-2fa5-11ea-a329-0bcf87a328f2. Accessed 18 Feb 2021

The Financial Times (31 March 2020b) Erdogan under pressure as Turkey's coronavirus toll mounts. https://www.ft.com/content/b0a9de7b-f618-45f4-a352-d658ce554cf3. Accessed 18 Feb 2021

The Guardian (17 March 2020) 'This enemy can be deadly': Boris Johnson invokes wartime language. https://www.theguardian.com/world/2020/mar/17/enemy-deadly-boris-johnson-invokes-wartime-language-coronavirus. Accessed 6 Oct 2021

The Telegraph (2020) Top bosses earn annual wage of average worker by end of today. (6 January 2020). https://www.telegraph.co.uk/news/2020/01/06/top-bosses-earn-annual-wage-average-worker-end-today/. Accessed 6 Oct 2021

World Happiness Index (2019) Countryeconomy.com. https://countryeconomy.com/demography/world-happiness-index/iceland. Accessed 6 Oct 2021

Zielonka J (2018) Counter-revolution in Europe: liberal retreat in Europe. Oxford University Press, Oxford

Chapter 2
Diversity of European Societies: Regimes, Freedoms, Rights, and the Rule of Law

2.1 Method of Analysis

Of the 45 states in Europe with over a 1,00,000 population, 24 went through the transition from the communist system towards some form of democracy. The challenging process has proven to be more complex for some of these countries. The processes of transition, institution and state-building, conflict resolution, post-conflict reconstruction, and reconciliation were almost simultaneous for those societies and states. The conflicts in several post-Soviet and post-Yugoslav countries have delayed many of these processes, particularly the democratisation, and ultimately contributed to the development of the societies that are not open and regimes that are not fully supportive of liberal democratic values. The levels of devastation and destruction of the material, social and political pattern are certainly contributing factor. However, for this study, a methodology has been developed applicable to all 45 countries. The causes of the country specifics had to be disregarded to compile a unique set of figures for the whole of Europe.

The COVID-19 pandemic has forced all European governments to act, suspend some of its policies, and impose restrictions on society to protect the population. Although the measures might have varied in strength and intensity, they provided a common point in time to measure the type of pre-pandemic state-power and society across the continent by using a diverse set of established indices. This point reflects the time after which changes will not revert to the pre-pandemic period, as argued earlier.

Understanding the irreversibility of changes is based on previous European historical experiences following pandemics described in more detail in the previous chapter. All countries are analysed under the same conditions and when normality has been interrupted by the pandemic. There would be no return to the same kind of normality. The resulting index of state-power and society truly reflects the country's comparative status precisely at the moment of interruption. Individual states' reactions differ and prove to be unreliable for predictions with a significant degree of

N. Andjelic, *Covid-19, State-Power and Society in Europe*, European Union and its Neighbours in a Globalized World 5, https://doi.org/10.1007/978-3-030-91073-0_2

certainty. However, the knowledge of the state "*ante bellum*" might enable more informed prediction and the understanding of potential changes in the future.

The methodology is based on the study of twenty global indices of democracy, economic, personal and media freedoms, the rule of law, corruption, and human rights.[1] International nongovernmental organisations, academic research centres, think tanks, newspapers and foundations provide a broad range of indices in this field. However, not all of them are all-inclusive to offer a reliable sample of entries for the comparative analysis across Europe. This was the first restriction that eliminated some of the indices with otherwise telling details and in-depth analysis but restricted to countries in "transformation processes toward democracy and a market economy"[2] or "nations in transit"[3] which covers just over half of the European states. This research, however, considers only indices that have been produced for all or almost all countries in Europe.

The specific data collection methods for each index might differ, but multiple indices considered together provide a solid base for valid conclusions about the relationship between state-power and society. As indices used different methodologies, samples, timeframes and naming of the resulting categories and descriptions, they were given numerical values in this study so they could be compared and corresponded to each other, and so the final results could be measured. Some indices have no descriptive findings and are only numerical. Therefore, they have been ascribed status corresponding to the numerical index to provide the aggregated findings and index. Once all the findings are put in place, it will be clear what kind of state-power has developed and what kind of society is to be found in the country.

---

[1]
- Economist Intelligence Unit. Democracy Index 2019;
- Center for Systemic Peace. Global Report 2017;
- V-Dem Institute. University of Gothenburg. Annual Democracy Report 2020;
- Freedom House. Freedom in the World 2020;
- Friedrich Neumann Stiftung. 2019. Freedom Barometer Index;
- Foundation for the Advancement of Liberty. (2019). World Electoral Freedom Index;
- Cato Institute (2019). Human Freedom Index;
- Civicus Monitor (2020). National Civic Space Ratings;
- The Heritage Foundation. (2020). Index of Economic Freedom;
- Fraser Institute. (2018). Economic Freedom Index;
- The World Bank. (2018). Index of Economic Freedom Score;
- World Economic Forum (2020) Social Mobility Index 2020;
- Transparency International. (2019). Corruption Perceptions Index;
- V-Dem Institute. University of Gothenburg. Political Corruption 2019;
- World Justice Project (2020). Rule of Law Index;
- Friedrich Neumann Stiftung. 2020. Human Rights Index;
- V-Dem Institute. University of Gothenburg. Freedom of Expression Index 2019;
- Reporters Without Borders. World Press Freedom Index 2020;
- Freedom House. Freedom and the Media 2019;
- Article 19. 2020. The Global Expression Report.

[2] Bertelsmann Stiftung (2020).

[3] Freedom House (2020), Nations in Transit.

The twenty different indices are grouped into five categories measuring regime, personal freedoms, economic freedoms, the rule of law with corruption and human rights, and media freedoms. All indices from the particular category are put together. The lower the resulting index, the better the country's score. Once the results within the categories have been established, they are computed together to produce the final result. The lowest possible score is 5, meaning that the country has achieved the best results in each of the five categories giving it the overall index of one, i.e., index of one in each of the five categories. Table 2.1 reflects this method.

Each category is measured separately. The regime index is developed by using three separate studies, and the indices these studies have established. The personal freedom index is based on five separate indices, while economic freedom consists of four aggregated indices. Media freedoms rely on four indices, and the rule of law, corruption perceptions and human rights index is based upon four separate indices within the category. This means that the lowest possible scores in each category might differ. The regime index score could be three because there are only three indices to calculate from. In comparison, the personal freedom category is based on five indices meaning the lowest possible score in this category is five.

However, each of these results means that the country is in the best group within the category. Therefore, it is given only one point in each category bringing the overall score in the study to 5, indexed 1, which is the lowest possible and awarded to only eleven countries where society is described as open. Ireland, Switzerland, Denmark, Finland, The Netherlands, Norway, Sweden, Germany, Luxembourg, Austria, and the United Kingdom are all considered Western Europe, if not geographically but precisely because of the types of state-power and societies developed.

Thirteen countries are in the next best category of a "fairly open society." It includes a mixture of post-communist countries that transitioned well and some traditional bastions of liberal democracy that failed to be indexed in the top group in one or two categories and therefore are considered in the second-best group of countries. The three Baltic republics, Estonia, Latvia and Lithuania, are in this group and four other EU newcomers in 2004, Czechia, Cyprus, Slovenia and Poland. The founding members of the EU, Belgium, France and Italy, share the same category with them and latecomers to the EU from the 1980s, Portugal and Spain. Iceland is the only non-EU member of this group of countries.

This group is followed by 12 countries with the "opening society" that include less successfully transitioned post-communist countries Slovakia, Romania, Croatia, Bulgaria, and Hungary that joined the EU in the twenty-first century together with Malta. Greece is another EU member state in this group. The EU outsiders, Georgia, Kosovo, Armenia, North Macedonia, and Albania make up the rest of the group. Most of these non-EU countries experienced a conflict following their independence, as did Croatia, making their results more remarkable. It is noticeable that the top half of this rather large group of countries is populated by EU member states while the Western Balkans countries dominate the bottom half. The state of a frozen conflict in some countries makes their state policies frequently changing, and the particular

Table 2.1 State-power and society

Position	Country	Ind-ex	Society	Total Points across fields 5–23	Total score across indices 20–96	Regime (3–13)	Personal Freedom (5–25)	Economic Freedom (4-18)	Rule of Law Corruption Human Right (4–20)	Media freedom (4–20)
1	Ireland	1	Open	5	20.00	1 (3 of 13)	1 (5 of 25)	1 (4 of 18)	1 (4 of 20)[a]	1 (4 of 20)
1	Switzerland	1	Open	5	20.00	1 (3 of 13)	1 (5 of 25)	1 (4 of 18)	1 (4 of 20)[a]	1 (4 of 20)
3	Denmark	1	Open	5	21.00	1 (3 of 13)	1 (5 of 25)	1 (5 of 18)	1 (4 of 20)	1 (4 of 20)
3	Finland	1	Open	5	21.00	1 (3 of 13)	1 (5 of 25)	1 (5 of 18)	1 (4 of 20)	1 (4 of 20)
5	Netherlands	1	Open	5	22.00	1 (3 of 13)	1 (6 of 25)	1 (5 of 18)	1 (4 of 20)	1 (4 of 20)
6	Norway	1	Open	5	23.00	1 (3 of 13)	1 (6 of 25)	1 (6 of 18)	1 (4 of 20)	1 (4 of 20)
6	Sweden	1	Open	5	23.00	1 (3 of 13)	1 (6 of 25)	1 (6 of 18)	1 (4 of 20)	1 (4 of 20)[a]
6	Germany	1	Open	5	23.00	1 (3 of 13)	1 (7 of 25)	1 (5 of 18)	1 (4 of 20)	1 (4 of 20)
9	Luxembourg	1	Open	5	24.33	1 (3 of 13)	1 (7 of 25)	1 (5 of 18)	1 (4 of 20)[a]	1 (5.3 of 20)[a]
10	Austria	1	Open	5	25.00	1 (3 of 13)	1 (7 of 25)	1 (5 of 18)	1 (4 of 20)	1 (6 of 20)
11	UK	1	Open	5	26.00	1 (3 of 13)	1 (7 of 25)	1 (6 of 18)	1 (5 of 20)	1 (5 of 20)
12	Estonia	1.2	Fairly open	6	25.00	2 (5 of 13)	1 (6 of 25)	1 (6 of 18)	1 (4 of 20)	1 (4 of 20)
13	Iceland	1.2	Fairly open	6	25.66	1 (4 of 13)[a]	1 (6 of 25)	1 (5 of 18)	1 (4 of 20)[a]	2 (6.7 of 20)[a]
14	Lithuania	1.4	Fairly open	7	28.66	2 (5 of 13)	1 (6 of 25)	1 (6 of 18)	2 (6.7 of 20)[a]	1 (5 of 20)
15	Portugal	1.4	Fairly open	7	30.00	1 (3 of 13)	1 (6 of 25)	3 (10 of 18)	1 (7 of 20)	1 (4 of 20)
16	Czechia	1.4	Fairly open	7	32.00	2 (5 of 13)	1 (7 of 25)	1 (6 of 18)	2 (8 of 20)	1 (6 of 20)
17	Latvia	1.4	Fairly open	7	33.33	2(5 of 13)	1(7 of 25)	1(6 of 18)	29.3 of 20[a]	1(6 of 20)
18	Slovenia	1.4	Fairly open	7	35.00	1 (4 of 13)	2 (8 of 25)	2 (9 of 18)	1 (8 of 20)	1 (6 of 20)
19	Belgium	1.6	Fairly open	8	29.00	2 (5 of 13)	2 (8 of 25)	2 (8 of 18)	1 (4 of 20)	1 (4 of 20)
20	Spain	1.6	Fairly open	8	32.00	1 (3 of 13)	2 (8 of 25)	2 (8 of 18)	2 (7 of 20)	1 (6 of 20)
21	France	1.6	Fairly open	8	33.00	1 (4 of 13)	2 (8 of 25)	2 (9 of 18)	2 (7 of 20)	1 (5 of 20)
22	Cyprus	1.6	Fairly open	8	33.33	1 (4 of 13)	2 (8 of 25)	2 (7 of 18)	2 (9.3 of 20)[a]	1 (5 of 20)

23	Italy	1.8	Fairly open	9	37.00	1 (4 of 13)	2 (8 of 25)	3 (10 of 18)	2 (9 of 20)	1 (6 of 20)
24	Poland	2.0	Fairly open	10	40.00	2 (5 of 13)	2 (9 of 25)	2 (9 of 18)	2 (8 of 20)	2 (9 of 20)
25	Slovakia	2.2	Opening	11	39.66	2 (5 of 13)	2 (9 of 25)	2 (8 of 18)	3 (10.7 of 20)[a]	2 (7 of 20)
26	Malta	2.2	Opening	11	41.33	2 (6 of 13)[a]	2 (9 of 25)	2 (7 of 18)	2 (10 of 20)[a]	3 (9.3 of 20)[a]
27	Romania	2.2	Opening	11	46.00	2 (6 of 13)	2 (9 of 25)	2 (9 of 18)	3 (14 of 20)	2 (8 of 20)
28	Croatia	2.4	Opening	12	46.00	2 (5 of 13)	2 (10 of 25)	3 (10 of 18)	3 (12 of 20)	2 (9 of 20)
29	Bulgaria	2.4	Opening	12	48.00	2 (5 of 13)	2 (10 of 25)	2 (8 of 18)	4 (15 of 20)	2 (10 of 20)
30	Georgia	2.6	Opening	13	45.00	3 (7 of 13)	3 (12 of 25)	2 (7 of 18)	3 (11 of 20)	2 (8 of 20)
31	Greece	2.6	Opening	13	50.00	2 (5 of 13)	2 (11 of 25)	4 (14 of 18)	3(13 of 20)	2(7 of 20)
32	Hungary	2.6	Opening	13	52.00	2(6 of 13)	3(13 of 25)	2 (9 of 18)	3 (13 of 20)	3 (11 of 20)
33	Kosovo	2.8	Opening	14	54.00	2 (6 of 13)[a]	3 (11.7 of 25)[a]	3 (10 of 18)[a]	4 (17.3 of 20)[a]	2 (9 of 20)
33	N. Macedonia	2.8	Opening	14	54.00	3 (7 of 13)	3 (12 of 25)	2 (8 of 18)	4 (17 of 20)	2 (10 of 20)
35	Armenia	2.8	Opening	14	54.33	4 (9 of 13)	3 (15 of 25)	2 (9 of 18)	3 (13.3 of 20)[a]	2 (8 of 20)
36	Albania	2.8	Opening	14	56.00	3 (8 of 13)	3 (13 of 25)	2 (9 of 18)	4 (16 of 20)	2 (10 of 20)
37	Montenegro	3.2	Suppressed	16	58.66	3 (8 of 13)	3 (13 of 25)	3 (10.66 of 18)[a]	4 (16 of 20)[a]	3 (11 of 20)
38	Moldova	3.2	Suppressed	16	60.00	3 (7 of 13)	3 (13 of 25)	3 (12 of 18)	4 (17 of 20)	3 (11 of 20)
39	Serbia	3.2	Suppressed	16	61.00	3 (7 of 13)	3 (14 of 25)	3 (11 of 18)	4 (17 of 20)	3 (12 of 20)
40	B & H	3.4	Suppressed	17	61.00	4 (9 of 13)[b]	3 (12 of 25)	3 (12 of 18)[a]	5 (18 of 20)	2 (10 of 20)
41	Ukraine	4.2	Closed	21	71.00	4 (9 of 13)	4 (17 of 25)	5 (16 of 18)	5 (18 of 20)	3 (12 of 20)
42	Turkey	4.4	Closed	22	82.00	4 (9 of 13)	5 (23 of 25)	3 (12 of 18)	5 (20 of 20)	5 (18 of 20)
43	Russia	4.4	Closed	22	83.00	4 (10 of 13)	5 (22 of 25)	3 (13 of 18)	5 (20 of 20)	5 (18 of 20)
44	Belarus	4.6	Closed	23	78.50	5 (11 of 13)	5 (22.50 of 25)[a]	4 (13.33 of 18)[a]	4 (14.7 of 20)[a]	5 (17 of 20)
45	Azerbaijan	4.6	Closed	23	86.00	5 (11 of 13)	5 (24 of 25)	3 (12 of 18)[a]	5 (20 of 20)[a]	5 (19 of 20)

[a]Some countries have been omitted from some data and therefore the average score had to be calculated for the particular feature, i.e., Freedoms or Rule of Law, etc.

[b]: Bosnia-Herzegovina is the only country classified as "occupied" by the Center for Systemic Peace. Cyprus, Kosovo, Ukraine, Georgia or Azerbaijan are not although they do not control the whole of their territories. It would be arbitrary correction of the data if their description of the country was ignored

indices might not reflect the current state of affairs. However, the indices reflect the state of play at the time when they have been measured.

Moldova is grouped with the three Western Balkans countries of Montenegro, Serbia, and Bosnia-Herzegovina in the second-worst category of a "suppressed society." As the three other Western Balkans countries are just above this category, it is appropriate to analyse the Western Balkans later together as many characteristics are shared by all or most of them. Moldova, both post-conflict and post-Soviet, fares better than its large post-Soviet European neighbours grouped in the category of a "closed society." Four of the countries with a "closed society" are former Soviet republics of Russia, Belarus, Ukraine, and Azerbaijan, while Turkey is the group's final member.

A "pure" index of one means state-power in the countries provided for an open society. Countries with an index between one and two are in the category of the "fairly open" society, while countries with an index between two and three are in the "opening society" category. The score between three and four positioned countries in the category of "suppressed societies." "Closed society" is the category of the countries with a score of four and above. (See Table 2.1)

The first four columns show position in the table, country, the overall index, and the type of the resulting society. The fifth column shows total points across the categories. The minimal number is five, i.e., one in each category, and the worst possible score is 25. Eleven countries achieved minimal score while only Belarus and Azerbaijan share the worst score of 23. As explained already, there are three to five indices in each category, making the total available score across the indices ranging between 20 and 96. Only Ireland and Switzerland scored 20 only while Azerbaijan has the worst score of 86. The final five columns show each particular group of indices, Regime Index, with the total available score ranging between 3 and 13 because three indices have been taken into consideration, and the lowest available score would be one in each of the indices making the minimum possible score of 3. The worst possible score is 13 across all three indices combined. The Personal Freedom category ranges between 5 and 25. This project's Economic Freedoms Index is based on four indices, making 4 the lowest score and 18 the highest. Both the Rule of Law, Corruption and Human Rights Index and Media Freedoms Index have a range between 4 and 20.

2.2 State of Play on the Eve of the Pandemic

The table with the overall findings reinforces the understanding of divided Europe. Liberal "old" coexists with a liberalising and increasingly authoritarian "new" Europe. The top eleven countries with "open society" are all part of what is usually perceived as "western Europe." In contrast, the following category of "fairly open" societies, consisting of thirteen countries, is filled with the rest of "western Europe" and six countries of the "new Europe" that transitioned well from communist regimes. The next category of "opening society" is dominated by six countries of the "new Europe" that joined the EU in 2004 and later, one older EU member-state and the five outsiders. The three of the Western Balkans six countries are at the bottom of this group. The other three countries of the WB6, Bosnia-Herzegovina, Serbia and Montenegro, together with Moldova, are in the group of "suppressed societies," just above the five countries with "closed society," four of which are former Soviet countries with the addition of Turkey, all of them situated on the eastern edges of Europe.

Therefore, it is possible to draw some general conclusions on regional developments as many similarities are found across each of the regions. Western European countries, together with Scandinavian states, enable an open society whereby state-powers are mainly being kept in check. Some western countries are yet to fully develop all democratic instruments to produce and protect an open society but are very close to it and have a fairly open society together with the most successful countries of central Europe that transitioned well. This is the category where part of the "new Europe" begins. "New Europe" dominates the middle category where many central European countries are found with their "opening societies." Most Western Balkans countries are at the bottom of the same category reinforcing the idea of "new" Europe. This vision is strengthened by the following group of post-conflict and post-communist countries grouped in the "suppressed society" category: Bosnia-Herzegovina, Serbia and Montenegro, from the western Balkans, and Moldova from the post-Soviet space. Finally, it is four former Soviet countries where society is closed. Turkish democratic decline adds the country to this group.

Altogether, regions could be understood as:

- western (old) Europe with an open society,
- mixture of "old" and "new" Europe is mainly central Europe with a fairly open society,
- countries on the fringes of central Europe with opening societies,
- less-successful post-conflict societies of western Balkans and post-Soviet space with the suppressed society,
- significant part of the post-Soviet space, including Eurasian Russia, together with Eurasian Turkey with closed societies.

Naturally, there are exceptions in each of the regions.

General observation reconfirms different levels of democratic models, levels of freedoms, the rule of law and human rights in the "old" and "new" Europe. The Western Balkans countries show remarkably similar results that are produced by the common recent history and result from the similar nature of the regimes and, perhaps, cultural similarities. This chapter provides restricted commentary on individual states but focuses on the general presentation of the findings. The elaboration of the findings of the whole region and the continent will follow in the subsequent chapters.

2.3 Democracy Under Threat

"Current autocratization trends are probably fuelled by societal changes,"[4] write Lührmann and Lindberg. Their finding supports this project's attempt to determine society's nature, determined by the resulting index based on the 20 indices in five different categories. It is possible to argue the inclusion of one index into a different category, but it would be possible again to argue against this. The categories might seem natural and artificial at the same time. After all, findings are considered together, following the determined methodology at the beginning of the project. They generally correspond to conclusions and works of leading social scientists specialising in particular regions of Europe.

Petrova critically observes the work of Lührmann and Lindberg on autocratization, finding that "it excludes another critical assault on democracy in the post-communist space—persistent efforts to undermine democratic checks and balances on government power."[5] While these efforts are not exclusive to the post-communist space, Turkey being the most obvious example, many democracies developed since the 1990s are experiencing suppression or complete removal of democratic processes that would keep governments in check. Petrova reinforces her argument by considering if "their measure combines indices reporting freedom of association, freedom of expression, and free and fair elections."[6] This critique of other efforts in this broad field supports this project's decision to combine 20 various indices and determine what kind of society is to be found in each of the 45 European countries with a population of over half a million.

The relevance of regional developments is confirmed by academic research. Daly argues that research "has shown that regional political environments that are supportive of democracy, as reflected in the preponderance of other democracies, strongly correlate with the durability of each democracy in the region."[7]"The converse is also true," Daly points, "authoritarian regimes that are perceived as successful tend to breed imitators."[8] The behaviour of states during the pandemic reinforces this conclusion. Suspension of democratic instruments seems to have been determined more by the country's region than by the democratic indices measuring the rule of law, freedoms, and human rights.

It proved to be difficult, if not impossible, to create an index on the suspension of democratic values. Both academic and activist organisations have made attempts to create indices on state reactions to the pandemic based on various indicators and set up the data. The Oxford UniversityBlavatnik School of Government has produced a very ambitious project measuring government's interventions globally and creating

[4]Lührmann A & Lindberg S in Aydın-Düzgit et al. (2019).

[5]Petrova T in Aydın-Düzgit et al. (2019).

[6]PetrovaT in Aydın-Düzgit et al. (2019).

[7]Daly, T G in Aydın-Düzgit et al. (2019).

[8]Daly, T G in Aydın-Düzgit et al. (2019).

the government stringency index for most sovereign states.[9] However, the academic team has changed some methodology and indexing practices during the process of collecting data. Thus, the index set up to measure the intervention on the scale from zero to hundred has soon been populated by several European countries reaching the index of hundred. The later version of the index has only two countries, Serbia and Georgia, reaching the index of 100 at the peak of the crisis.[10] Therefore, the general consideration of the index should be in its later form. Even this form might only be considered conditionally with the reappearance of state interventionism in Autumn 2020 and thus the second, and later the third wave, of the pandemic.

The International Centre for Not-for-Profit Law has also produced data on state actions caused by the pandemic.[11] Their findings are used as raw data supporting the research and findings of the study. The activist website Pandemic Big Brother, founded by several reputable NGOs in the field of freedom of expression, provided additional resources for studying the state's intrusion into citizens' privacy. The OSCE showed concerns in the field of state-intervention during the COVID pandemic and have produced their research.[12] The International Monetary Fund has been updating its data on state interventionism in national economies.[13] Even some internet-based specialist organisations offered their data on state interventionism in digital fields during the pandemic.[14] The findings provide valuable data, but they do not offer indices, and the data cannot be indexed for the lack of concurrent categories for all countries. Another academic institution, V-Dem Institute at the University of Gothenburg, has developed its indices that include a Pandemic Violations of Democratic Standards Index[15] and the Pandemic Backsliding Index.[16]

In addition to the original research, these sources provide the basis for the analysis of state-power and its imposition over society during the pandemic. However, it is not possible to produce an aggregated index based on diverse findings because the findings cannot be transferred into numerical values, the focus of the research was diverse, and several countries have been omitted from the results. The Blavatnik index has omitted three countries (see Table 2.2), while the V-Dem indices have no information about eight countries. Both organisations have not offered specific table-summarised findings. The following tables result from this project's attempt to present some form of their findings to support the main arguments that states have developed their stringent measures regardless of the regime's nature.

The resulting table based on the Blavatnik School of Government research project supports the impression that the type of the regime and society have minimal, if any,

---

[9] Hale et al. (2020).

[10] Our World in Data (2021a, b) and Hale et al. (2020).

[11] The International Centre for Not-for-Profit Law (2020).

[12] OSCE Office for Democratic Institutions and Human Rights (ODIHR) (2020).

[13] International Monetary Fund (updated 5 February 2021).

[14] Top Ten VPN (2020).

[15] V-Dem Institute (2020d).

[16] V-Dem Institute (2020c).

Table 2.2 Stringency index according to the Oxford University's Blavatnik School of Government (Hale et al. 2021; Our World in Data 2021a, b)

Position	Country	Society	Stringency index at its peak	Period of the highest stringency
1	Serbia	Suppressed	100	21/03–20/04
1	Georgia	Opening	100	31/03–26/04
3	Azerbaijan	Closed	96.30	21/06–17/07
3	Croatia	Opening	96.30	23/03–26/04
5	Cyprus	Fairly open	94.44	16/04–03/05
6	Italy	Fairly open	93.52	12/04–03/05
7	Kosovo	Opening	92.59	24/03–17/05
7	Bosnia-Herzegovina	Suppressed	92.59	10/04–23/04
9	France	Fairly open	90.74	17/03–10/05
9	Ireland	Open	90.74	06/04–17/05
11	Albania	Opening	89.81	18/04–17/05
11	Slovenia	Fairly open	89.81	30/03–19/04
13	Portugal	Fairly open	89.74	09/04–13/04 & 01/05–03/05
14	Malta	Opening	87.04	08/04–21/05
14	Romania	Opening	87.04	31/03–10/05
14	Moldova	Suppressed	87.04	24/03–17/04
14	Russia	Closed	87.04	30/03–05/04
14	Slovakia	Opening	87.04	08/04–13/04
14	Lithuania	Fairly open	87.04	10/04–13/04
20	Spain	Fairly open	85.19	30/03–03/05
20	Austria	Open	85.19	16/03–13/04
22	Greece	Opening	84.26	23/03–03/05
23	Poland	Fairly open	83.33	09/04–24/05
24	Czechia	Fairly open	82.41	23/03–01/04
25	Belgium	Fairly open	81.48	20/03–04/05
26	Netherlands	Open	79.63	31/03–10/05
26	Luxembourg	Open	79.63	17/03–19/04
26	Norway	Open	79.63	24/03–19/04
29	Estonia	Fairly open	77.78	29/03–26/04
29	Turkey	Closed	77.78	11/04–12/04 & 18/04–19/04
31	Hungary	Opening	76.85	28/03–03/05
32	Ukraine	Closed	75.93	03/04–21/05
32	United Kingdom	Open	75.93	26/03–11/05
34	Germany	Open	73.15	22/03–03/05
34	Switzerland	Open	73.15	17/03–26/04
34	Bulgaria	Opening	73.15	21/03–30/03 & 15/04–15/05
37	Denmark	Open	72.22	18/03–14/04
38	Latvia	Fairly open	65.74	27/03–10/05
39	Finland	Open	60.19	28/03 – 14/04
40	Iceland	Fairly open	53.70	20/03–03/05

(continued)

Table 2.2 (continued)

Position	Country	Society	Stringency index at its peak	Period of the highest stringency
41	Sweden	Open	40.74	04/04–12/06
42	Belarus	Closed	19.44	04/04–19/04
No data	Armenia	Opening	No data	No data
No data	Montenegro	Suppressed	No data	No data
No data	North Macedonia	Opening	No data	No data

reflection in the state reaction to the pandemic. When putting parallel the findings of this project on the state-power and society and the stringency index results, the resulting table (Table 2.3) supports the argument of no correlation between the regime's nature and the level of stringency of state measures. Nevertheless, the very top of the stringency index is not populated by open societies. If Ireland is understood as an exception in ninth place and Austria in position 19, all other countries with the open society are positioned from 25th place onwards. Nevertheless, the least stringent measures were introduced in Belarus, where the society is closed, and the president has almost dictatorial powers.

The lack of a direct correlation is reconfirmed by the mixture of findings that position closed societies of Turkey and Ukraine, together with the least liberal EU member Hungary, between traditionally liberal Norway and open societies of the United Kingdom, Germany, and Switzerland. This kind of mixture is present among the 42 measured states. It is closer to conclude that regional positioning influenced stringency measures. Thus, the Western Balkans countries are all in the top 11 positions, although two were not included in the index, as Table 2.2 shows. As the argument states that the general relation between the state-power and society somewhat reflects regional divisions in Europe, especially the perception of the co-existence of the "old" and "new" Europe, the impression of regionally correlated stringency measures might be considered. However, there are far too many exceptions that populated places between the countries of the same region that the overall conclusion of the correlation would be challenging to make.

The V-Dem Institute has developed the whole project on consequences for democracy during the pandemic.[17] Their research results between March and December 2020 are based on imposition and levels of discriminatory measures, abusive enforcement of these measures, derogation of otherwise non-derogable rights, limitations imposed on the legislature, no time-limit, restrictions of media, and official disinformation campaigns. The valuable information provides for the analyses of 144 countries globally and ranks each country individually. Table 2.4 is based on the results of the V-Dem's project and restricted to European countries

[17] V-Dem Institute, University of Gothenburg (2020a), The Pandemic Backsliding Project (PanDem), Version 5.

Table 2.3 Parallel tables

State-power and society			Blavatnik stringency index		
Country	Index	Society	Country	Stringency index at its peak	Society
Ireland	1	Open	Serbia	100	Suppressed
Switzerland	1	Open	Georgia	100	Opening
Denmark	1	Open	Azerbaijan	96.30	Closed
Finland	1	Open	Croatia	96.30	Opening
Netherlands	1	Open	Cyprus	94.44	Fairly open
Norway	1	Open	Italy	93.52	Fairly open
Sweden	1	Open	Kosovo	92.59	Opening
Germany	1	Open	B & H	92.59	Suppressed
Luxembourg	1	Open	France	90.74	Fairly open
Austria	1	Open	Ireland	90.74	Open
UK	1	Open	Albania	89.81	Opening
Estonia	1.2	Fairly open	Slovenia	89.81	Fairly open
Iceland	1.2	Fairly open	Portugal	89.74	Fairly open
Lithuania	1.4	Fairly open	Malta	87.04	Opening
Portugal	1.4	Fairly open	Romania	87.04	Opening
Czechia	1.4	Fairly open	Moldova	87.04	Suppressed
Latvia	1.4	Fairly open	Russia	87.04	Closed
Slovenia	1.4	Fairly open	Slovakia	87.04	Opening
Belgium	1.6	Fairly open	Lithuania	87.04	Fairly open
Spain	1.6	Fairly open	Spain	85.19	Fairly open
France	1.6	Fairly open	Austria	85.19	Open
Cyprus	1.6	Fairly open	Greece	84.26	Opening
Italy	1.8	Fairly open	Poland	83.33	Fairly open
Poland	2.0	Fairly open	Czechia	82.41	Fairly open
Slovakia	2.2	Opening	Belgium	81.48	Fairly open
Malta	2.2	Opening	Netherlands	79.63	Open
Romania	2.2	Opening	Luxembourg	79.63	Open
Croatia	2.4	Opening	Norway	79.63	Open
Bulgaria	2.4	Opening	Estonia	77.78	Fairly open
Georgia	2.6	Opening	Turkey	77.78	Closed
Greece	2.6	Opening	Hungary	76.85	Opening
Kosovo	2.6	Opening	Ukraine	75.93	Closed
Hungary	2.6	Opening	United Kingdom	75.93	Open
N. Macedonia	2.8	Opening	Germany	73.15	Open
Armenia	2.8	Opening	Switzerland	73.15	Open
Albania	2.8	Opening	Bulgaria	73.15	Opening
Montenegro	3.2	Suppressed	Denmark	72.22	Open
Moldova	3.2	Suppressed	Latvia	65.74	Fairly open
Serbia	3.2	Suppressed	Finland	60.19	Open
B & H	3.4	Suppressed	Iceland	53.70	Fairly open
Ukraine	4.2	Closed	Sweden	40.74	Open

(continued)

Table 2.3 (continued)

State-power and society			Blavatnik stringency index		
Country	Index	Society	Country	Stringency index at its peak	Society
Turkey	4.4	Closed	Belarus	19.44	Closed
Russia	4.4	Closed	Armenia	No data	Opening
Belarus	4.6	Closed	Montenegro	No data	Suppressed
Azerbaijan	4.6	Closed	North Macedonia	No data	Opening

[a]The first three columns are taken from the "State-Power and Society" Index of this research, while the latter three columns show the stringency index based on the Blavatnik School of Government's project. (Hale et al. 2021; Our World in Data 2021a, b)

only. The highest-ranked European country is Switzerland, with an index of 0 that it shares with eight other European countries, all EU member states.

The group of countries where governments led to minor violations of democratic standards is not a monolith as the group with no violations. The level of minor violations is putting in the same group Sweden, Norway and the UK with open societies and Ukraine, where the findings have determined closed society. Between these countries is a diverse group with "fairly open," "opening", and "suppressed" societies like Romania, Lithuania, Italy, Georgia, France, Belgium, Moldova, Czechia, and Armenia. None of the countries with open societies is below this group.

The group of countries where not only minor but "some violations" occurred is also diverse. The best positioned are countries with fairly open societies like Spain, Slovenia, and Poland, but Azerbaijan with a closed society is also in this group together with several post-communist countries, both the EU-members and non-EU states.

Major violations of democratic standards took place in closed societies of Russia, Belarus, and Turkey. Greece, Bosnia-Herzegovina, and Serbia are the remaining countries in this lowest-positioned group. The index is not provided for eight of the 45 European countries.

The Pandemic Backsliding Index developed by the same institute relies on the factors found in the same fields as its Pandemic Violations of Democratic Standards Index. Table 2.5 is based on this index. Twenty-three European countries are with a low risk of backsliding according to this index. All the countries with open societies are part of this group and several other EU member-states, the three states in southern Caucasus, and Ukraine and Moldova. A slightly higher risk of backsliding is found in Russia with the closed society, while this risk is significantly higher in Poland, where society is fairly open. In-between and within this group are diverse states including EU members with a fairly open society like Slovenia and Czechia, opening society like Slovakia, Greece, Hungary and Croatia and non-EU states of the western Balkans like Albania, North Macedonia and Bosnia-Herzegovina. Belarus and Turkey, with closed societies, are also in this group. The only country found in this survey with a high risk of backsliding is Serbia.

Table 2.4 Pandemic violations of democratic standards index

Position	Country	Status	Index	Global rank (of 144)
1	Switzerland	No violations	0	143
2	Portugal	No violations	0	142
3	Netherlands	No violations	0	140
4	Ireland	No violations	0	139
5	Germany	No violations	0	138
6	Finland	No violations	0	137
7	Denmark	No violations	0	136
8	Austria	No violations	0	131
9	Sweden	Minor violations <0.2	0.10	127
10	Romania	Minor violations <0.2	0.10	125
11	Norway	Minor violations <0.2	0.10	124
12	Lithuania	Minor violations <0.2	0.10	122
13	Italy	Minor violations <0.2	0.10	120
14	Georgia	Minor violations <0.2	0.10	119
15	France	Minor violations <0.2	0.10	118
16	Belgium	Minor violations <0.2	0.10	114
17	UK	Minor violations <0.2	0.15	111
18	Ukraine	Minor violations <0.2	0.15	109
19	Moldova	Minor violations <0.2	0.15	106
20	Czechia	Minor violations <0.2	0.15	101
21	Armenia	Minor violations <0.2	0.15	98
22	Spain	Some violations <0.35	0.20	93
23	Slovenia	Some violations <0.35	0.20	92
24	Bulgaria	Some violations <0.35	0.20	83
25	Azerbaijan	Some violations <0.35	0.20	82
26	Poland	Some violations <0.35	0.25	77
27	Albania	Some violations <0.35	0.25	56
28	Slovakia	Some violations <0.35	0.30	50
29	N. Macedonia	Some violations <0.35	0.30	48
30	Hungary	Some violations <0.35	0.30	40
31	Croatia	Some violations <0.35	0.30	36
32	Russia	Major violations ≥0.35	0.35	28
33	Greece	Major violations ≥0.35	0.35	22
34	B & H	Major violations ≥0.35	0.35	18
35	Belarus	Major violations ≥0.35	0.35	17
36	Turkey	Major violations ≥0.35	0.50	8
37	Serbia	Major violations ≥0.35	0.60	5
–	Cyprus	No Data		
–	Estonia	No Data		
–	Iceland	No Data		
–	Latvia	No Data		
–	Luxembourg	No Data		

(continued)

Table 2.4 (continued)

Position	Country	Status	Index	Global rank (of 144)
–	Kosovo	No Data		
–	Malta	No Data		
–	Montenegro	No Data		

V-Dem Institute, University of Gothenburg (2020d), Pandemic Violations of Democratic Standards

When the two indices are put together next to each other, it is evident that the top nine positions in both surveys are identical, while the rest are similar (see Table 2.6). The exception is Poland that actually has the same index in both surveys but is positioned differently. The Backsliding Index puts Poland second worst, just above Serbia, in Europe and on the 19th worst position out of 144 countries globally with the high risk of backsliding. In the Violations of Democratic Standards Index, Poland occupies 26th position in Europe and 77th globally.

Belarus has the 17th worst record globally for violations of democratic standards, with only Turkey and Serbia performing worse in Europe. Its Backsliding Index positions it eight places better. Russia shares the index for violations of democratic standards with Belarus. However, it is positioned three places above as it is three places higher than the neighbouring country in the Backsliding Index. Lithuania is also eight positions better off in the Violations of Democratic Standards Index than in the Backsliding Index. The most significant difference for any country has been found for Azerbaijan. It is 15th in the Backsliding Index, but the violations put it at the 25th place in the other index. Azerbaijan occupies the last, 45th place in the State-Power and Society Index, thus reconfirming the lack of strong causal relations between state regimes, societies, and government measures during the pandemic.

The details of the relation between state-power and society across Europe, at the time of the suspension of democratic institutions in all European states, show a clear division. The more developed democratic institutions, the more open society is to be found in these countries. Historically, the whole of Europe has never suspended democracy at the same time. This unique development caused by the COVID-19 pandemic provided a temporary opportunity to use the available data of leading institutions and create a telling comparable index. Generally, Western Europe, consisting of states in the west and north of the continent, has developed an "open society." It is generally eastern Europe, made up of large post-Soviet states and Turkey, that have developed a "closed society." The categories in-between the open and the closed society are populated by countries of Central Europe, few underperformers of Western Europe and some Eastern European countries. The Western Balkans shows signs of a successful transition towards Western values. Nevertheless, it also clearly shows some ruling elites' tendencies to apply the governing style not uncommon in the continent's East.

Regardless of the nature of their societies, the reaction of the states did not generally correspond to the indices measuring the state of play before the pandemic. States were looking to effectively respond to the crisis and protect their citizens. More open societies often experienced a similar pressure from the state-power as did

Table 2.5 Pandemic backsliding index

Position	Country	Status	Index	Global rank (of 144)
1	Switzerland	Low risk <0.1	0	143
2	Portugal	Low risk <0.1	0	142
3	Netherlands	Low risk <0.1	0	140
4	Ireland	Low risk <0.1	0	139
5	Germany	Low risk <0.1	0	138
6	Finland	Low risk <0.1	0	137
7	Denmark	Low risk <0.1	0	135
8	Austria	Low risk <0.1	0	131
9	Sweden	Low risk <0.1	0.02	127
10	Italy	Low risk <0.1	0.02	126
11	Romania	Low risk <0.1	0.03	124
12	Georgia	Low risk <0.1	0.03	123
13	Norway	Low risk <0.1	0.04	121
14	Belgium	Low risk <0.1	0.04	119
15	Azerbaijan	Low risk <0.1	0.04	117
16	Armenia	Low risk <0.1	0.05	116
17	France	Low risk <0.1	0.07	103
18	Ukraine	Low risk <0.1	0.07	101
19	UK	Low risk <0.1	0.08	97
20	Lithuania	Low risk <0.1	0.08	96
21	Spain	Low risk <0.1	0.08	93
22	Moldova	Low risk <0.1	0.08	92
23	Bulgaria	Low risk <0.1	0.10	80
24	Russia	<0.20	0.11	70
25	Czechia	<0.20	0.13	67
26	Slovakia	<0.20	0.14	64
27	Belarus	<0.20	0.14	60
28	Slovenia	<0.20	0.16	50
29	Turkey	<0.20	0.18	45
30	Albania	<0.20	0.18	43
31	N. Macedonia	<0.30	0.21	32
32	Greece	<0.30	0.21	36
33	Hungary	<0.30	0.22	28
34	B & H	<0.30	0.23	25
35	Croatia	<0.30	0.23	23
36	Poland	<0.30	0.25	19
37	Serbia	High risk ≥0.30	0.30	9
-	Cyprus	No data		
-	Estonia	No data		
-	Iceland	No data		
-	Latvia	No data		
-	Luxembourg	No data		

(continued)

Table 2.5 (continued)

Position	Country	Status	Index	Global rank (of 144)
-	Kosovo	No data		
-	Malta	No data		
-	Montenegro	No data		

V-Dem Institute, University of Gothenburg (2020c), Pandemic Backsliding Index

societies in states with more authoritarian regimes. The correlation of increased authoritarianism in less open societies during the pandemic compared with the suspension of democratic principles in more open societies shows the states behaved similarly regardless of the regime and the society. Thus, democratic standards and institutions, all kinds of freedoms, the rule of law, and human rights have been undermined in all 45 states.

The state actions are legal as constitutions have provisions for executive authority to monopolise powers when faced with a threat to the state or the nation. Researchers have found that "eighty democracies approved legal provisions for a state of emergency" between 1800 and 2012.[18] The same researchers found that "only 55 percent of emergency provisions mandate that emergencies terminate within a specific time frame."[19] The emergencies declared in 2020 affected European countries in various forms and often had no time restrictions, as shown and found by researchers creating the Stringency Index[20] and the Backsliding Index.[21]

There is, however, a distinction found in the study of pre-pandemic measures of emergency in democracies. A "temporary institutional derogation" is found in democracies that "constrained [newly provided powers] to truly existential threats to the nation."[22] The state's opposite behaviour is found when emergency powers are used as justification to authorise a single power-holder further. The process that "constitutes a dramatic institutional shift,"[23] Lührmann and Rooney name "autocratization" which Cassani and Tomini understand as an "umbrella concept for all the processes of regime change that share a direction towards autocracy."[24]

It was Huntington who determined three waves of democratization and the two reversing effects.[25] Lührmann and Lindberg, using a different methodology, added the third reversing tendency that they call "the third wave of autocratization."[26] The authors prove the decline of democracy since 1994 when the third wave started but

[18] Lührmann and Rooney (2020), p. 2.

[19] Lührmann and Rooney (2020), p. 6.

[20] Hale et al. (2020).

[21] V-Dem Institute, University of Gothenburg (2020a), The Pandemic Backsliding Project (PanDem), Version 5.

[22] Lührmann and Rooney (2020), p. 9.

[23] Lührmann and Rooney (2020), p. 9.

[24] Cassani and Tomini (2019), p. 15.

[25] Huntington (1991).

[26] Lührmann and Lindberg (2019), p. 1104.

Table 2.6 Democracy during the pandemic: parallel tables

Position	Country	Violations of democratic standards	Country	Backsliding
1	Switzerland	No violations	Switzerland	Low risk <0.1
2	Portugal	No violations	Portugal	Low risk <0.1
3	Netherlands	No violations	Netherlands	Low risk <0.1
4	Ireland	No violations	Ireland	Low risk <0.1
5	Germany	No violations	Germany	Low Risk <0.1
6	Finland	No violations	Finland	Low risk <0.1
7	Denmark	No violations	Denmark	Low risk <0.1
8	Austria	No violations	Austria	Low risk <0.1
9	Sweden	Minor violations <0.2	Sweden	Low risk <0.1
10	Romania	Minor violations <0.2	Italy	Low risk <0.1
11	Norway	Minor violations <0.2	Romania	Low risk <0.1
12	Lithuania	Minor violations <0.2	Georgia	Low risk <0.1
13	Italy	Minor violations <0.2	Norway	Low risk <0.1
14	Georgia	Minor violations <0.2	Belgium	Low risk <0.1
15	France	Minor violations <0.2	Azerbaijan	Low risk <0.1
16	Belgium	Minor violations <0.2	Armenia	Low risk <0.1
17	UK	Minor violations <0.2	France	Low risk <0.1
18	Ukraine	Minor violations <0.2	Ukraine	Low risk <0.1
19	Moldova	Minor violations <0.2	UK	Low risk <0.1
20	Czechia	Minor violations <0.2	Lithuania	Low risk <0.1
21	Armenia	Minor violations <0.2	Spain	Low risk <0.1
22	Spain	Some violations <0.35	Moldova	Low risk <0.1
23	Slovenia	Some violations <0.35	Bulgaria	Low risk <0.1
24	Bulgaria	Some violations <0.35	Russia	<0.20
25	Azerbaijan	Some violations <0.35	Czechia	<0.20
26	Poland	Some violations <0.35	Slovakia	<0.20
27	Albania	Some violations <0.35	Belarus	<0.20
28	Slovakia	Some violations <0.35	Slovenia	<0.20
29	N. Macedonia	Some violations <0.35	Turkey	<0.20
30	Hungary	Some violations <0.35	Albania	<0.20
31	Croatia	Some violations <0.35	N. Macedonia	<0.30
32	Russia	Major violations ≥0.35	Greece	<0.30
33	Greece	Major violations ≥0.35	Hungary	<0.30
34	B & H	Major violations ≥0.35	B & H	<0.30
35	Belarus	Major violations ≥0.35	Croatia	<0.30
36	Turkey	Major violations ≥0.35	Poland	<0.30
37	Serbia	Major violations ≥0.35	Serbia	High risk ≥0.30
No Data	Cyprus			
No Data	Estonia			
No Data	Iceland			
No Data	Latvia			
No Data	Luxembourg			

(continued)

Table 2.6 (continued)

Position	Country	Violations of democratic standards	Country	Backsliding
No Data	Kosovo			
No Data	Malta			
No Data	Montenegro			

V-Dem Institute, University of Gothenburg (V-Dem Institute, University of Gothenburg 2020b), Pandemic Backsliding: Democracy During Covid-19 (March to December 2020) Violations of Democratic Standards

also provide, as Daly argues, "a useful corrective to a burgeoning supply of panic literature" that "tends to lament the so-called death of democracy (or the death of liberalism, or even the death of the West or of Europe)."[27] Titles like "Suicide of the West," referenced in Daly's text, are "The New York Times Bestseller" arguing that "democracies are in peril because they have lost the will to defend the values and institutions that sustain freedom and prosperity."[28]

The importance of the findings of the research on autocratization is undoubted. This project, however, is not concerned with a process that develops over time. The timeframe for this project is particular to the beginning of the pandemic in 2020. It looked at possible regression of democratic norms and found no correlation between authoritarian tendencies and suspension of democratic principles. Similarities within a particular region have been found. However, they cannot lead to the argumentative conclusion of the reliance on regional influence, cross-border processes that would determine democratic developments in the country, and the state-power and society's relation.

References

Aydın-Düzgit S, Daly TG, Godfrey K, Lindberg SI, Lührmann A, Petrova T, Youngs R (2019) Post–cold war democratic declines: the third wave of autocratization. Carnegie Europe. https://carnegieeurope.eu/2019/06/27/post-cold-war-democratic-declines-third-wave-of-autocratization-pub-79378. Accessed 6 Oct 2021

Bertelsmann Stiftung (2020) Bertelsmann transformation index. https://www.bti-project.org/en/index/political-transformation.html. Accessed 6 Oct 2021

Cassani A, Tomini L (2019) What autocratization is. In: Autocratization in post-Cold War political regimes. Challenges to democracy in the 21st century. Palgrave Macmillan, Cham, pp 15–35

Cato Institute (2019) Human freedom index. https://www.cato.org/sites/cato.org/files/2021-03/human-freedom-index-2020.pdf. Accessed 1 May 2021

Civicus Monitor (2020) National civic space ratings. https://findings2020.monitor.civicus.org/europe-central-asia.html. Accessed 1 May 2021

[27] Daly, T G in Aydın-Düzgit et al. (2019).

[28] Goldberg (2018).

Foundation for the Advancement of Liberty (2019) World electoral freedom index. https://fundalib.org/world-election-freedom-index-wefi-2020/?lang=en. Accessed 6 Oct 2021

Fraser Institute (2018) Economic freedom index. https://www.fraserinstitute.org/economic-freedom/dataset?geozone=world&year=2018&page=dataset&min-year=2&max-year=0&filter=0. Accessed 1 May 2021

Freedom House (2020) Nations in transit. https://freedomhouse.org/report/nations-transit/2020/dropping-democratic-facade. Accessed 27 Mar 2021

Goldberg J (2018) Suicide of the West: how the rebirth of tribalism, populism, nationalism, and identity politics is destroying American Democracy. Crown Forum, New York

Hale T, Webster S, Petherick A, Phillips T, Kira B (2020) Oxford COVID-19 government response tracker. Blavatnik School of Government. https://covidtracker.bsg.ox.ac.uk/. Accessed 7 Sept 2020

Hale T, Angrist N, Goldszmidt R, Kira B, Petherick A, Phillips T, Webster S, Cameron-Blake E, Hallas L, Majumdar S, Tatlow H (2021) A global panel database of pandemic policies (Oxford COVID-19 Government Response Tracker). Nat Human Behav. https://doi.org/10.1038/s41562-021-01079-8. Accessed 1 May 2021

Huntington SP (1991) The third wave of democratization in the late twentieth century. University of Oklahoma Press, London

International Monetary Fund (updated 5 February 2021) Policy Responses to COVID-19. https://www.imf.org/en/Topics/imf-and-covid19/Policy-Responses-to-COVID-19#B. Accessed 24 Feb 2021

Lührmann A, Lindberg SI (2019) A third wave of autocratization is here: what is new about it? Democratization 26(7):1095–1113

Lührmann A, Rooney B (2020) Autocratization by decree: states of emergency and democratic decline. Working Paper, V-Dem Institute/University of Gothenburg. https://www.v-dem.net/media/filer_public/31/1d/311d5d45-8747-45a4-b46f-37aa7ad8a7e8/wp_85.pdf. Accessed 6 Oct 2021

OSCE Office for Democratic Institutions and Human Rights (ODIHR) (2020) OSCE human dimension commitments and state responses to the Covid-19 pandemic. https://www.osce.org/odihr/human-rights-states-of-emergency-covid19. Accessed 6 Oct 2021

Our World in Data (2021a). https://ourworldindata.org/grapher/covid-stringency-index?time=2020-12-31&region=Europe&country=MLT~AFG. Accessed 6 Oct 2021

Our World in Data (2021b) Covid-19: Government stringency index. https://ourworldindata.org/grapher/covid-stringency-index?tab=chart&stackMode=absolute&time=2020-01-22..2020-09-05&country=ALB~AUT~AZE~BLR~BEL~BIH~BGR~HRV~CYP~CZE~DNK~EST~FIN~FRA~GEO~DEU~GRC~HUN~ISL~IRL~ITA~OWID_KOS~LVA~LTU~LUX~MDA~NLD~NOR~POL~PRT~ROU~RUS~SRB~SVK~SVN~ESP~SWE~CHE~TUR~UKR~GBR&region=Europe. Accessed 6 Oct 2021

The Heritage Foundation (2020) Index of economic freedom. https://www.heritage.org/index/. Accessed 6 Oct 2021

The International Centre for Not-for-Profit Law (2020) Covid-19 civic freedom tracker. https://www.icnl.org/covid19tracker/. Accessed 22 Sept 2020

The World Bank (2018) Index of economic freedom score. https://tcdata360.worldbank.org/indicators/idx.econ.free.scr?country=BRA&indicator=747&viz=line_chart&years=2013,2018. Accessed 6 Oct 2021

Top Ten VPN (2020) COVID-19 digital rights tracker. https://www.top10vpn.com/research/investigations/covid-19-digital-rights-tracker/. Accessed 6 Oct 2021

Transparency International (2019) Corruption perceptions index. https://images.transparencycdn.org/images/2019_CPI_Report_EN.pdf. Accessed 6 Oct 2021

V-Dem Institute, University of Gothenburg (2020a) The pandemic backsliding project (PanDem), Version 5. https://github.com/vdeminstitute/pandem. Accessed 3 Mar 2021

V-Dem Institute, University of Gothenburg (2020b) Pandemic backsliding: democracy during Covid-19 (March to December 2020) violations of democratic standards. https://www.v-dem.net/en/analysis/PanDem/. Accessed 3 Mar 2021

V-Dem Institute, University of Gothenburg (2020c) Pandemic backsliding index. https://www.v-dem.net/en/analysis/PanDem/. Accessed 27 Feb 2021

V-Dem Institute, University of Gothenburg (2020d) Pandemic violations of democratic standards. https://www.v-dem.net/en/analysis/PanDem/. Accessed 27 Feb 2021

World Economic Forum (2020) Social mobility index 2020. http://www3.weforum.org/docs/Global_Social_Mobility_Report.pdf. Accessed 1 May 2021

World Justice Project (2020) Rule of law index. https://worldjusticeproject.org/our-work/research-and-data/wjp-rule-law-index-2020. Accessed 1 May 2021

Chapter 3
Western Balkans Regimes Between European Democracy and Autocracy

3.1 Findings on European Democracy

The category of the regime is based on three research indices that have delivered different descriptions to their findings and were, therefore, numericized, thus enabling the determination of a common average denominator for each regime. The Democracy Index[1] and the Global Report[2] both mark 13 European regimes as "full democracy", while the same countries are described as "liberal democracy" in the Democracy Report.[3] The Regime Index of this project converts this into a numerical value of 1, enabling the creation of the final common index. The next category is even more diversely named in different indices as "flawed democracy," "democracy", and "electoral democracy". It reconfirms the need and the method of converting categories in their numerical values. In this case, it is 2, and eventually creating the Regime Index of this project with five categories of liberal democracy, liberalising democracy, populist democracy, populist autocracy and full autocracy, as Table 3.1 shows.

In addition to the 13 countries found by all three indices to be at the top level of democracy, five countries are placed in the second-best category by just one of the three indices. The result is 18 countries categorised as "liberal democracy" in the Regime Index of this project. The differences among the 13 countries with the best performance according to all three indices are minimal, and the actual order among them is based on the additional numerical scores of the Economist Intelligence Unit's index and V-Dem's index. All 13 countries are long-established liberal democracies, and this just determined the order of naming them in the same category. The rest of Western Europe follows Scandinavian countries that top the list with Belgium being a notable exception. Five more countries have two indices

[1] Economist Intelligence Unit (2020).

[2] Center for Systemic Peace (2017).

[3] V-Dem Institute (2020).

N. Andjelic, *Covid-19, State-Power and Society in Europe*, European Union and its Neighbours in a Globalized World 5, https://doi.org/10.1007/978-3-030-91073-0_3

Table 3.1 Regime type

Democracy index[a]		Global report index[b]		Annual democracy report[c]		Final		
Status	Index	Status	Index	Status	Index	Points 3–13	Status	Index
Fool democracy	1	Full democracy	1	Liberal democracy	1	3–4	Liberal democracy	1
Flawed democracy	2	Democracy	2	Electoral democracy	2	5–6	Liberalising democracy	2
Hybrid regime	3	Open anocracy Closed anocracy	3	Electoral autocracy	3	7–8	Populist democracy	3
Authoritarian	4	Autocracy	4	Closed autocracy	4	9–10	Populist autocracy	4
		Occupied/Failed[d]	5			11–13	Full autocracy	5

[a]Economist Intelligence Unit (2020)
[b]Center for Systemic Peace (2017)
[c]V-Dem Institute (2020)
[d]Bosnia-Herzegovina is the only country with the status of "occupied" country although the justification is wrong. Azerbaijan, Cyprus, Georgia, Kosovo and Ukraine were not given the same status

putting them in the top category, making the group of 18 liberal democracies. Cyprus and Slovenia are added to the Western world in this category (See Table 3.2).

The next category of "liberalising democracy" is made of 14 countries, 11 of them post-communist. Belgium, Greece, and Malta make up the rest of the category. Kosovo is at the bottom of the 14 countries as an average score had to be calculated for it because the EIU's index does not cover this country. In reply to the query, the EIU stated, "Kosovo is not included because the Index was launched in 2006, before Kosovo's declaration of independence in 2008." The EIU continued clarification of the reasons for non-inclusion for other countries, like "they were microstates; were at war; or were lacking data."[4] They failed to notice that Serbia and Montenegro became independent states in June 2006, and yet they are included in the index although they did not exist as states for half of the first year the EIU measured levels of democracy. The same process was used for Malta which was not included in the Center for Systemic Peace's index. Unlike the EIU, they never replied to the queries.

States of the Western Balkans, except for Bosnia-Herzegovina, follow immediately after Kosovo and are categorised as "populist democracy" together with Moldova and Georgia. The common feature for them, and the following category of "populist autocracy", is a recent experience of violent conflict. From Kosovo in the 32nd position, all the countries to the bottom of the list in 45th position experienced war except for Albania and Belarus. The Western Balkans, Caucasus, and post-Soviet countries on the eastern edge of Europe belong to this group. Turkey, the only country with no history of communist regime among the bottom three groups, was also recently involved in internal and external conflicts. Therefore, it is possible to argue that a recent history of violent conflict is the most serious obstacle to developing functioning democratic institutions in a country. Slovenia, a liberal democracy, represent the exception to this rule and, to some extent Croatia in 28th place.

The geographic spread of different regimes confirms the West, which includes not only the geographic West, as a liberal democratic space. With some countries that geographically do not belong to *Mitteleuropa*, Central Europe dominates the following category of liberalising democracies. The Western Balkans, with some post-Soviet states, is dominated by populist democracies. Populist autocracies are found generally in the eastern edges of Europe among diverse countries of post-Soviet states, Turkey and Bosnia-Herzegovina. Another two post-Soviet states, Azerbaijan and Belarus, are full autocracies in the Regime Index of this project based on the three different indices that broadly measure the level of democracy in the state.

The table shows that Bosnia-Herzegovina is the only country marked as "occupied" in the Global Report, making it the only country in the lowest category of that index. It is symptomatic that the countries immediately above Bosnia-Herzegovina and immediately below in the final Regime Index of this project are categorised as an anocracy in the Global Report.[5] This gives them a numerical value of 3, while

[4] EIU Customer Services/The Economist Intelligence Unit (2021).

[5] Center for Systemic Peace (2017).

Table 3.2 Regime type index

Position	Country	Index	Status	Points	Democracy Index 2019[a]	Global Report 2017[b]	Democracy Report 2020[c]
1	Norway	1	Liberal democracy	3	One 9.87 full democracy	One full democracy	One liberal democracy 0.825
2	Sweden	1	Liberal democracy	3	One 9.39 full democracy	One full democracy	One liberal democracy 0.829
3	Denmark	1	Liberal democracy	3	One 9.22 full democracy	One full democracy	One liberal democracy 0.858
4	Finland	1	Liberal democracy	3	One 9.25 full democracy	One full democracy	One liberal democracy 0.813
5	Switzerland	1	Liberal democracy	3	One 9.03 full democracy	One full democracy	One liberal democracy 0.827
6	Ireland	1	Liberal democracy	3	One 9.24 full democracy	One full democracy	One liberal democracy 0.799
7	Netherlands	1	Liberal democracy	3	One 9.01 full democracy	One full democracy	One liberal democracy 0.784
8	Luxembourg	1	Liberal democracy	3	One 8.81 full democracy	One full democracy	One liberal democracy 0.787
9	Germany	1	Liberal democracy	3	One 8.68 full democracy	One full democracy	One liberal democracy0.779
10	Spain	1	Liberal democracy	3	One 8.29 full democracy	One full democracy	One liberal democracy 0.815
11	UK	1	Liberal democracy	3	One 8.52 full democracy	One full democracy	One liberal democracy 0.852
12	Portugal	1	Liberal democracy	3	One 8.03 full democracy	One full democracy	One liberal democracy 0.817
13	Austria	1	Liberal democracy	3	One 8.29 full democracy	One full democracy	One liberal democracy 0.721
14	Iceland	1	Liberal democracy	4	One 9.58 full democracy	One full democracy	Two electoral democracy 0.765
15	France	1	Liberal democracy	4	One 8.12 full democracy	Two democracy	One liberal democracy 0.783
16	Italy	1	Liberal democracy	4	Two 7.52 flawed demo.	One full democracy	One liberal democracy 0.772
17	Cyprus	1	Liberal democracy	4	Two 7.59 flawed demo.	One full democracy	One liberal democracy 0.710
18	Slovenia	1	Liberal democracy	4	Two 7.50 flawed demo.	One full democracy	One liberal democracy 0.714
19	Estonia	2	Liberalising democracy	5	Two 7.90 flawed demo.	Two democracy	One liberal democracy 0.840
20	Belgium	2	Liberalising democracy	5	Two 7.64 flawed demo.	Two democracy	One liberal democracy 0.822
21	Greece	2	Liberalising democracy	5	Two 7.43 flawed demo.	One full democracy	Two electoral democracy 0.762
22	Lithuania	2	Liberalising democracy	5	Two 7.50 flawed demo.	One full democracy	Two electoral democracy 0.732
23	Czechia	2	Liberalising democracy	5	Two 7.69 flawed demo.	One full democracy	Two electoral democracy 0.697
24	Latvia	2	Liberalising democracy	5	Two 7.49 flawed demo.	Two democracy	One liberal democracy 0.712
25	Slovakia	2	Liberalising democracy	5	Two 7.17 flawed demo.	One full democracy	Two electoral democracy 0.717
26	Poland	2	Liberalising democracy	5	Two 6.62 flawed demo.	One full democracy	Two electoral democracy 0.500

27	Malta	2	Liberalising democracy	6[d]	Two 7.95 flawed demo.	[d]	Two electoral democracy 0.560
28	Croatia	2	Liberalising democracy	6	Two 6.57 flawed demo.	Two democracy	Two electoral democracy 0.545
29	Bulgaria	2	Liberalising democracy	6	Two 7.03 flawed demo.	Two democracy	Two electoral democracy 0.488
30	Romania	2	Liberalising democracy	6	Two 6.49 flawed demo.	Two democracy	Two electoral democracy 0.434
31	Hungary	2	Liberalising democracy	6	Two 6.63 flawed demo.	One full democracy	Three electoral autocracy 0.402
32	Kosovo	2	Liberalising democracy	6[d]	[d]	Two democracy	Two electoral democracy 0.413
33	Georgia	3	Populist democracy	7	Three 5.42 hybrid regime	Two democracy	Two electoral democracy 0.504
34	N. Macedonia	3	Populist democracy	7	Three 5.97 hybrid regime	Two democracy	Two electoral democracy 0.432
35	Moldova	3	Populist democracy	7	Three 5.75 hybrid regime	Two democracy	Two electoral democracy 0.445
36	Serbia	3	Populist democracy	7	Two 6.41 flawed demo.	Two democracy	Three electoral autocracy 0.254
37	Albania	3	Populist democracy	8	Three 5.89 hybrid regime	Two democracy	Three electoral autocracy 0.431
38	Montenegro	3	Populist democracy	8	Three 5.65 hybrid regime	Two democracy	Three electoral autocracy 0.349
39	Armenia	4	Populist autocracy	9	Three 5.54 hybrid regime	Three open anocracy	Three electoral autocracy 0.641
40	Ukraine	4	Populist autocracy	9	Three 5.90 hybrid regime	Three open anocracy	Three electoral autocracy 0.292
41	Turkey	4	Populist autocracy	9	3 4.09 hybrid regime	3 closed anocracy	3 electoral autocracy 0.101
42	B & H	4	Populist autocracy	10	Three 4.86 hybrid regime	5[e] occupied	Two electoral democracy 0.345
43	Russia	4	Populist autocracy	10	Four 3.11 authoritarian	Three open anocracy	Three electoral autocracy 0.099
44	Belarus	5	Full autocracy	11	Four 2.48 authoritarian	Four autocracy	Three electoral autocracy 0.115
45	Azerbaijan	5	Full autocracy	11	Four 2.75 authoritarian	Four autocracy	Three electoral autocracy 0.070

[a]Economist Intelligence Unit (2020)
[b]Center for Systemic Peace (2017)
[c]V-Dem Institute (2020)
[d]Some countries have been omitted from some data and therefore the average score had to be calculated for the particular feature
[e]Bosnia-Herzegovina is the only country classified as "occupied" by the Center for Systemic Peace. Cyprus, Kosovo, Ukraine, Georgia or Azerbaijan,although with no control over their whole territory, are not. It would be arbitrary to correct the data if their index's description of the country was ignored

Bosnia-Herzegovina's numerical value is 5. The rest of the Western Balkans are described as "democracy" in the Global Report, with the numerical value of 2. If Bosnia-Herzegovina were also given a value of 2 or 3, it would be described as "populist democracy" in the final index like other Western Balkans countries, as shown in Table 3.2.

The Global Report attempts to clarify this status claiming, "Bosnia remains an "occupied state" (−66) since the December 1995 Dayton Agreement established the Office of the High Representative and the Peace Implementation Council," and arguing that the "*de facto* authority has largely been assumed by the ethnic enclaves."[6] Different indices provide slightly different findings, but they generally do not significantly stray from each other's results. This is one of the rare cases when this has happened. It reaffirms the method of computing the three indices together into the same category as this is a corrective if one of the indices employed a somewhat unusual method.

None of the other countries with recent experience of violent conflict is described as such. Cyprus, Moldova, Azerbaijan, Georgia, Ukraine, and Kosovo lack control over some parts of their sovereign territory, while Bosnia-Herzegovina's consociational regime has the whole country's territory under control. The presence of international organisations and their interventionist nature of actions shows elements of supervised sovereignty, but, yet again, this is not the only country with some form of international troops, mediators and almost permanent internationally imposed institutions that oversee the transition away from post-conflict society towards democracy. The UN is present in Cyprus, and has been since the 1970s, yet the Global Report describes it as "full democracy." With a heavy international presence and supervised sovereignty ever since it declared independence, Kosovo is named "democracy."

Another example of the curious categorisation is Serbia in the EIU's Democracy Index that describes it as "flawed democracy" while the rest of Western Balkans are in the category of "hybrid regime," with Kosovo being omitted from the index.[7] Meanwhile, the V-Dem index describes Serbia as an "electoral autocracy", like Albania and Montenegro, while Kosovo, North Macedonia and Bosnia-Herzegovina are a category higher with "electoral democracy."[8] It is not a simple question of the category, but Serbia is, according to the V-Dem Institute, in the top-10 most autocratizing countries globally. Like first-placed Hungary, Serbia in the fourth place went from liberal democracy in 2009 to electoral autocracy in 2019. Turkey, the second most autocratizing state, dropped from electoral democracy to electoral autocracy, while Poland, in the third place, was autocratized from liberal democracy to electoral democracy.[9] The strength of the process of autocratization is measured

[6]Center for Systemic Peace (2017), p. 32.

[7]EIU (2020), pp. 10–14.

[8]V-Dem Institute (2020), p. 26.

[9]V-Dem Institute (2020), p. 16.

and not the final destination in the list in 2019. In Serbia, the report found "electoral integrity suffered and this nation slipped back to authoritarianism in 2015."[10]

The three indices show a country either in the same numerical category, or one of the three indices puts a country one category higher or lower. Thus, a general conclusion of the country's regime is supported. The exceptions are Hungary and Bosnia-Herzegovina categorised differently by each of the indices. The Global Report named Hungary a "full democracy," but their latest report was 2 years older than other indices. The EIU index has it as "flawed democracy," but the V-Dem index describes it as "electoral autocracy." Hungary's deterioration is shown further in the EIU's index for the consequent year, during the pandemic, when it was the only EU member-state described as "transitional or hybrid regime"[11] by the "Nations in Transit" index of the Freedom House. As this index focuses only on post-communist states, it does not affect this research's index, but their findings are telling.

Hungary is in the same category, according to the Freedom House index, as all the countries of Western Balkans and equals the results of Serbia, which is the best-placed Western Balkans country followed by Montenegro, Albania, North Macedonia, Bosnia-Herzegovina, and Kosovo, all described as "transitional or hybrid regime."[12]

3.2 Failings of Democratic Development in the Western Balkans

Another index restricted to nations in transition, the Bertelsmann Transformation Index, places five countries of the Western Balkans in the category of defective democracy. They are ordered according to their political transformation progress: Montenegro, North Macedonia, Albania, Serbia, and Kosovo. Hungary is placed between Serbia and Kosovo according to this index.[13] Bosnia-Herzegovina is the only state of the Western Balkans in the category of "highly defective democracy."[14] The processes and practices of "illiberal politics and subnational autocratization"[15] that Kapidžić described in Bosnia-Herzegovina, pushed the country into this category.

Both the Freedom House and the Bertelsmann indices help study states and societies but are restricted to the countries in transition. Therefore, they have not been included in the index resulting from this project, but they both strengthen the

[10] V-Dem Institute (2020), p. 17.

[11] Freedom House (2020a, b), p. 12.

[12] Freedom House (2020a, b), p. 24.

[13] Bertelsmann Transformation Index (2020).

[14] Bertelsmann Transformation Index (2020).

[15] Kapidžić (2020), p. 83.

argument that the EIU index overrates Serbia's democracy, as the rest of the indices see its performance on the same level with other troubled democracies in the Western Balkans. The problem is underlined when some countries are omitted from one of the three indices, like Kosovo, and therefore an average score of the two indices provides the imaginary value of the third, thus removing a possibility of the corrective. In Kosovo's case, corrective was needed because specialised indices, like Freedom House and Bertelsmann, put Kosovo in the category of "transitional or hybrid regime" or "defective democracy" together with its neighbours. Furthermore, Kosovo is the worst placed country of the Western Balkans in the Freedom House index[16] and second worst in the Bertelsmann index.[17] This all proves deficiencies of the indexing processes. The method must be strictly applied regardless of the occasional deficiency if the project's final aim is to be pursued strenuously.

A general tendency of the six countries in the Western Balkans is the deterioration and decline of democratic institutions. The EIU index, as shown in Table 3.3, provides a historical overview since 2006, which confirms the slide towards autocracy across the region. Regimes of all six countries reflect a populist nature, but only Bosnia-Herzegovina is categorised as a populist autocracy in the overall findings, while all other countries are populist democracies. Kosovo is positioned even higher as a liberalising democracy partly due to the reasons already explained. Except for Albania that suffered the state collapse in 1997, all other countries are, to varying degrees and in different ways, post-conflict societies. Thus, all the states of the Western Balkans have a common feature of recent historic upheaval.

There is a heavy presence of international organisations in Kosovo, their involvement in the judiciary and strong influence over executive power-holders. Kosovo's status that just over half of the international community recognises as independent has made it more challenging to create indices, and it is therefore missing from some projects. This study calculates an average index when one element is missing and consequently set the country in a specific category. The final result justifies the method as it reflects several academic findings and reiterates the conclusion that the whole of the Western Balkans is in a very similar position, although corrective measures were restricted in Kosovo's case because of its omittance from some indices.

The Economist Intelligence Unit somehow found all Western Balkans to have hybrid regimes, except for Serbia which, according to them, is placed in the higher category of "flawed democracy." If one relied on only the Economist Intelligence Unit's index, Serbia would be in the same category with thirteen latest European Union members, Greece and two founding members of the EU, Belgium and Italy.[18] It would be difficult finding a scholar of post-communist countries and comparative politics that would put in the same category Serbia and most, if not all, of these countries.

[16] Freedom House (2020a, b), p. 24.

[17] Bertelsmann Transformation Index (2020).

[18] Economist Intelligence Unit (2020).

Table 3.3 The EIU Democracy Index 2006–2019: Western Balkans Six[a]

Country	2006	2008	2010	2011	2012	2013	2014	2015	2016	2017	2018	2019
Albania	5.91	5.91	5.86	5.81	5.67	5.67	5.67	5.91	5.91	5.98	5.98	5.89
B & H	5.78	5.70	5.32	5.24	5.11	5.02	4.78	4.83	4.87	4.87	4.98	4.86
Montenegro	6.57	6.43	6.27	6.15	6.05	5.94	5.94	6.01	5.72	5.69	5.74	5.65
N. Macedonia	6.33	6.21	6.16	6.16	6.16	6.16	6.25	6.02	5.23	5.57	5.87	5.97
Serbia	6.62	6.49	6.33	6.33	6.33	6.67	6.71	6.71	6.57	6.41	6.41	6.41
Kosovo	x	x	x	x	x	x	x	x	x	X	x	x

[a]EIU Democracy Index (Economist Intelligence Unit 2020), pp. 16–17

Foreign Policy described the whole region in the text under the title "The Budding Autocrats of the Balkans."[19] Journalists also do not describe the country in terms of democracy. Voice of America headlined their report in 2018, "Thousands Protest Serbian President's Autocratic Rule."[20] A year later, The Globe Post titled their opinion piece "Orbanization of Serbia: Vučić's Path towards Competitive Authoritarianism."[21] The National explained in 2020, "How Serbia's lockdown led to an outcry against the authoritarianism."[22] The Guardian saw Serbia's president in 2021 as "a bulldozing leader whose dominance of institutions ... led a watchdog to conclude Serbia is no longer a democracy."[23] The Foreign Policy article describes "the Balkans' fledgling autocrats" who oversee democratic processes that give "free rein to the budding autocrats of the Balkans."[24] This all shows that different sources have consistently seen the nature of the regime in Serbia as authoritarian, autocratic, hybrid, or, as Nations in Transit Index shows, both Serbia and Montenegro "are no longer categorised as democracies" after "years of increasing state capture, abuse of power, and strongman tactics."[25]

Leading academics are almost unanimous in seeing Serbia, like other Western Balkans countries, as less than democratic regimes. The levels of autocracy or naming of the types might be diverse, but the regimes' character is evident. Bieber considers "three examples of clear competitive authoritarian regimes: Serbia since 2012, Montenegro, and Macedonia between 2006/8 and 2017."[26] The remaining three, Bieber sees as "partially competitive authoritarian regimes."[27] Radeljić describes "the increasing semi-authoritarianism in post-Democrats-led Serbia and post-independence Kosovo."[28] The electoral successes, Vachudova analysed, were "giving Vučić virtually total power over the Serbian government—and this was only deepened when he was elected President in 2017."[29] Kmezić points at "serious and persistent gaps between European standards in the judiciary and media freedom and the realities on the ground in Serbia and Macedonia."[30] Pavlović describes "the local reality of authoritarian rule and corruption", naming such regimes as "stabilitocracy", and provides "the examples of Montenegro, Macedonia, Serbia, and Kosovo."[31]

---

[19] Foreign Policy (15 April 2016).

[20] Voice of America (8 December 2018).

[21] The Globe Post (29 April 2019).

[22] National (12 July 2020).

[23] The Guardian (25 March 2021).

[24] Foreign Policy (15 April 2016).

[25] Freedom House (2020a, b), p. 2.

[26] Bieber (2018a, b), p. 340.

[27] Bieber (2018a, b), p. 340.

[28] Radeljić (2019), p. 163.

[29] Vachudova (2019), p. 75.

[30] Kmezić (2019), p. 104.

[31] Pavlović (5 May 2017).

Serbia in the EIU index is not the only example of the importance of combining the indices regardless of different methodologies and structures. After putting different findings together and converting the results into numerical values, it is possible to create the final overall index that would realistically reflect the country's state of affairs (See Table 3.2). This method allows for one index to "stray" and to provide a surprising result because the other indices, it is two indices in the case of regimes, serve as correctives.

Bosnia-Herzegovina in the Regime Index ended in the same category with Russia, Turkey, Ukraine, and Armenia, all named "populist autocracy" because Global Report Index contentiously described it as occupied.[32] Armenia is in this category as some indices used markers from before the change of government in 2018. Other indicators describe Bosnia-Herzegovina in more similar terms as its fellow countries from the Western Balkans. If the Center for Systemic Peace in its Global Report Index did not characterise it as "occupied,"[33] but like a form of anocracy, Bosnia-Herzegovina would be found a "populist democracy" and join the group of countries like Montenegro, Serbia, North Macedonia, Albania, Georgia, and Moldova.

The fact is that there is no single all-powerful leader in Bosnia-Herzegovina around whom the system is organised, but the consociational political model has provided for three such leaders who almost independently run their sub-national territories. This would justify marking Bosnia-Herzegovina as a "populist autocracy" or a collection of populist autocracies. Kapidžić points at the core of the problem in the country: "Measuring democracy at the national level can, therefore, be misleading as both the electoral contest and the tools to affect it are largely present at the level of the two subnational entities."[34]

Even the international community, acting in the collective form of the Office of High Representative, the EU permanent representative to the country, the American Ambassador, and Quint, a group of five leading western ambassadors, often call on meetings with the three nationalist leaders regardless of their current institutional position in the state power-structure. If things have to be done in the country, the representatives of liberal democracies rely upon the three nationalist leaders and not state institutions. Therefore, yet another fact is offered to support the idea that the state functions as a populist autocracy rather than democracy despite the periodical elections and formally set up democratic institutions. The actual decision-making is in the hands of the three nationalist leaders.

Unlike autocracies that develop a state around the strong leader and provide an impression of a strong state, Bosnia-Herzegovina is a weak state with the three strong leaders who draw their strength from the subnational levels of governance or non-institutional rule, thus undermining the state and making it even weaker. This creates an anomaly of Bosnia-Herzegovina as an autocracy and weak state, while

[32] Center for Systemic Peace (2017).

[33] Center for Systemic Peace (2017).

[34] Kapidžić (2020), p. 82.

other autocracies in the Balkans have strengthened state-functions to support an autocratic leader's outreach.

The rule of the three ethnic nationalist leaders in the country is secured similarly as they all share the same system of developing patronage politics organised in a pyramidal shape, with one of them at the top of each of the three pyramids. There is not a state-wide pyramid but the three subnational systems of pyramidal patronage. Kapidžić pointed at the relationship between nationalist leaders and state-owned enterprises (SOE). Milorad Dodik, Bosnian Serb nationalist leader of the Alliance of Independent Social-Democrats (SNSD), secures his power-structure by "selectively distributing public funding, favouring business allies and controlling large state-owned enterprises (SOEs)." The dominant Croat nationalist party, Dragan Čović-led Croatian Democratic Union, "HDZ BiH has established deep patronage networks, linking 'party-affiliated SOEs [that] employ a significant share of the local Croat population and in return create loyal voters'." Despite the more developed intra-ethnic political competition within the Bosniak community, the power-structures are dominated by the Party of Democratic Action (SDA) leader, Bakir Izetbegović. He has a modus operandi of "managing SOEs and running public procurement procedures with patronage in mind" while relying on a "close-knit network of family and party officials to distribute public resources in order to maximise electoral gain."[35]

All three leaders control their parties, and through the pyramidal patronage schemes, their communities regardless of their state-position within the political system. It is irrelevant whether they head the state institution, entity-level government, or some other elected position; their grip on the leading nationalist party's power-structures provides them with the overall control at the subnational level of power. This is all that matters as the state is weak and is lacking resources.

Bosnia's uniqueness rests on its political system's complexity, but the methods of the top-leaders are more common across the Western Balkans. Aleksandar Vučić in Serbia, Edi Rama in Albania, and Milo Đukanović in Montenegro might provide impression and evidence of their authoritarian powers despite their countries being categorised in the general index as "populist democracies." Austrian scholar Oliver Schmitt offers interesting comparisons of Rama and Vučić who both "override the democratic structures and free media," and are using the conflict between Serbs and Albanians, primarily over Kosovo, to "draw political capital from it." Rama, according to Schmitt, "acts as the leader of all Albanians" thus undermining the authority of Kosovo leaders.[36]

An opposition politician in Albania described Rama as "authoritarian, arrogant and not transparent,"[37] while a journalist report describes an "increasingly authoritarian grasp on the country."[38] A German thinktank similarly saw the government

[35] Kapidžić (2020), p. 87.

[36] Der Standard (3 April 2019).

[37] The Guardian (10 June 2019).

[38] Hajdari (2020).

"operating in an increasingly authoritarian way."[39] Rama's "autocratic bent," a magazine report presented, "came to the fore at the onset of the ongoing pandemic when he became the first European leader to send the army onto the streets... to maintain security – and to show force."[40] An academic blog set Albanian example by pointing at "the region's recent history [that] abounds with 'strong and stable' leaders that squandered their mandate away through autocratic, anti-democratic and otherwise ill-conceived policies and actions."[41] The Economist found in neighbouring Montenegro that "some 71% of Montenegrins want their leader 'strong and resolute.'"[42] It seems Albanians are not different in their taste of state leadership.

Nikola Gruevski governed North Macedonia with similar powers until he was forced out of office in 2016, and the more liberal political forces formed the new government in 2017. Based on the overall findings of the three indices combined, the general index set them together in the category of populist democracies. Yet, when focussing on just one of the indices,[43] North Macedonia, Bosnia-Herzegovina and Kosovo are all described as "electoral democracy", which is one level below "liberal democracy," but above Serbia, Montenegro, and Albania in the category of "electoral autocracy." This is another argument supporting the need to combine findings of different institutions and create a general index that would create an average result.

All three leaders, Rama, Đukanović and Vučić, are, intentionally or by accident, sometimes misunderstood as liberals when it suits European institutions or security alliances of the West. They contribute to this impression despite the strict rule at home. Even Rama's unusual fashion style misleads. Reports describe him "dressed, as is his habit, in a T-shirt and trainers,"[44] when giving an official interview, or when posing for group photo "alongside with leaders from Balkan and EU ... Rama combined his formal suit with white Addidas [Sic!] sneakers," or when meeting "Federica Mogherini, he was spotted wearing a stamped T-shirt and sporty pants and shoes."[45]

Vučić's fashion style might differ, but the government is similarly under his complete personal control. He was described in Foreign Policy as "Europe's favorite [Sic!] autocrat," his governing form as "soft autocracy" with the argument that "the EU is undermining its credibility by choosing stability over democracy in Serbia."[46] Indeed, a new term has been developed – stabilitocracy – used increasingly by

39 Rüttershoff (19 May 2020).

40 Hajdari (2020).

41 Fras (30 June Fras 2017).

42 The Economist (11 April The Economist 2019).

43 V-Dem Institute (2020).

44 The Guardian (10 June The Guardian 2019).

45 Mejdini (14 July Mejdini 2017).

46 Eror (9 March Eror 2018).

academic thinktanks like Balkans in Europe Policy Advisory Group,[47] academics like at LSE blog[48] or in a monograph,[49] or expert magazines[50] and journals like Foreign Policy,[51] and many authors.[52] *Deutsche Welle* titled the opinion piece on Serbian elections "Aleksandar Vucic: Serbia's stabilocrat".[53] The term was initially used in a study of Albania[54] in the form of "stabilocracy", as Bieber[55] pointed out. Vučić, not unlike Đukanović in Montenegro, contributes to this impression. Pavlović describes the rule in Montenegro, Macedonia, Serbia, and Kosovo as "a façade democracy while diminishing the role of parliament, holding unfair elections, criminalising the local political arena, assuming dictatorial powers, enacting predatory laws aimed at eliminating political competition, and stifling dissent as well as plundering a country's resources for the benefit of political leaders and their closest associates."[56]

The rule in the Western Balkans is characterised by nationalist policies and rhetoric, a strong man as a leader and a state capture. This description only partly fits Montenegro as the ruling nationalism in the state, unlike elsewhere in the Western Balkans, was until 2020 of an inclusive type developed during the state-building process and relying on ethnic minorities in addition to the ruling party supporters who dominantly see themselves as ethnic Montenegrins. The minorities have their ethnic parties that are standard members of the ruling coalition regardless of whether the Democratic Party of Socialists (DPS) needs such a coalition for the majority in the Parliament. Đukanović always relied on support from minority political parties, i.e., ethnic Bosniak, Albanian and Croat. The irony is that only Serbs, by far the largest minority group, strongly opposed his rule and loudly complained of discrimination.

Whatever office he occupied, "power remained with Đukanović, who determined if and when he would return to office, . . . power has always followed him."[57] Only some royals in Europe are in power, titular or actual, for a more extended period. The Economist described him as the "Monarch of Montenegro," "King Milo", and as "Europe's most durable ruler."[58] He dominates the country's politics regardless of the position he holds. The Independent described him in 2010 as "mysteriously

[47] Kmezić and Bieber (March 2017).

[48] Pavlović (5 May 2017).

[49] Kmezić (2019).

[50] Heinrich-Böll-Stiftung Office Sarajevo (November 2019).

[51] Eror (9 March Eror 2018).

[52] Bieber (2018a), pp. 337–354; also: Pavlović (23 December 2016).

[53] Deutsche Welle (22 June 2020).

[54] Primatarova and Deimel (2012).

[55] Bieber (2018b) The Rise (and Fall) of Balkan Stabilitocracies; also, Bieber (2018a) Patterns of competitive authoritarianism in the Western Balkans. p. 338.

[56] Pavlović (5 May 2017).

[57] Bieber (2020), p. 120.

[58] The Economist (11 April 2019).

wealthy", estimating his wealth at "£10m" and placing him in the 20th place of the wealthiest politicians in the world.[59] As most politicians on the list were royals, Đukanović was effectively the eighth richest elected politician on the Independent's list.

The Organised Crime and Corruption Reporting Project (OCCRP) named Đukanović a "person of the Year" in 2015 "for his work in creating an oppressive political atmosphere and an economy choked by corruption and money laundering," and "for his work in promoting crime, corruption and uncivil society."[60] Vladimir Putin was awarded in 2014 with "runners-up in the competition including Hungarian Prime Minister Viktor Orbán and Montenegrin Prime Minister Milo Djukanovic [Sic!]."[61] The winners' list includes Azerbaijani leader Ilham Aliyev, Nicolas Maduro of Venezuela and Philippine President Rodrigo Duterte.[62]

A lengthy period of Đukanović in power has led to an "emergence of dozens of parties that are indistinguishable copies of one another,"[63] especially within the pro-Serbian bloc. The tendency to divide the existing and set up new political parties is widespread. As Bieber found, there was one political party per 20,000 citizens for the elections in 2016. This ratio was surpassed in Bosnia-Herzegovina in 2020 when 21 political parties contested the local elections in Sarajevo Centar. The borough had 60,326 citizens registered with the right to vote, creating a ratio of one political party per less than 3000 people.[64] When finally, during the pandemic in 2020, the parties opposing Đukanović's Democratic Party of Socialists (DPS) made a truce, his party, albeit still the strongest in the Parliament, lost for the first time since the multi-party system was introduced in 1990. An Italian author offered an analysis of the regime in Montenegro in the text titled "Milo Đukanović: the defeat of the last "king of Montenegro."[65]

Montenegro has been described as a hybrid regime, democracy and electoral autocracy thus fitting into the final category as populist democracy. This is the third out of five categories in the regime type index and typical for the region. The covid-era elections in the region, where they have been organised, reconfirmed the power-holders except for Montenegro. However, instead of the Montenegrin inclusivist form of nationalism, Serb exclusivist nationalism succeeded in the 2020 elections. The Serbian Orthodox Church proved itself once more as the crucial element in securing and preserving Serbian identity and its political influence. States in the Balkans, in general, are not secular. When Đukanović attempted to secure the state from this influence, it was, besides the widespread allegations of corruption,

[59] The Independent(19 May 2010).

[60] The Organised Crime and Corruption Reporting Project (2015).

[61] Radio Free Europe (1 January 2015).

[62] The Organised Crime and Corruption Reporting Project (2015).

[63] Bieber (2020), p. 114.

[64] Centralna izborna komisija BiH (2020).

[65] Martino (2020).

Table 3.4 Unemployment rates

Country	Eurostat[a]	World Bank & WIIW[b]	ILO[c]	Viborc[d]	ILO (youth)[e]
Albania	12.3%	12.4%	12.5%	11.5%	27.0%
B & H	18.5%	18.4%	15.7%	15.7%	33.8%
Kosovo	29.4%	29.2%	25.6%	25.3%	49.5%
Montenegro	15.2%	14.4%	15.1%	14.3%	25.2%
N. Macedonia	20.7%	21.1%	17.3%	17.5%	35.6%
Serbia	12.8%	11.9%	9.0%	10.3%	26.6%

[a]Eurostat Statistics Explained (Feb Eurostat Statistics Explained 2020), Enlargement countries – labour market statistics
[b]World Bank& WIIW Vienna Institute for International Economic Studies (March World Bank and WIIW Vienna Institute for International Economic Studies 2019)
[c]The International Labour Organisation (ILO) (2020)
[d]Viborc (2020)
[e]The International Labour Organisation (ILO) (2020)

arguably the main factor of mobilising support for the opposition. The mass protests against the regime for reasons of corruption were nothing new.

The autocrats' rule in the Western Balkans states is secured by citizens who are under the permanent risk of job-loss. Their welfare depends on the state that is ruled by autocrats or authoritarian regimes. The unemployment levels are among the highest in Europe. The only comparable rates to Western Balkans countries "were observed in Greece (16.6% in October 2019) and Spain (13.7%)."[66] Besides the Western Balkans, Turkey, Armenia, and Georgia, they are the only countries with a double-digit unemployment rate. The EU-28 rate in December 2019 was 6.2%, and the Euro area of 19 countries had an average rate of 7.4%.[67] This shows (see Table 3.4) around twice as bad unemployment rates in the Western Balkans six as in the EU countries.

Eurostat and the World Bank provided statistics for 2018, while the ILO and data analytics platform Viberc refer to their findings in 2019. Although the figures vary slightly between different organisations, they tend to have high unemployment rates across the region. Youth unemployment is around double the general rate. Women find it even harder to find jobs as employment rates in 2018 "were below 50% in North Macedonia, Bosnia-Herzegovina and Kosovo. In the EU-27, the rate was 66.5%."[68] The ILO provided details of the average monthly salary of those employed, regrettably not for all the countries at the same time but close enough to support the idea of hardship. (see Table 3.5) The values are recalculated from local currencies into Euros so they could be compared.

After considering high unemployment rates and low average salaries, it is not surprising that significant numbers of citizens of all countries in the region are emigrating primarily to the European Union. "Every two minutes one citizen from

[66]Eurostat News Release Euroindicators (31 January 2020).
[67]Eurostat News Release Euroindicators (31 January 2020).
[68]Eurostat Statistics Explained (Feb 2020).

Table 3.5 Average monthly earnings of the employed[a]

Country	Local currency		Period	Euros
Albania	52,380	Albanian Lek	2019	438.87
B & H	829.1	Bosnian Mark	2019	424.09
Kosovo	474	Euro	2017	474
Montenegro	773	Euro	2019	773
N. Macedonia	30,416	Macedonian Denar	2014	492.96
Serbia	74,160	Serbian Dinar	2019	633.79

[a]The International Labour Organisation (ILO) (2020)

Table 3.6 Number of legal arrivals from Western Balkans to the EU in 2018[a]

Country	Number of citizens
Albania	62,525
Bosnia-Herzegovina	53,764
Kosovo	34,778
Montenegro	3,077
North Macedonia	24,442
Serbia	52,049

[a]Bonomi et al. (2020), p. 9. See also: Töglhofer (2019), p. 3

the Western Balkans migrates legally to the EU (first permits of residence in the EU in 2018)," states a research paper supported by the Italian Foreign Ministry.[69] As the Table 3.6 shows, a total of 230,635 citizens have legally arrived in the EU from Western Balkans during 2018.[70]

This all creates a situation whereby those in employment depend on the survival of state-controlled or state-owned companies. Some private companies provide the bulk of the rest of employment opportunities, but they, in turn, rely on state contracts. Thus a "democratised" state in the Western Balkans is a domestically powerful state usually controlled by an autocrat or, in more "liberal" cases, by the leadership of the dominant political party that goes unchallenged. Widespread clientelism partly inherited from the communist era, and patronage networks perpetuate the power-structure. Control over the media and the judiciary cements autocrats in power seemingly for ever. Even where power is successfully challenged on occasions, weak institutions, and the control over the resources prevent alternatives from producing functioning democratic change before the original clique secures its return to power.

"The political, administrative, and economic backwardness of the Western Balkan" Vachudova concludes, "is largely the fault of rent-seeking elites for whom the status quo offers power and wealth at the expense of reform."[71] Radeljić adds to the "the elites' behaviour in Serbia and Kosovo [that] is undoubtedly

[69]Bonomi et al. (2020), p. 9.

[70]Töglhofer (2019), p. 3.

[71]Vachudova (2019), p. 64.

semi-authoritarian," the failure of "the EU [that] has largely refrained from confronting it."[72] "The EU has contributed to semi-authoritarian practices in the Western Balkans,"[73] Radeljić points out. At the same time, Serbian and Montenegrin presidents, "Vučić and Đukanović are now alike," describes Vachudova, as "they employ strongly nationalist appeals, claiming to be defending the nation against its internal enemies while also striving toward the EU."[74] This is how stabilitocracy has been developed across the Western Balkans.

"From Croatia to Albania," argues Pula, "the region has plenty of grim stories of autocrats cloaking themselves in democrats' clothing."[75] "Regimes," writes Pavlović, that "are willing to protect and sustain western geo-political, security, military, economic, or energy related interests" are secured from western interference, thus leaving "local autocrats" to "do whatever suits their needs in their private domains."[76] "Regimes that consolidated themselves," similarly, concludes Bieber, "combine a formal commitment to democracy and European integration with informal authoritarian practices."[77] The tactics are widespread in the Western Balkans, even in Bosnia-Herzegovina with more than one autocrat, where "elites believe they have learned to manipulate the EU to get around its requirements"[78] and "appear to be cooperating fully in preserving a status quo that immiserates all Bosnians."[79] "While turnovers in government do happen," Kapidžić observes, "it is largely the same political parties that win elections."[80] The development of liberal democracy, while theoretically possible, is prevented by processes that Kapidžić describes as "segmental autonomy, in the form of territorial ethnic self-governance, and ethnic party systems."[81]

Serbian President Aleksandar Vučić has developed an authoritarian regime that controls democratic institutions and faces little challenges from the fragmented opposition. In Montenegro, the regime led by Milo Đukanović faces challenges from the opposition, and his party even lost the elections after 30 years, but the challengers are not liberals. It does not mean Đukanović's regime is liberal as a system of cronyism and control over institutions has been in place for decades. The consociational model in Bosnia-Herzegovina has not produced liberal democracy but the rule of three autarchic leaders over three communities making up the state. Another consociational model in North Macedonia has provided for security. However, some leading liberals in the EU, like Emmanuel Macron, did not see it as a full

[72] Radeljić (2019), p. 163.
[73] Radeljić (2019), p. 174.
[74] Vachudova (2019), p. 76.
[75] Pula (15 April 2016).
[76] Pavlović (2017).
[77] Bieber (2020), p. 139.
[78] Vachudova (2019), p. 80.
[79] Vachudova (2019), p. 76.
[80] Kapidžić (2020), p. 81.
[81] Kapidžić (2020), p. 82.

transition to liberal democracy. Kosovo has experienced the most robust western intervention in nation-building and state-building, but these efforts have not resulted in a liberal democracy. However, they have produced the system to be run by a series of leaders that relied on clientelist structures in governance and eventually enabled populists to triumph at two consecutive elections. Albania is ruled by another strong man who supersedes institutional powers by influencing and dominating political structures.

Pula described "the budding autocrats of the Balkans," that are "aware of their indispensability to strategic goals and interests beyond democratization and the rule of law," because of the Western "overriding concerns with issues of security and political stability." They "have masterfully exploited the political and diplomatic cover offered by strengthened EU and U.S. ties to attack and undermine domestic opponents."[82] Hoxhaj describes stabilitocracies as the condition when "autocrats capture the state and claim to secure stability, pretend to champion EU integration and rely on informal, clientelist structures, control of the media, and the regular production of artificial political crises to undermine democracy and the rule of law."[83] This means that "only a handful of people control the economy and the distribution of political power."[84] All six Western Balkans countries are run or have been recently governed by autocrats creating suppressed societies.

References

Bertelsmann Stiftung (2020) Bertelsmann transformation index. https://www.bti-project.org/en/index/political-transformation.html. Accessed 6 Oct 2021

Bieber F (2018a) Patterns of competitive authoritarianism in the Western Balkans. East Eur Politics 34(3):337–354

Bieber F (2018b) The rise (and fall) of Balkan Stabilitocracies. Horizons Winter 2018 (10). https://www.cirsd.org/en/horizons/horizons-winter-2018-issue-no-10/the-rise-and-fall-of-balkan-stabilitocracies. Accessed 6 Oct 2021

Bieber F (2020) The rise of authoritarianism in the Western Balkans. Palgrave Macmillan, London

Bonomi M, Hackaj A, Reljić D (2020) Avoiding the trap of another paper exercise: why the Western Balkans need a human development-centred EU enlargement model. Istituto Affari Internazionali, Rome. https://www.iai.it/en/pubblicazioni/avoiding-trap-another-paper-exercise. Accessed 6 Oct 2021

Center for Systemic Peace (2017) Global Report 2017. http://www.systemicpeace.org/vlibrary/GlobalReport2017.pdf. Accessed 1 May 2021

Der Standard (3 April 2019) Wölfl A: Interview Schmitt O J: Aus dem Konflikt ziehen Serben und Albaner Kapital. https://www.derstandard.at/story/2000100547410/aus-konflikt-zwischen-serben-und-albanern-ziehen-beide-seiten-kapital. Accessed 6 Oct 2021

[82] Pula (15 April 2016).

[83] Hoxhaj (2019).

[84] Hoxhaj (2019).

Deutsche Welle (22 June 2020) Mappes-Niediek N, Opinion: Aleksandar Vucic: Serbia's stabilocrat.https://www.dw.com/en/opinion-aleksandar-vucic-serbias-stabilocrat/a-53901545. Accessed 6 Oct 2021

Economist Intelligence Unit (2020) Democracy index 2019. https://www.eiu.com/topic/democracy-index/. Accessed 1 May 2021

EIU Customer Services/The Economist Intelligence Unit (2021) e-mail correspondence on 25 February at 1130

Eror A (9 March 2018) How Aleksandar Vucic became Europe's favorite autocrat. Foreign Policy. https://foreignpolicy.com/2018/03/09/how-aleksandar-vucic-became-europes-favorite-autocrat/. Accessed 6 Oct 2021

Eurostat News Release (31 January 2020) Euro area unemployment at 7.4%. Euroindicators. https://ec.europa.eu/eurostat/documents/2995521/10159296/3-30012020-AP-EN.pdf/b9a98100-6917-c3ea-a544-ce288ac09675. Accessed 6 Oct 2021

Eurostat Statistics Explained (Feb 2020) Enlargement countries – labour market statistics. https://ec.europa.eu/eurostat/statistics-explained/index.php/Enlargement_countries_-_labour_market_statistics#Unemployment_rates. Accessed 6 Oct 2021

Foreign Policy (2016, 15 April) The Budding Autocrats of the Balkans. https://foreignpolicy.com/2016/04/15/the-budding-autocrats-of-the-balkans-serbia-macedonia-montenegro/. Accessed 6 October 2021

Fras M (30 June 2017) Prime Minister Edi Rama takes total control in Albania, but who can keep him in check? LSE Blog. https://blogs.lse.ac.uk/europpblog/2017/06/30/edi-rama-takes-control-albania/?utm_source=feedburner&utm_medium=feed&utm_campaign=Feed%3A+Europp+%28EUROPP+-+European+Politics+and+Policy+at+LSE%29. Accessed 6 Oct 2021

Freedom House (2020a) Freedom in the World 2020. https://freedomhouse.org/report/freedom-world/2020/leaderless-struggle-democracy. Accessed 1 May 2021

Freedom House (2020b) Nations in transit. https://freedomhouse.org/report/nations-transit/2020/dropping-democratic-facade. Accessed 27 Mar 2021

Hajdari U (2020) Life under a flamboyant autocrat's rule in Albania. Summer of Solidarity project. https://www.summerofsolidarity.eu/home/life-under-flamboyant-autocrats-rule-albania-edi-rama. Accessed 6 Oct 2021

Heinrich-Böll-Stiftung Office Sarajevo (November 2019) 'Stabilitocracy' and/or radicalism. Perspectives, Issue No 7. Heinrich-Böll-Stiftung Office Sarajevo (Bosnia and Herzegovina, North Macedonia, Albania). https://rs.boell.org/sites/default/files/importedFiles/2020/04/03/perspectives%2520-%252011-2019%2520-%2520web.pdf. Accessed 27 Mar 2021

Hoxhaj A (2019) Civil society needs support to fight corruption and organised crime in the Western Balkans. LSE Blog. https://blogs.lse.ac.uk/europpblog/2019/10/30/civil-society-needs-support-to-fight-corruption-and-organised-crime-in-the-western-balkans/. Accessed 6 Oct 2021

Izbori 2020: Centar Sarajevo (2020) Centralna izborna komisija BiH. https://www.izbori.ba/Rezultati_izbora/?resId=27&langId=1#/9/136/0/0. Accessed 6 Oct 2021

Kapidžić D (2020) Subnational competitive authoritarianism and power-sharing in Bosnia and Herzegovina. Southeast Eur Black Sea Studies 20(1):81–101

Kmezić M (2019) EU rule of law conditionality: democracy or 'Stabilitocracy' promotion in the Western Balkans? In: Džankić J, Keil S, Kmezić M (eds) The Europeanisation of the Western Balkans: a failure of EU conditionality? Palgrave Macmillan, London, pp 87–110

Kmezić M, Bieber F (March 2017) The crisis of democracy in the Western Balkans: an anatomy of stabilitocracy and the limits of EU democracy promotion. Balkans in Europe Policy Advisory Group Graz. https://biepag.eu/publication/policy-study-the-crisis-of-democracy-in-the-western-balkans-an-anatomy-of-stabilitocracy-and-the-limits-of-eu-democracy-promotion/. Accessed 6 Oct 2021

Martino F (2020) Milo Đukanović: the defeat of the last "king of Montenegro". Osservatoria Balkani e Caucaso Transeuropa. https://www.balcanicaucaso.org/eng/Areas/Montenegro/Milo-Dukanovic-the-defeat-of-the-last-king-of-Montenegro-204578. Accessed 6 Oct 2021

Mejdini F (14 July 2017) Stylish Rama' Sending Message' To Europe About Albania. BalkanInsight. https://balkaninsight.com/2017/07/14/albanian-pm-conveys-political-messages-to-europe-in-sneakers-07-13-2017/. Accessed 6 Oct 2021

Pavlović S (23 December 2016) Montenegro's 'stabilitocracy': The West's support of Đukanović is damaging the prospects of democratic change. LSE blog. https://blogs.lse.ac.uk/europpblog/2016/12/23/montenegros-stabilitocracy-how-the-wests-support-of-dukanovic-is-damaging-the-prospects-of-democratic-change/. Accessed 6 Oct 2021

Pavlović S (5 May 2017) West is best: how 'stabilitocracy' undermines democracy building in the Balkans. LSE blog. https://blogs.lse.ac.uk/europpblog/2017/05/05/west-is-best-how-stabilitocracy-undermines-democracy-building-in-the-balkans/. Accessed 6 Oct 2021

Primatarova A, Deimel J (2012) Bridge over Troubled Waters? The role of the internationals in Albania. Center for Liberal Strategies, Sofia. https://www.yumpu.com/en/document/read/41598019/bridge-over-troubled-waters-the-role-of-the-internationals-in-. Accessed 6 Oct 2021

Pula B (15 April 2016) Foreign policy. The budding autocrats of the Balkans. https://foreignpolicy.com/2016/04/15/the-budding-autocrats-of-the-balkans-serbia-macedonia-montenegro/. Accessed 6 Oct 2021

Radeljić B (2019) Tolerating Semi-authoritarianism? Contextualising the EU's Relationship with Serbia and Kosovo. In: Džankić J, Keil S, Kmezić M (eds) The Europeanisation of the Western Balkans: a failure of EU conditionality? Palgrave Macmillan, London, pp 157–180

Radio Free Europe/Radio Liberty (1 January 2015) Investigative journalists Name Putin Corruption's "Person of the Year". https://www.rferl.org/a/putin-russia-corruption-person-of-the-year/26772361.html. Accessed 6 Oct 2021

Rüttershoff T (19 May 2020) Albania: autocratic measures in the shadows of corona. Konrad Adenauer Stiftung. https://www.kas.de/en/country-reports/detail/-/content/albania-autocratic-measures-in-the-shadows-of-corona. Accessed 6 Oct 2021

The Economist (11 April 2019) The Monarch of Montenegro: why Milo Djukanovic is Europe's most durable ruler. https://www.economist.com/europe/2019/04/11/why-milo-djukanovic-is-europes-most-durable-ruler. Accessed 6 Oct 2021

The Globe Post (29 April 2019) Orbanization of Serbia: Vucic's path towards competitive authoritarianism. https://theglobepost.com/2019/04/29/serbia-vucic-orbanization/. Accessed 6 Oct 2021

The Guardian (10 June 2019) Walker, S: Edi Rama, Albania's unconventional PM who wants to escape the 'curse of history'. https://www.theguardian.com/world/2019/jun/10/edi-rama-albania-pm-escape-curse-of-history. Accessed 6 Oct 2021

The Guardian (25 March 2021) 'I am begging you, get the vaccine': Pockets of fear emerge in Serbia. https://www.theguardian.com/world/2021/mar/25/i-am-begging-you-get-the-vaccine-pockets-of-fear-emerge-in-serbia. Accessed 6 Oct 2021

The Independent (19 May 2010) Rich and powerful: Obama and the global super-elite. The Independent. https://www.independent.co.uk/news/world/politics/rich-and-powerful-obama-and-the-global-super-elite-1976403.html. Accessed 6 Oct 2021

The International Labour Organisation (ILO) (2020) Ilostat. https://ilostat.ilo.org/data/country-profiles/. Accessed 27 May 2021

The National (12 July 2020) How Serbia's lockdown led to an outcry against the authoritarianism. https://www.thenational.scot/news/18577823.serbias-lockdown-led-outcry-authoritarianism/. Accessed 6 Oct 2021

The Organised Crime and Corruption Reporting Project (2015) Person of the year 2015: Milo Djukanovic. https://www.occrp.org/en/poy/2015/. Accessed 6 Oct 2021

Töglhofer T (2019) No time to lose for the EU overcoming the accession stalemate in the Western Balkans", In: *DGAP Policy Briefs*, No. 8 (December 2019), p. 3, https://dgap.org/en/node/33272. Accessed 6 Oct 2021

Vachudova MA (2019) EU enlargement and state capture in the Western Balkans. In: Džankić J, Keil S, Kmezić M (eds) The Europeanisation of the Western Balkans: a failure of EU conditionality? Palgrave Macmillan, London, pp 63–86

V-Dem Institute (2020) University of Gothenburg. Annual Democracy Report 2020
Viborc (2020) Unemployment rates in Europe and Balkans for 2019. https://viborc.com/unemployment-rates-europe-unemployment-rates-balkans/. Accessed 6 Oct 2021
Voice of America (8 December 2018) Thousands protest Serbian President's autocratic rule. https://www.voanews.com/a/thousands-protest-serbian-president-autocratic-rule/4692828.html. Accessed 6 Oct 2021
World Bank & WIIW Vienna Institute for International Economic Studies (March 2019) Western Balkans labour market trends. http://documents1.worldbank.org/curated/en/351461552915471917/pdf/135370-Western-Balkans-Labor-Market-Trends-2019.pdf. Accessed 6 Oct 2021

Chapter 4
Personal Freedoms

4.1 Consideration of the Category and the Term

The categories of this research are artificially created, and it takes effort, often in vain, to justify why specific indices are grouped in the category of personal freedoms while others are in the category of human rights. The shortest answer is that after considering each of the indices' specific features, it became clear that some of them share more characteristics than the others, and therefore, it would follow the logic that they are measured against the same or similar categories. Therefore, five categories have been created, although it was possible to create more groups or even fewer. Whatever the decision, it would always be possible to argue the other way. One solution to this problem would have been to remove all five groups and just have the project as a collection of 20 indices. The final result would be similar to the current one, with just a few countries moving positions slightly but remaining in the same overall categories. This method, however, would deprive the researcher of an insight into the more specific category like economic freedoms or regime, for example. This has led to developing a method of grouping indices that share significant research elements and eventually to this project's five categories.

The first issue arising from this particular category, eventually titled personal freedoms, is how to name it to reflect a group of five indices understood to relate closely to each other. Another issue is to justify excluding some other indices from this group and placing them into the groups like economic freedoms or human rights, or media freedoms. This issue is easier to clarify because the five indices in this group are more closely related than other indices that have been considered within the groups like media freedoms or human rights. Furthermore, some of the indices in this group include elements of economic freedoms but they are just one of the elements for collecting data in creating the particular index. Therefore, these five indices are part of the group of personal freedoms as factors other than economic freedoms dominate the indices' focuses. Admittedly, the issue of aligning political and economic freedoms remains unsolved by this approach. The tables showing

N. Andjelic, *Covid-19, State-Power and Society in Europe*, European Union and its Neighbours in a Globalized World 5, https://doi.org/10.1007/978-3-030-91073-0_4

personal and economic freedoms present us with some surprising results where some states are near the top of the economic freedoms table, but this is not reflected in personal freedoms based mainly on political freedoms.

This all leads back to the issue of naming this group of five indices. During this work, the formulation has been changed several times without a conclusive result. Each time, arguments have been developed against the change. The indices are about citizens' freedom but naming them as such would not reflect specifics of this category and would require the inclusion of several other indices. Individual freedoms might have been the solution, but this brings into question how to address freedoms enjoyed collectively. Private freedoms would be an even more radical attempt to solve the issue and, therefore, not acceptable for this project. The use of human freedom as a term would lead to defining it as "a social concept that recognizes the dignity of individuals and is defined here as negative liberty or the absence of coercive constraint."[1] This index named human freedom "encompasses personal, civil, and economic freedom."[2] If the same name were adopted for the whole group of five indices, it would not adequately reflect the group, nor would it distinguish correctly from other groups.

"Civil liberty," as Hayek suggests, "is too liable to be confused with ... "political liberty","[3] and therefore unhelpful for the creation of the categorised indices of this research. In his *The Constitution of Liberty*, Hayek quotes Abraham Lincoln, who said, "The World has never had a good definition of the word liberty."[4] Hayek later defines "liberty or freedom" as "that condition of men in which coercion of some by others is reduced as much as is possible in society."[5] Karl Popper reiterates, "... there is no freedom if it is not secured by the state; and conversely, only a state which is controlled by free citizens can offer them any reasonable security at all",[6] which leads to the core idea of this project. The state, albeit providing citizens with some freedoms, inevitably coerces its citizens to some extent. In open societies, this coercion is lesser and results in greater freedoms. Therefore, states could be classified in a range between open and closed societies, according to the level of freedoms, rights, citizens engagement, and the rule of law developed and protected by the state. Hayek's thoughts and definitions are providing this research with a critical specific definition: "The state in which a man is not subject to coercion by the arbitrary will of another or others is often also distinguished as "individual" or "personal" freedom."[7]

This work has no space to go significantly out of the focus of the research on state-power and society based on the findings of the 20 indices, thus leaving aside

---

[1] Vásquez and McMahon (2020).

[2] Vásquez and McMahon (2020).

[3] Hayek (2006), p. 11.

[4] Hayek (2006), p. 11.

[5] Hayek (2006), p. 11.

[6] Popper (2020), p. 106.

[7] Hayek (2006), p. 11.

debates that have been present in academia and society for centuries. Among others, John Lock and Immanuel Kant contributed to our understanding of sovereign people, i.e., a group, that "acts against violations of individual liberty and despotic power."[8] "The content and meaning of what we call freedom," Havighurst wrote at the beginning of the Cold War, "changes from one culture to another."[9] "One of the meanings of freedom is absence of constraint," he wrote and added, "freedom from constraint is less important than freedom to act in desired directions."[10] At a similar time, Isiah Berlin delivered his famous lecture and explained the concept of "positive and negative liberty", underlining that no man's activity is so completely private as never to obstruct the lives of others in any way.[11]

After considering different leading authors using terms interchangeably, it is possible to develop a diverse understanding of what are personal, individual, human, or civil freedoms or liberties. This work has opted for the term personal freedom to distinguish it from other freedoms considered for the indices like economic or media freedoms. While terminology might be problematic, the understanding is transparent and based largely on the works and ideas cited.

4.2 The Findings

The Personal Freedom Index has reconfirmed the geographic spread of open and free societies in Western Europe, including all Scandinavian countries and most of the geographic West, and findings gradually decreasing towards the east of the continent. The same four countries, albeit in a different order, Switzerland, Ireland, Finland, and Denmark, are on the top of the general index and the Personal Freedom Index. While the general index has found 11 states with an open society, the Personal Freedom Index has produced 17 "free" societies. Additional 13 countries are found to be "mostly free". This group includes the remaining Western European states and the EU member states, except for Hungary. All the Western Balkans countries are grouped as "moderately free" together with Hungary and three post-Soviet countries Georgia, Moldova, and Armenia. Ukraine is found to have "endangered freedom", and four countries, Russia, Turkey, Belarus, and Azerbaijan, are "not free".

The Personal Freedom Index is compiled from five indices measuring diverse elements under the broad description of personal freedoms. Freedom House has produced an index with only three categories: free, partly free, and not free. They were given numerical values in the overall Personal Freedom Index of one, three and five because the remaining indices have either numerical only values or between four and six categories that were also numericized to enable calculation of the overall

[8] Queiroz (2018).
[9] Havighurst (1952), p. 230.
[10] Havighurst (1952), p. 231.
[11] Berlin (1959), p. 121.

values of freedom. The Freedom House index focused on political rights and civil liberties and "assesses the real-world rights and freedoms enjoyed by individuals, rather than governments or government performance per se."[12]

The Friedrich Naumann Stiftung has produced the Freedom Barometer Index with numerical values. This "is a composite index, which means it consists of data from secondary sources, namely other indices that measure specific aspects of freedom."[13] It is based on three categories, political freedom, the rule of law and economic freedom, with each of them having subcategories that result in numerical values. The multicoloured heatmap of this global index shows European countries in only three colours. For this project, numerical values are used to categorise them into five groups, with none of the countries belonging to the lowest category.

The Foundation for the Advancement of Liberty produced the World Electoral Freedom Index with eight categories; four of them are positive; "Outstanding, Very High, High and Acceptable electoral freedom." The negative categories are "Insufficient, Low, Very Low or Remarkably Low electoral freedom."[14] The marks are based on four sub-indices: political development, active suffrage, passive suffrage, and elector empowerment. Only five European countries are in negative groups of this global index, three of them marked as low, Belarus, Turkey, and Azerbaijan, and two, Armenia and Russia, are found to have insufficient electoral freedom. On the other end, only Ireland and Switzerland are marked as outstanding. The rest of Europe is ranked as with very high or high electoral freedom.

By looking into the Political Development Index, one of the contributing indicators to *The World Electoral Freedom Index*, authored by José Antonio Peña, the order remains almost unchanged. The Western Balkans countries remain in similar positions; Montenegro in 31st, followed by Kosovo in 33rd and then from 35th to 38th place Serbia, Albania, North Macedonia, and Bosnia-Herzegovina.[15]

Some different results, especially regarding Kosovo and Montenegro, are found in the same index 1 year later. However, their lowered scores and the resulting drop in the category of *The World Electoral Freedom Index* of 2020 did not affect these countries overall standing in the Personal Freedoms Index of this project. If these results were applied to the table, Kosovo and Montenegro would be ranked several places lower but remain in the same category as the "Moderately Free" countries.

The Human Freedom Index "presents a broad measure of human freedom, understood as the absence of coercive constraint," based on "76 distinct indicators of personal and economic freedom" in diverse areas such as the rule of law, security and safety, freedoms of movement, religion, assembly, expression, various aspects of legal protection, and economic rights.[16] They marked countries into four categories ranging from "most free" to "least free". The countries of Europe are organised

[12]Freedom House (2019), p. 1.

[13]Friedrich Naumann Foundation (2021).

[14]Peña (2019), p. 42.

[15]Peña (2019), pp. 50–57.

[16]Vásquez and Porčnik (2019).

within two distinct regions, i.e., Eastern and Western Europe. Western Europe is "most free", while there is a mixture in Eastern Europe. The Personal Freedom Index considers countries with an eight and higher index to be in the top category and those between seven and eight in the second-highest group. The Civicus coalition of civil society organisations provided Index on Civic Space with five categories, ranging from "open" to "closed". They "defined [it] as the respect in policy and practice for the freedoms of association, peaceful assembly and expression."[17] This lengthy elaboration of the organising of the Personal Freedom measurements and the index is shown in Table 4.1.

After considering all five indices, taking into account their classification and giving them numerical values, the results have been computed to this project's Personal Freedom Index. It consists of five categories: "Free", "Mostly Free", "Moderately Free", with the "Endangered Freedom", and "Not Free". While there are only four countries that have been classified into the top category by all five indices, there are other 13 countries that all together share the category of "Free". Seven of them have slipped one level in one index, and six have been categorised in the second-best group in two of the five indices. Four former communist countries joined traditionally considered western countries in this group, the three Baltic republics and Czechia.

The next group of "mostly free" countries is a mixture of the rest of western countries and the transitioned central Europe. The following group, titled "moderately free" in this index, are dominated by the Western Balkans, all six countries are here, three post-Soviet states and the worst positioned EU member state, Hungary. Ukraine is the only country with "endangered freedom". The four countries that are found not to be free are Russia, Belarus, Turkey, and Azerbaijan, as shown in Table 4.2.

The countries are commonly put in the same or similar categories across the indices. Most of them are thus in the two neighbouring categories in the indices. However, indices of eleven countries are less homogenous and are spread across three numerically different groups. Belgium's electoral freedom[18] and Italy's freedom barometer[19] are in the third category, which has prevented them from being entirely "free" as the three other indices have these countries in the top category and one in the second-best. Unlike the remaining four indices placing these countries in one of the top two categories, the Freedom Barometer Index has put Malta, Poland, Slovakia, Romania, Croatia, Bulgaria, and Greece into the third category.[20] The Human Freedom Index[21] is unusual in two cases. Armenia stands out because this index puts it in the second-best category, while all other indices put the country in category three or four. The same index found Ukraine in the worst category, unlike

[17] Civicus Monitor (2020).

[18] Peña (2019).

[19] Despotović et al. (2019).

[20] Despotović et al. (2019).

[21] Vásquez and Porčnik (2019).

Table 4.1 Personal freedom

Freedom house Index[a]		Freedom Barometer Index[b]		World Electoral Freedom Index[c]		Human Freedom Index[d]		Civic Space Index[e]		Final		
Status	Index	Status	Index	Status	Index	Status	Index	Status	Index	Index	Status	Point 5–25
Free	1	>80	1	Outstanding/Very high	1	Most free	1	Open	1	1	Free	5–7
		70–80	2	High	2	II	2	Narrowed	2	2	Mostly free	8–11
Partly Free	3	50–70	3	Acceptable	3			Obstructed	3	3	Moderately free	12–15
		40–50	4	Insufficient	4	III	4	Repressed	4	4	Endangered freedom	16–20
Not free	5	<40	5	Low	5	Least free	5	Closed	5	5	Not free	21–25

[a]Freedom House (2020a)
[b]Friedrich Naumann Stiftung (2019a)
[c]Foundation for the Advancement of Liberty (2019)
[d]Cato Institute (2019)
[e]Civicus Monitor (2020)

Table 4.2 Personal Freedom Index

Position	Country	Index	Status	Points	Freedom House Index[a]	Freedom Barometer Index[b]	World Electoral Freedom Index[c]	Human Freedom Index[d]	Civic Space Index[e]
1	Switzerland	1	Free	5	One free	One 84.81	One outstand. 80.77	One 8.82	One open
2	Ireland	1	Free	5	One free	One 81.47	One outstand. 80.98	One 8.52	One open
3	Finland	1	Free	5	One free	One 82.12	One very high 79.96	One 8.53	One open
4	Denmark	1	Free	5	One free	One 81.35	One very high 77.83	One 8.56	One open
5	Sweden	1	Free	6	One free	One 80.44	Two high 74.72	One 8.50	One open
6	Iceland	1	Free	6	One free	Two 79.98	One very high 75.96	One 8.41	One open
7	Estonia	1	Free	6	One free	Two 78.91	One very high 76.50	One 8.46	One open
8	Netherlands	1	Free	6	One free	One 81.10	Two high 72.71	One 8.50	One open
9	Norway	1	Free	6	One free	One 80.67	Two high 73.44	One 8.44	One open
10	Lithuania	1	Free	6	One free	Two 75.51	One very high 75.85	One 8.32	One open
11	Portugal	1	Free	6	One free	Two 74.90	One very high 76.28	One 8.27	One open
12	UK	1	Free	7	One free	Two 79.85	One very high 75.37	One 8.47	Two narrowed
13	Luxembourg	1	Free	7	One free	Two 79.19	Two high 74.80	One 8.56	One open
14	Austria	1	Free	7	One free	Two 77.12	Two high 72.79	One 8.48	One open
15	Germany	1	Free	7	One free	Two 79.09	Two high 70.05	One 8.53	One open
16	Czechia	1	Free	7	One free	Two 74.01	Two high 74.60	One 8.34	One open
17	Latvia	1	Free	7	One free	Two 72.43	One very high 76.38	One 8.29	Two narrowed
18	Slovenia	2	Mostly free	8	One free	Two 73.63	One very high 76.34	Two 7.97	Two narrowed
19	Belgium	2	Mostly free	8	One free	Two 75.94	Three accept. 67.96	One 8.29	One open
20	Spain	2	Mostly free	8	One free	Two 72.88	Two high 71.11	One 8.12	Two narrowed
21	France	2	Mostly free	8	One free	Two 71.79	Two high 72.31	One 8.02	Two narrowed
22	Italy	2	Mostly free	8	One free	Three 67.24	One very high 75.72	One 8.04	Two narrowed
23	Cyprus	2	Mostly free	8	One free	Two 73.40	Two high 70.58	Two 7.93	One open
24	Malta	2	Mostly free	9	One free	Three 69.97	Two high 74.96	One 8.37	Two narrowed
25	Poland	2	Mostly free	9	One free	Three 69.08	One very high 75.91	Two 7.78	Two narrowed

(continued)

Table 4.2 (continued)

Position	Country	Index	Status	Points	Freedom House Index[a]	Freedom Barometer Index[b]	World Electoral Freedom Index[c]	Human Freedom Index[d]	Civic Space Index[e]
26	Slovakia	2	Mostly free	9	One free	Three 69.61	Two high 72.11	One 8.02	Two narrowed
27	Romania	2	Mostly free	9	One free	Three 69.67	Two high 70.14	One 8.11	Two narrowed
28	Croatia	2	Mostly free	10	One free	Three 66.51	Two high 71.51	Two 7.86	Two narrowed
29	Bulgaria	2	Mostly free	10	One free	Three 66.06	Two high 71.21	Two 7.79	Two narrowed
30	Greece	2	Mostly free	11	One free	Three 64.50	Three accept. 68.09	Two 7.33	Two narrowed
31	Kosovo	3	Mod. free	11.7	Three part free	*	Two high 71.22	*	Two narrowed
32	N. Macedonia	3	Mod. free	12	Three part free	Three 59.59	Two high 71.52	Two 7.34	Two narrowed
33	B & H	3	Mod. free	12	Three part free	Three 54.68	Two high 71.17	Two 7.37	Two narrowed
34	Georgia	3	Mod. free	13	Three part free	Three 69.05	Three accept. 66.34	Two 7.74	Two narrowed
35	Montenegro	3	Mod. free	13	Three part free	Three 60.64	Three accept. 67.21	Two 7.43	Two narrowed
36	Hungary	3	Mod. free	13	Three part free	Three 63.37	Two high 71.12	Two 7.65	Three obstructed
37	Albania	3	Mod. free	13	Three part free	Three 62.85	Three accept. 66.10	Two 7.84	Two narrowed
38	Moldova	3	Mod. free	13	Three part free	Three 56.54	Two high 71.70	Three 6.93	Two narrowed
39	Serbia	3	Mod. free	14	Three part free	Three 58.75	Three accept. 67.88	Two 7.30	Three obstructed
40	Armenia	3	Mod. free	15	Three part free	Three 60.15	Four insuff. 61.71	Two 7.42	Three obstructed
41	Ukraine	4	Endangered	17	Three part free	Three 55.84	Three accept. 68.65	Five 6.26	Three obstructed
42	Russia	5	Not free	22	Five not free	Four 45.54	Four insuff. 60.40	Five 6.34	Four repressed
43	Belarus	5	Not free	22.50	Five not free	*	Five low 56.76	Four 6.65	Four repressed
44	Turkey	5	Not free	23	Five not free	Four 50.03	Five low 58.51	Five 6.21	Four repressed
45	Azerbaijan	5	Not free	24	Five not free	Four 44.46	Five low 55.44	Five 6.22	Five closed

[a]Freedom House (2020a, b)
[b]Friedrich Naumann Stiftung (2019a, b)
[c]Foundation for the Advancement of Liberty (2019)
[d]Cato Institute (2019)
[e]Civicus Monitor (2020)

all other indices that have put Ukraine in the third, medium, group. These specific cases of eleven countries categorised by one of the indices significantly different from the other four prove once more the validity of computing different indices and finding a common value, thus potentially serving as a correction of the findings.

4.3 The Western Balkans

Three indices put all six countries of the Western Balkans in the same group. The Freedom House Index found them all "part free",[22] the Freedom Barometer Index has all the countries in the third quality group with values in the range of 54.68 for Bosnia-Herzegovina to 62.85 for Albania as the best ranked,[23] and the Human Freedom Index has all countries in the second-best group, except for Kosovo that was not measured. Serbia was found the worst with an index of 7.30 and Albania the best with an index of 7.84.[24] The Freedom Barometer and Human Freedom indices did not include Kosovo and averages had to be calculated for the country based on the other three indices. The World Electoral Freedom Index has found North Macedonia, Kosovo, and Bosnia-Herzegovina within the second-best group of "high freedom" and Serbia, Montenegro, and Albania in the third category of "acceptable freedom".[25] The Civic Space Index have all the countries with "narrowed civic space" and only Serbia a category lower with "obstructed".[26] The computed results for the six Western Balkans countries are shown in Table 4.3.

"In Montenegro and Serbia," the Freedom House found, "independent journalists, opposition figures, and other perceived foes of the government faced ongoing harassment, intimidation, and sometimes violence. Public frustration with the entrenched ruling parties boiled over into large protests in both countries," the report continues, "but they failed to yield any meaningful change."[27] The report was published before the parliamentary elections in both countries that resulted in an even firmer hold on power by President Vučić in Serbia but, in Montenegro, Đukanović's party lost the majority for the first time in 30 years.

Electoral freedoms are a cause of concern in Albania where "many problems with elections, such as voting irregularities and abuse of administrative resources, remained as an issue."[28] Furthermore, "a weak separation of powers in practice" and the ruling party dominating "over legislative and executive", and having "capabilities to influence the judicial sector", contribute to "undermining democratic

[22] Freedom House (2020a, b).

[23] Despotović et al. (2019).

[24] Vásquez and Porčnik (2019).

[25] Peña (2019).

[26] Civicus Monitor (2020).

[27] Freedom House (2020a, b).

[28] Despotović et al. (2019), p. 34.

Table 4.3 Personal Freedoms in the Western Balkans Index

Position	Country	Index	Status	Points	Freedom House Index[a]	Freedom Barometer Index[b]	World Electoral Freedom Index[c]	Human Freedom Index[d]	Civic Space Index[e]
31	Kosovo	3	Mod. Free	11.7	Three part free	*	Two high 71.22	*	Two narrowed
32	N. Macedonia	3	Mod. Free	12	Three part free	Three 59.59	Two high 71.52	Two 7.34	Two narrowed
33	B & H	3	Mod. Free	12	Three part free	Three 54.68	Two high 71.17	Two 7.37	Two narrowed
35	Montenegro	3	Mod. Free	13	Three part free	Three 60.64	Three accept. 67.21	Two 7.43	Two narrowed
37	Albania	3	Mod. Free	13	Three part free	Three 62.85	Three accept. 66.10	Two 7.84	Two narrowed
39	Serbia	3	Mod. Free	14	Three part free	Three 58.75	Three accept. 67.88	Two 7.30	Three obstructed

[a]Freedom House (2020a, b), p. 24
[b]Friedrich Naumann Stiftung (2019a, b)
[c]Foundation for the Advancement of Liberty (2019)
[d]Cato Institute (2019)
[e]Civicus Monitor (2020)

institutions and decision-making in Albania" where the state officials are "the biggest threat."[29]

The change of government in North Macedonia was forced by protests first and only then, with subtle support of the West, put into place and legitimised. Thus, the country is the only European state among the top gainers. It came forth gainer globally, in the Freedom House Report.[30] However, it is a question of the level of democracy in the country if the people's will expressed in the referendum on the name change was not respected. The recently established liberal elite did not get support for the name change at the referendum in September 2018 because of the insufficient turnout. Nevertheless, the parliamentary majority adopted the change of the name. The West showed their support by a follow-up process of adopting the country into the NATO alliance.

In Kosovo, "many corrupt officials . . . continued to occupy public sector positions." The "reported instances of senior officials engaging in corruption or acting with impunity" are underlined in a report.[31] Years of domination of Kosovo politics by parties accused of corruption resulted in a shift towards populism and a consequent victory of Vetëvendosje (Movement for self-determination). Despite the previous numerous violent incidents in the parliament, some of which have been instigated by this party's members, it was the electoral process that brought about the change.

The "high freedom" status of the electoral freedom in Bosnia-Herzegovina proves frequency and generally peaceful periodical elections, but the change of government proved to be impossible. "Strong societal division along ethnic lines is constantly maintained by the established nationalistic parties, alongside of the political system created by Dayton agreement which favors [Sic!] those parties, ensuring their constant dominance at almost all executive levels of power,"[32] the barometer found. The electoral process is overseen by the commission that is supposed to act independently. However, the members are appointed by institutions made up of ruling parties' members, and the decisions often correspond to the parties' will. The judiciary is also filled with appointments approved by the dominating nationalist movements. The media is under constant pressure and often dependant on the ruling elites for government contracts. The collaborative pro-government media are spared of frequent tax, health and safety, or other forms of inspections. These inspections are being used as an instrument of pressure on independent media. This all contributes to a deadlock in the country that cannot be broken without the legislative change and the new constitutional set up.

[29] Despotović et al. (2019), p. 35.

[30] Freedom House (2020a, b), p. 11.

[31] U.S. Department of State (2020) Country Reports on Human Rights Practices: Kosovo.

[32] Despotović et al. (2019), p. 52.

4.4 Struggle for New Liberties and Equality in Western Balkans

The lack of rights of the population of minority sexual orientation is symptomatic of all minority groups. After several years of banning the "gay-pride" parade in Belgrade because of hostile messages from right-wing organisations and police declaring an inability to protect marchers, Aleksandar Vučić in 2014 promised safety for marchers. He made state institutions do their job and secure the parade, provide safety to all citizens, and enable civil liberties, at least for one afternoon. Montenegrin police, a year earlier, rescued the first gay-pride demonstrators from angry crowds while the then Prime-Minister Đukanović condemned the violence saying, "if the government's policy is to support the rights of all people, if we adopt strategies to protect the rights of all minorities, including sexual, then we have to act that way too."[33] In 2017, the pride parade in Belgrade was attended by the new Prime Minister, Ana Brnabić, the first women and the first lesbian heading the government in Serbia and who was appointed by President Vučić earlier that year.

These symbolic, rather than substantial gestures, are made to please western powers upon whom all Western Balkan countries are dependant. Even when securing the incident-free pride festivals, the strong leaders make sure their electorate understands their personal opposition to such sexual orientation. After making sure the pride would go ahead in 2014, Vučić had "other things to do instead of marching." He stressed that "even if I did not have other things to do, I would not march. That is my choice. It is my choice if I go out with my kids on Sunday or to go . . . to work."[34]

Western diplomats make their point by joining the marchers, making authorities oblige to provide security and prevent hostile reactions. The diplomats marched in Tirana in 2013, the Pristina based diplomats were joined at the beginning of the march by President Hashim Thaçi in 2017, and western diplomats marched in Skopje and Sarajevo in 2019. Unlike in Rama's Albania and North Macedonia under the post-Gruevski government, there was no political office in Bosnia-Herzegovina that secured the parade in Sarajevo, the last Western Balkans capital to stage the pride parade.

The Islamic Community pulled triggers behind the scenes and used its influence over the Bosniak nationalist SDA party that ensured the incident free pride. The political vision of Muslim religious leaders in Sarajevo proved to be probably more progressive and certainly more pragmatic than that of the nationalist SDA party, which positions itself as a conservative party based on traditional values and whose powerholders did nothing for years when activists attempted to stage the parade. The Islamic Community officially underlined its opposition to "non-traditional" lifestyles and called on the faithful not to attend the parade, but, at the same time,

---

[33] Reuters (24 July 2013).

[34] Balkan Insight (25 September 2014).

local imams were ordered to instruct their followers to be civil and non-violent toward those with whom they disagree on particular lifestyle choices. Bosnia-Herzegovina officially has a secular setup, but the practices from education to public life show religious leaders' critical role. They have influence "in shaping public opinion and have got significant influence on decision making."[35]

The unusual, albeit unofficial, position of the Islamic Community in Sarajevo that effectively enabled an incident-free parade stands in contrast with most religious leaders elsewhere in the Western Balkans. The Patriarch of Serb Orthodox Church, Irinej, called on Belgrade authorities in 2012 to ban the parade by calling it a "tragicomic parade of shame."[36] Religious leaders usually support counter-events on such occasions. Some of the faithful followed Friday prayers in Sarajevo mosques by a protest march on the eve of the pride. Elsewhere in North Macedonia, "Christian priests from various denominations, members of the Muslim community, and Roman Catholic nuns attended"[37] the counter-event in Skopje showing their opposition to the set of liberal values and equality.

Both the government, except for a minor coalition party, and the opposition supported the parade in Tirana. However, the Muslim community representative argued that "such public demonstration is an abuse of human rights and freedoms and presents a danger for the morals and tradition of the Albanian family." At the same time, the Catholic Church spokesman observed that "homosexuality is opposed to the natural order and the morals of society."[38] Thus religious leaders across the Western Balkans reflect the perception of a "conservative region."[39] Even politicians whose policies are liberal and who are perceived as such, like Zoran Zaev in North Macedonia, contribute to the idea of the dominance of conservative ideas. When asked about a case of corruption involving a detained businessman, the Prime Minister said he would not allow "a few criminals, one vain journalist and, I apologize in advance to the LGBTI community, a faggot, to topple the government."[40]

The legislation in all the Western Balkans countries is positively addressing equality, liberties, and rights. The practices, however, show the real problems. The discussion of the rights and freedoms of persons with different sexual preferences is reminiscent of all minority policies and gender inequality. Incidents committed by elected politicians across the political spectrum confirm that the political class either imposes its values upon the society while paying lip service to universal values and adopting legislation to step up European integrations or is reflecting the society and the traditional values found in the community.

---

[35] Despotović et al. (2019), p. 53.

[36] B92 (3 October 2012).

[37] DW – Deutsche Welle (29 June 2019).

[38] Pink News UK (26 March 2012).

[39] DW – Deutsche Welle (29 June 2019).

[40] Balkan Insight (14 August 2019).

Bosniak nationalist leader Bakir Izetbegović attracts criticisms for his policies that are often reflected in observations about his wife, Sebija, a Sarajevo hospital general manager. She is compared to Elena Ceausescu in Romania and Mira Marković in Serbia.[41] "It is only your wife that you lost control of,"[42] was a remark by an opposition politician following public concerns with tackling the pandemic and high mortality rates in Sarajevo. Besides the plentiful and evident failings that the Izetbegović couple showed in their public work, it was the gender that provided the basis of some instances of criticism. On another occasion, it was alleged that following the conclusions of Izetbegović's party's highest political body; he came home to hear his wife saying, "forget the conclusions. I will tell you what to do."[43]

During just 1 month, Reporting Diversity Network reported 20 instances "related to sexist and misogynist narratives across Western Balkan media that targeted female politicians, journalists and other public figures, perpetuated rape victim-blaming and placed women on usual margins of media reporting and society."[44] The report provides examples from all the countries. Following the several actresses coming out with stories of rape, they were faced in Serbia with "perpetuated continuous targeting and victimisation" and "victim blaming narratives" in media. A female Prime Minister, therefore, does not change the general situation. A leading journalist in Montenegro was described as a "biological entity with human shape and female attributes". Women groups in North Macedonia demanded action from the Public Prosecutor in the case of a sexist social media group. A female candidate for the president of Kosovo faced sexist verbal attacks. Perhaps some progress might be observed as she was eventually elected. Entertainment shows provide public with plenty of examples of sexism in Albania and Serbia. As the media is watched across national borders and entertainers were the first to follow criminals in cross-border activities, the influence is pan-regional. The report concludes that it "looked at other diversity categories as well, sexism has been a cross cutting issue that was detected in all the countries."[45]

The situation found at the start of the pandemic even deteriorated across the globe, as the UN Secretary-General stated. "The virus is also infecting political and civil rights, and further shrinking civic space," wrote António Guterres in The Guardian. He pointed that "divisive approaches, authoritarianism and nationalism make no sense against a global threat."[46] However, this kind of rule is widespread in the Western Balkans and is on the rise globally.

[41] Dnevni avaz (13 December 2020a, b).

[42] Dnevni avaz (3 April 2021).

[43] Press Media (27 November 2020).

[44] Reporting Diversity Network 2.0 (2021).

[45] Reporting Diversity Network 2.0 (2021).

[46] Guterres (22 February 2021).

References

B92 (2012) Serbian patriarch calls for ban of gay parade, exhibit. https://www.b92.net/eng/news/society.php?yyyy=2012&mm=10&dd=03&nav_id=82467. (3 October 2012) Accessed 6 Oct 2021

Balkan Insight (25 September 2014) Serbian PM to give gay pride a miss. https://balkaninsight.com/2014/09/25/vucic-says-no-to-belgrade-pride-march/. Accessed 6 Oct 2021

Balkan Insight (14 August 2019) North Macedonia's Zaev Condemned for Calling Detainee "Faggot". https://balkaninsight.com/2019/08/14/north-macedonias-zaev-condemned-for-calling-detainee-faggot/. Accessed 6 Oct 2021

Berlin I (1959) Two concepts of liberty, in four essays on liberty. Oxford University Press, Oxford, pp 118–172

Cato Institute (2019) Human freedom index. https://www.cato.org/sites/cato.org/files/2021-03/human-freedom-index-2020.pdf. Accessed 1 May 2021

Civicus Monitor (2020) National civic space ratings. https://findings2020.monitor.civicus.org/europe-central-asia.html. Accessed 1 May 2021

Despotović I, Gamser D, Gajić M (2019) Freedom barometer Europe. Friedrich Neumann Foundation for Liberty. http://freedombarometer.org/files/download/Freedom_Barometer_Europe_2019.pdf. Accessed 6 Oct 2021

Deutsche Welle - DW (29 June 2019) First gay pride rally held in North Macedonia. https://www.dw.com/en/first-gay-pride-rally-held-in-north-macedonia/a-49413815. Accessed 6 Oct 2021

Dnevni Avaz (19 July 2020a) Podaci zvaničnih institucija otkrivaju: Uvoz testova za koronu postaje unosan biznis. https://avaz.ba/vijesti/bih/582690/podaci-zvanicnih-institucija-otkrivaju-uvoz-testova-za-koronu-postaje-unosan-biznis. Accessed 6 Oct 2021

Dnevni avaz (13 December 2020b) Hoće li Sebija ugasiti SDA i karijeru supruga Bakira kao što su Elena i Mira srušile vlast svojih muževa. https://avaz.ba/vijesti/bih/616063/hoce-li-sebija-ugasiti-sda-i-karijeru-supruga-bakira-kao-sto-su-elena-i-mira-srusile-vlast-svojih-muzeva. Accessed 6 Oct 2021

Dnevni avaz (3 April 2021) Muzur odgovorio Izetbegoviću: Ovdje je jedino tebi tvoja žena iskliznula iz ruku.https://avaz.ba/vijesti/bih/642271/muzur-odgovorio-izetbegovicu-ovdje-je-jedino-tebi-tvoja-zena-iskliznula-iz-ruku. Accessed 6 Oct 2021

Foundation for the Advancement of Liberty (2019) World electoral freedom index. https://fundalib.org/world-election-freedom-index-wefi-2020/?lang=en. Accessed 6 Oct 2021

Freedom House (2019) Freedom and the Media 2019. https://freedomhouse.org/report/freedom-and-media/2019/media-freedom-downward-spiral. Accessed 1 May 2021

Freedom House (2020a) Freedom in the World 2020. https://freedomhouse.org/report/freedom-world/2020/leaderless-struggle-democracy. Accessed 1 May 2021

Freedom House (2020b) Nations in transit. https://freedomhouse.org/report/nations-transit/2020/dropping-democratic-facade. Accessed 27 Mar 2021

Friedrich Naumann Foundation (2021) Methodology of freedom barometer: measuring freedom. http://freedombarometer.org/about-us/methodology/. Accessed 6 Oct 2021

Friedrich Naumann Stiftung (2019a) Freedom Barometer index. http://freedombarometer.org/files/download/Freedom_Barometer_Europe_2019.pdf. Accessed 1 May 2021

Friedrich Naumann Stiftung (2019b) Human Rights Index. https://www.freiheit.org/sites/default/files/import/2020-02/21969-humanrightsindex2019.pdf. Accessed 1 May 2021

Guterres A (2021) The world faces a pandemic of human rights abuses in the wake of Covid-19. The Guardian. (22 February 2021) https://www.theguardian.com/global-development/2021/feb/22/world-faces-pandemic-human-rights-abuses-covid-19-antonio-guterres. Accessed 6 Oct 2021

Havighurst R (1952) Personal freedom: its meaning for international understanding. Bull Am Assoc Univ Professors (1915–1955) 38(2):230–243. https://doi.org/10.2307/40220888

Hayek F (2006) The constitution of liberty. Routledge, London

Peña JA (2019) World electoral freedom index. Foundation for the advancement of liberty. Available from https://fundalib.org/wp-content/uploads/2020/10/IMLE-2020.pdf. Accessed 3 Oct 2021

Pink News UK (2012) Albania: Proposed gay pride march provokes homophobic comments. (26 March 2012). https://www.pinknews.co.uk/2012/03/26/albania-proposed-gay-pride-march-provokes-homophobic-comments/. Accessed 6 Oct 2021

Popper K (2020) Open society and its enemies. Princeton classics paperback edition

Press Media (2020) Vrh SDA dogovorio da adekvatno odgovori na afere, a onda je Bakir Izetbegović otišao kući gdje ga je dočekala supruga Sebija... (27 November 2020). https://pressmedia.ba/vijesti/2020/27/11/vrh-sda-dogovorio-da-adekvatno-odgovori-na-afere-a-onda-je-bakir-izetbegovic-otisao-kuci-gdje-ga-je-docekala-supruga-sebija/?fbclid=IwAR1I-reTw6yaat2OGODrLkqweK5GjEedXbTNLGwHAYKHw-PMSudzkn1TVUg. Accessed 6 Oct 2021

Queiroz R (2018) Individual liberty and the importance of the concept of the people. Palgrave Communications. https://doi.org/10.1057/s41599-018-0151-3

Reporting Diversity Network 2.0 (2021) Monthly monitoring highlight: sexism in the Western Balkans. https://www.reportingdiversity.org/sexism-in-the-western-balkans-monthly-monitoring-highlight/. Accessed 6 Oct 2021

Reuters (2013) Violent protests disrupt Montenegro's first gay pride parade. (24 July 2013) https://uk.reuters.com/article/montenegro-gay-parade/violent-protests-disrupt-montenegros-first-gay-pride-parade-idINDEE96N0CC20130724. Accessed 6 Oct 2021

U.S. Department of State (2020) Country reports on human rights practices: Kosovo. https://www.state.gov/reports/2020-country-reports-on-human-rights-practices/kosovo/. Accessed 6 Oct 2021

Vásquez I, McMahon F (2020) Human freedom index. Cato Institute and Fraser Institute, Washington, D.C., Vancouver. https://www.cato.org/human-freedom-index/2020 Accessed 31 Mar 2021

Vásquez I, Porčnik T (2019) Human freedom index. Cato Institute, Fraser Institute, Friedrich Naumann Foundation for Freedom, Washington, D.C., Vancouver, Potsdam. https://www.fraserinstitute.org/sites/default/files/human-freedom-index-2019-rev.pdf. Accessed 31 Mar 2021

Chapter 5
Dissonant Findings of Economic Freedoms and Social Mobility

5.1 Diversity of Economic Freedoms in European Countries

Sixteen countries are found in the top category of this project's Economic Freedoms and Social Mobility Index. Like in most categories, Switzerland and Ireland are heading the list and are followed by many Scandinavian and western countries. The three Baltic republics and Czechia make up the rest of this index's "Free" category. The next category of "Mostly Free" is made up of 14 countries. There is no geographical determination of this diverse group that includes island nations in the Mediterranean, three western countries, several post-communist countries in central Europe, Caucasus, and North Macedonia and Albania from the Western Balkans. Eleven even more diverse countries hold a "Moderately Free" status as the group includes Turkey and Russia, besides states from other regions. The remaining four countries from the Western Balkans are in this group. "Mostly Unfree" is the status given to Belarus and Greece, while Ukraine is the only country in the category "Least Free".

This particular index is created by computing the indices titled as indices of "economic freedoms". Unlike several other indices that take some elements of economic freedoms in producing a human freedom index or other personal freedom indices, there are only three specifically economic freedom indices that cover all European countries. The Heritage Foundation produces the Index of Economic Freedom[1] and the Fraser Institute publishes the Economic Freedom of the World Index.[2] The World Bank provides data developed from several diverse indicators that include the Index of Economic Freedom Score[3] that, in turn, is based on the Heritage Foundation's index. This is not an uncommon feature as some other organisations rely on data and indices, or some elements of them, produced, like

[1] The Heritage Foundation (2020) Index of Economic Freedom.

[2] Gwartney et al. (2019) Economic Freedom of the World: 2019 Annual Report.

[3] The World Bank (2018) Index of Economic Freedom Score.

N. Andjelic, *Covid-19, State-Power and Society in Europe*, European Union and its Neighbours in a Globalized World 5, https://doi.org/10.1007/978-3-030-91073-0_5

in this case, by institutions not dissimilar to the Heritage Foundation or, in the case of the Article 19th's Freedom of Expression Index, compiled and produced by the V-Dem Institute. The fourth index is somewhat incompatible and contrasting. The World Economic Forum's Social Mobility Index[4] is focused on different measures than economic indices. However, it is of importance to have slightly dissonant findings in one of the indices.

The three economic indices based on the two data are ideologically looking into the least constrained economic conditions where the state avoids interference into economic freedoms. As such, conditions inevitably lead towards a specific ideological position that is personified in the teachings and policies of some leading economists, like Milton Friedman, who successfully advised several right-wing governments globally. The resulting positive economic achievements also led to a rise in inequality and polarisation of societies following the introduction of such policies and economic freedoms. Therefore, it was necessary to introduce a "counter-index" like the one on social mobility that possibly balances some of the more socially painful aspects of economic freedoms. The libertarian ideology that partly resulted from Friedman and some other leading economists in advisory roles to Ronald Reagan and Margaret Thatcher has in some ways worked negatively towards the open society. After all, it was Thatcher who said, "there is no such thing as society."[5] This dominant libertarian ideological position, for some time, might mislead the findings on the condition of the society and the role of the state.

Therefore, an additional index focussed on social mobility, as an important feature of individual freedoms, was added to the indices on purely economic freedoms. When considered together, the four indices produce results that offer a broader understanding of the society than the view based on purely economic freedoms. Additional indicators taken into account by the World Economic Forum's index provide the necessary correction that does not have to be understood in simple ideological terms. However, they add elements that enable a more thorough understanding of the state-power and society. Authors of this index have taken into account "policies, practices and institutions that collectively determine the extent to which everyone in society has a fair chance to fulfil their potential, regardless of their socio-economic background, the origin of their parents, or the place where they were born."[6]

The Index of Economic Freedom is developed on four pillars: the rule of law, government size, regulatory efficiency, and open markets.[7] Authors of the Economic Freedom of the World Index used this definition: "The cornerstones of economic freedom are personal choice, voluntary exchange, freedom to enter markets and compete, and security of the person and privately owned property."[8] The Fraser

[4] World Economic Forum (2020) Social Mobility Index 2020.

[5] Thatcher (8 April 2013).

[6] World Economic Forum (2020).

[7] The Heritage Foundation (2019).

[8] Gwartney et al. (2019).

Institute's index is based upon and developed on "objective components [that] are preferred to those that involve surveys or value judgments."[9] Even the highly sophisticated set of measures and a clear research position of this index was self-challenged to recognise that pure numerical findings might not necessarily provide a complete and clear picture of the state of affairs. While the creators recognised that "it was necessary to remove ideological strictness of the economic indices that rely on free given the multi-dimensional nature of economic freedom and the importance of legal and regulatory elements," they also acknowledged that "it is sometimes necessary to use data based on surveys, expert panels, and generic case studies."[10]

The Heritage Foundation clarifies their methods and understandings of "the goal of economic freedom [that] is not simply the absence of government coercion or constraint, but rather the creation and maintenance of a mutual sense of liberty for all."[11] It is "societal norms, not government laws and regulations," the same authors argue, that "are the primary regulator of behavior (Sic!)."[12] The argument follows that government-imposed constraints in democracy "is no less a constraint than one imposed by an absolute ruler or oligarch," which inevitably leads towards the conclusion that "the degree of economic freedom" is determined by "the extent to which government has limits beyond which it may not, or at least does not, go," regardless of the type of government.[13]

This all provides the basis of the argument that liberty for all, as a goal of economic freedom, cannot be genuinely achieved even with minimal governmental and societal constraints if significant parts of the society have restricted social mobility due to economic freedoms. Therefore, the Social Mobility Index "corrects" the reputable economic freedom indices and contributes to this project's Economic Freedom and Social Mobility Index that is contributing to the final Index of State-Power and Society. "As such," authors of the Human Freedom Index argue, "economic freedom is not just inherently valuable; it empowers individuals to exercise other freedoms."[14] A possible conclusion on the nature of the state and the quality of the society must be looked at in the context of and interaction with other freedoms.

Frankly, an open society cannot exist if social mobility is significantly restricted to large groups of individuals within the society. If the price for providing greater social mobility is a particular element of government's coercion, it will affect economic freedoms understood per se in purely economic measures and create less free societies understood on this basis. However, the same measures, if providing for greater social mobility, would be understood positively and contribute to greater liberty for all. They would help develop and create an open society as a symbol of the

[9] Gwartney et al. (2019), p. 2.

[10] Gwartney et al. (2019), p. 2.

[11] The Heritage Foundation (2019), p. 8.

[12] The Heritage Foundation (2019), p. 8.

[13] The Heritage Foundation (2019), p. 8.

[14] Vásquez and McMahon (2020) Human Freedom Index.

greatest possible levels of individual and collective freedoms in the systems based on a nation-state, as shown by Table 5.1.

Over the quarter of a century during which the Index of Economic Freedom has been published annually, some countries, like Georgia and Lithuania, were making huge strides in economic freedom. However, Azerbaijan and Bosnia-Herzegovina increased their number of points most significantly as their initial position was far lower in 1995.[15] The Baltic republics, "all of which have become "mostly free" economies, have reformed their economies, shrunk the size of their governments, opened their markets, and let the talents of their people emerge."[16]

The same index has categorised only two European countries, Greece, and Ukraine, that "have economies that are rated 'mostly unfree'."[17] This reflects the political and security situation in Ukraine. Greece's economic freedoms have been affected by the sovereign debt crisis, imposed austerity measures under the dictate from Brussels, and the rule until mid-2019 by the left-wing coalition government led by *Syriza*. Russia scored just above these two countries, and yet the researchers have found that the Russian "government pursues statist, nationalist, and protectionist economic policies." The same report describes further "subservient judiciary, rampant corruption, and links among bureaucrats and organized criminal groups."[18]

There are 22 other countries in the same group as Russia, according to this index. Such a large group, just over a half of all countries indexed, is diverse and includes some European Union founding members and many new members with the past marked by planned economies, and several non-EU countries with a similar communist past. Although they have different numerical scores, they belong to the same group that starts with Malta and ends with Russia. The differences between the 23 countries could be understood better by using another index where only five European states are in the same group as Russia.[19] Greece is one of them, but it does not share the group in the Heritage's index. This leaves Turkey, Azerbaijan, Bosnia-Herzegovina, and Belarus as countries that, together with Russia, share the same categories in two indices, and many of the descriptions about Russia could be applied to them. When the World Bank's index is added, that is based on the Heritage Foundation's index but is not categorised in the same way, and the countries are only given numerical values of the index,[20] there are only Belarus and Russia of these countries in the same group.

The combination of the indices provides a possibility for a more detailed view into the economic freedoms found in the countries and groups together those who share more similarities. This particular case, based around Russia's findings, narrowed these to the two. Moldova and Greece are the most similar to Russia and

[15]The Heritage Foundation (2019), p. 4.

[16]The Heritage Foundation (2019), p. XI.

[17]The Heritage Foundation (2020), p. 84.

[18]The Heritage Foundation (2020), p. 90.

[19]Gwartney et al. (2019).

[20]The World Bank (2018).

Table 5.1 Economic freedoms and social mobility indexing

Index of Economic Freedom[a]		Economic Freedom Index[b]		Index of Economic Freedom Score[c]		Social Mobility Index[d]		Final		
Status	Index	Status	Index	Status	Index	Status	Index	Points 4–18	Status	Index
Free	1	Most free	1	70+	1	75–85	1	4–6	Free	1
Mostly free	2	II Quartile	2	65–70	2	65–75	2	7–9	Mostly free	2
Moderately free	3	III Quartile	3	60–65	3	55–65	3	10–12	Moderately free	3
Mostly unfree	4	Least free	4	55–60	4	45–55	4	13–15	Mostly unfree	4
Repressed	5			50–55	5			16–18	Least free	5

[a]The Heritage Foundation (2020) Index of Economic Freedom
[b]Fraser Institute (2018) Economic Freedom Index
[c]The World Bank (2018) Index of Economic Freedom Score
[d]World Economic Forum (2020) Social Mobility Index 2020

Belarus in the World Bank's index. This makes two out of three indices finding the state of economic freedoms similar in these countries. The same findings, but according to the different two indices, is to be found in Azerbaijan and Bosnia-Herzegovina. Turkey also shares findings with Russia in two indices, but the third index puts it two categories above Russia.

This all defines the state of economic freedoms in Russia as the most similar to the situation in Belarus. There are many similarities to be found in Moldova, Azerbaijan, Bosnia-Herzegovina, and Greece. Economic freedoms in Turkey should be slightly distinguished when the research deploys three indices. Belarus, Azerbaijan and Bosnia-Herzegovina were not measured by the Social Mobility Index. Nevertheless, Russia shares the score with Greece and Moldova, while Turkey fares worse than Russia. This index adds a few more countries in this same category, but as they did not share findings with Russia in other categories, the focus is not on them. Altogether, the inclusion of the three indices and combining their findings sets up the data for the analysis. As explained earlier, the fourth index brings the whole process into the broader context of this project and addresses elements of individual liberties in the open society. Could society be free if a group of individuals have restricted opportunities for social mobilities?

If the fourth index were not added, countries like Sweden and Norway would not end up in the group with the highest economic freedoms and would not be in the top category of the "open society" in the overall Index of State-Power and Society because of this. Nevertheless, these two countries certainly are states with an open society as they came joint sixth in the overall table. Several other countries also improved their score when the social mobility aspect was added to the index.

The UK was found by the economic indices to be third, just below Ireland and Switzerland, but the social mobility factor lowered its overall ranking to the tenth position. It certainly reflects the strong presence of the tradition of class society, and it would not be a just result if this were not incorporated into the findings. Georgia's position was scaled even more from sixth to 18th place, but more importantly, the country was not in the top category any longer. Armenia remained in the same category but was dropped from the 18th to 30th position in the table. Slovenia and France improved their category with the addition of the Social Mobility Index. Overall, the majority of the countries have similar results in the indices of this category. The World Economic Forum did not include six countries in their Social Mobility Index, four of which are from the Western Balkans. Therefore, average results for the other indices had to be calculated from their findings, as presented in Table 5.2.

5.2 Economic Freedoms in the Western Balkans

The World Economic Forum has included only Albania and Serbia as the countries from the Western Balkans in their Social Mobility Index. Serbia achieved a better score, i.e., 63.8, to Albania's 55.6 in the index where the top country, Denmark's

Table 5.2 Economic freedoms and Social Mobility Index

Position	Country	Index	Status	Points	Index of Economic Freedom[a]	Economic Freedom Index[b]	Index of Econ. Freedom Score[c]	Social Mobility Index[d]
1	Switzerland	1	Free	4	One 82.0 free	One 8.43 most free	One 81.7	One 82.1
2	Ireland	1	Free	4	One 80.9 free	One 8.13 most free	One 80.4	One 75.0
3	Denmark	1	Free	5	Two 78.3 mostly free	One 8.10 most free	One 76.6	One 85.2
4	Iceland	1	Free	5	Two 77.1 mostly free	One 7.71 most free	One 77.0	One 82.7
5	Netherlands	1	Free	5	Two 77.0 mostly free	One 7.82 most free	One 76.2	One 82.4
6	Finland	1	Free	5	Two 75.7 mostly free	One 7.76 most free	One 74.1	One 83.6
7	Luxembourg	1	Free	5	Two 75.8 mostly free	One 7.75 most free	One 76.4	One 79.8
8	Germany	1	Free	5	Two 73.5 mostly free	One 7.85 most free	One 74.2	One 78.8
9	Austria	1	Free	5	Two 73.3 mostly free	One 7.80 Most Free	One 71.8	One 80.1
10	UK	1	Free	6	Two 79.3 mostly free	One 8.08 most free	One 78.0	Two 74.4
11	Sweden	1	Free	6	Two 74.9 mostly free	Two 7.58 II Quartile	One 76.3	One 83.5
12	Estonia	1	Free	6	Two 77.7 mostly free	One 7.96 most free	One 78.8	Two 73.5
13	Norway	1	Free	6	Two 73.4 Mostly Free	Two 7.60 II Quartile	One 74.3	One 83.6
14	Lithuania	1	Free	6	Two 76.7 mostly free	One 8.10 most free	One 75.3	Two 70.5
15	Czechia	1	Free	6	Two 74.8 mostly free	One 7.81 most free	One 74.2	Two 74.7
16	Latvia	1	Free	6	Two 71.9 mostly free	One 7.89 most free	One 73.6	Two 69.0
17	Malta	2	Mostly free	7	Three 69.5 mod. free	One 7.94 most free	Two 68.5	One 75.0
18	Georgia	2	Mostly free	7	Two 77.1 mostly free	One 8.18 most free	One 76.2	Three 55.6
19	Cyprus	2	Mostly free	7	Two 70.1 mostly free	One 7.84 Most Free	Two 67.8	Two 69.4
20	Belgium	2	Mostly free	8	Three 68.9 mod. free	Two 7.56 II Quartile	Two 67.5	One 80.1
21	Bulgaria	2	Mostly free	8	Two 70.2 Mostly Free	One 7.74 Most Free	Two 68.3	Three 63.8
22	Spain	2	Mostly free	8	Three 66.9 mod. free	One 7.73 most free	Two 65.1	Two 70.0
23	Slovakia	2	Mostly free	8	Three 66.8 mod. free	One 7.63 most free	Two 65.3	Two 68.5
24	N. Macedonia	2	Mostly free	8*	Three 69.5 mod. free	Two 7.15 II Quartile	One 71.3	*

(continued)

Table 5.2 (continued)

Position	Country	Index	Status	Points	Index of Economic Freedom[a]	Economic Freedom Index[b]	Index of Econ. Freedom Score[c]	Social Mobility Index[d]
25	Slovenia	2	Mostly free	9	Three 67.8 mod. free	Two 7.33 II Quartile	Three 64.8	One 76.4
26	France	2	Mostly free	9	Three 66.0 mod. free	Two 7.40 II Quartile	Three 63.9	One 76.7
27	Romania	2	Mostly free	9	Three 69.7 mod. free	One 7.83 most free	Two 69.4	Three 63.1
28	Poland	2	Mostly free	9	Three 69.1 mod. free	Two 7.04 II Quartile	Two 68.5	Two 69.1
29	Hungary	2	Mostly free	9	Three 66.4 mod. free	Two 7.44 II Quartile	Two 66.7	Two 65.8
30	Armenia	2	Mostly free	9	Two 70.6 mostly free	One 7.92 Most Free	Two 68.7	Four 53.9
31	Albania	2	Mostly free	9	Three 66.9 mod. free	One 7.80 most free	Two 64.5	Three 55.6
32	Portugal	3	Mod. free	10	Three 67.0 mod. free	Two 7.60 II Quartile	Three 63.4	Two 72.0
33	Italy	3	Mod. free	10	Three 63.8 mod. free	Two 7.51 II Quartile	Three 62.5	Two 67.4
34	Croatia	3	Mod. free	10	Three 62.2 mod. free	Two 7.36 II Quartile	Three 61.0	Two 66.7
35	Kosovo	3	Mod. free	10*	Three 67.4 mod. free	*	Two 66.6	*
36	Montenegro	3	Mod. free	10.66*	Three 61.5 mod. free	Two 6.94 II Quartile	Three 64.3	*
37	Serbia	3	Mod. free	11	Three 66.0 mod. free	Two 7.05 II Quartile	Three 62.5	Three 63.8
38	Moldova	3	Mod. free	12	Three 62.0 mod. free	Two 6.99 II Quartile	Four 58.4	Three 59.6
39	Turkey	3	Mod. free	12	Three 64.4 mod. free	Three 6.62 III Quartile	Two 65.4	Four 51.3
40	Azerbaijan	3	Mod. free	12*	Three 69.3 mod. free	Three 6.37 III Quartile	Three 64.3	*
41	B & H	3	Mod. free	12*	Three 62.6 mod. free	Three 6.90 III Quartile	Three 61.4	*
42	Russia	3	Mod. free	13	Three 61.0 Mod. Free	Three 6.74 III Quartile	Four 58.2	Three 64.7
43	Belarus	4	Mostly unfree	13.33	Three 61.7 mod. free	Three 6.35 III Quartile	Four 58.1	*
44	Greece	4	Mostly unfree	14	Four 59.9 mostly unfree	Three 6.71 III Quartile	Four 57.3	Three 59.8
45	Ukraine	5	Least free	16	Four 54.9 mostly unfree	Four 6.06 least free	Five 51.9	Three 61.2

[a]The Heritage Foundation (2020)
[b]Fraser Institute (2018)
[c]The World Bank (2018)
[d]World Economic Forum (2020)

score is 85.2, and the lowest-ranked country globally 34.5. The lowest score of the indexed European country is Turkey's at 51.3.[21] Both countries were found to have the best indicators in the first pillar that covers health. Albania's score was 78.9 out of 100,[22] and Serbia's was 78.0. The latter came close to this score in the third pillar covering Education Quality and Equity with a score of 74.2.[23]

The overall Index of Economic Freedoms and Social Mobility was not affected, and Albania is found to be "mostly free" while Serbia is "moderately free". The index for other countries has to rely on the three economic indices, except for Kosovo that is not covered by the Fraser Institute's index. The same index has found Albania in the top group of countries with economic freedom, Bosnia-Herzegovina is placed in the "III Quartile", and the rest of the Western Balkans is in between, part of the "II Quartile". The Index of Economic Freedom placed all these countries in the same group. This leaves the World Bank's findings to differentiate these countries. North Macedonia has the best score in this index, followed by Kosovo and Albania. Montenegro and Serbia are further distant with their scores, and Bosnia-Herzegovina is the lowest placed Western Balkans country.

This has all been reflected in the overall Economic Freedoms and Social Mobility Index. Almost all countries from the region are, like in other indices, grouped closely together, shows Table 5.3. Albania is in the 31st position. Kosovo, Montenegro, and Serbia are placed from 35th to 37th, and Bosnia-Herzegovina is in 41st place. It is only North Macedonia in 24th place that is distinguished from the rest of the region. The change of nationalist government has undoubtedly influenced this improvement.

Economic policies of all the countries in the Western Balkans are largely dependent on international organisations and powerful individual states. The countries require foreign investment for domestic development reasons. The urgency of post-conflict reconstruction and redevelopment following the collapse of the communist regimes add to the needs and requirements. State building is a feature in five of the six countries. Following the dissolution of Yugoslavia, the new political map shows four former Yugoslav republics and one province as newly developed states in the Western Balkans. The sixth country, Albania, experienced a state collapse in 1997. Thus, all the Western Balkans countries have been recently in the process of state-building that, in many ways, is still in progress.

The situation has resulted in state capture, suppression of many of the freedoms and government's coercion, both institutionalised and subtle, in the field of economic freedoms. Property security as an important indicator of economic freedoms has been affected in all the countries by the nature of the post-WWII regimes that heavily nationalised property. The restitution processes following the collapse of these regimes did not bring satisfaction to many previous owners. Despite their strong influence on governments, religious communities were not able to reclaim all their property.

---

[21] World Economic Forum (2020).

[22] World Economic Forum (2020), pp. 38–39.

[23] World Economic Forum (2020), pp. 168–169.

Table 5.3 Western Balkans only: Economic Freedoms and Social Mobility Index

Position	Country	Index	Status	Points	Index of Economic Freedom[a]	Economic Freedom Index[b]	Index of Econ. Freedom Score[c]	Social Mobility Index[d]
24	N. Macedonia	2	Mostly free	8*	Three 69.5 mod. free	Two 7.15 II Quartile	One 71.3	*
31	Albania	2	Mostly free	9	Three 66.9 mod. free	One 7.80 most free	Two 64.5	Three 55.6
35	Kosovo	3	Mod. free	10*	Three 67.4 mod. free	*	Two 66.6	*
36	Montenegro	3	Mod. free	10.66*	Three 61.5 mod. free	Two 6.94 II Quartile	Three 64.3	*
37	Serbia	3	Mod. free	11	Three 66.0 mod. free	Two 7.05 II Quartile	Three 62.5	Three 63.8
41	B & H	3	Mod. free	12*	Three 62.6 mod. free	Three 6.90 III Quartile	Three 61.4	*

[a]The Heritage Foundation (2020)
[b]Fraser Institute (2018)
[c]The World Bank (2018)
[d]World Economic Forum (2020)

"Thousands of claims for private and religious property confiscated during the communist era remained unresolved"[24] in Albania. The same report focussed on the restitution of property in Serbia only on Holocaust-era claims, thus suggesting the 1990s did not affect property issues in the country in the same way as in other states. Another organisation found that the main challenges to the protection of private property in Serbia "lie in the strong influence of political actors over the judiciary and the Prosecutor's Office, which severely limits their independence."[25]

In Bosnia-Herzegovina, "in the absence of a state restitution law governing the return of nationalized properties, many government officials used such properties as tools for ethnic and political manipulation."[26] The lack of legislation has resulted in partial restitution on an ad hoc basis led by authorities at lower levels of governance. The process only adds to the confusion about property rights, legal security, and the judicial system. Several government institutions are housed in property claimed by one of the four main religious communities. The 1990s war additionally complicates issues of property restitution. Mass migration, both forced and voluntary following the conflict, has created a legally chaotic situation and a sense of insecurity among the population who struggled to return their pre-war property.

Of the Western Balkans countries, Kosovo is in the most similar position to Bosnia-Herzegovina with the experience of violent conflict. The significant movement of the population in the 1990s has resulted in changing ownership and possession of the property and the struggle to establish the rightful owners in a situation resulting from the mix of several unfulfilled restitution processes and legislative changes during the twentieth century. The U.S. government's report found "a complex mix of laws, regulations, administrative instructions, and court practices, as well as the illegal reoccupation of properties and multiple claims for the same property," additionally hampering "resolution of the property restitution."[27] The ethnic issue is reflected, the same report claims, in the fact that "more than 96 percent of these claims were filed by ethnic Serbs."

"A large number of restitution claims for private and religious properties," in Montenegro, "confiscated during the communist era remained unresolved."[28] In addition to individual claims, it was a concern of the Serbian Orthodox Church and the faithful, fearing a possible loss of parts of their religious property that amounted to public protests and, with few other issues, eventually brought about the change of government at the elections.

Complex relations between religious communities and the state have been reported in North Macedonia where the Islamic Community "continued to claim the government used a "selective justice" approach and that it failed to provide

---

[24] U.S. Department of State (2020a) Country Reports on Human Rights Practices: Albania.

[25] Despotović et al. (2019), p. 113.

[26] U.S. Department of State (2020b) Country Reports on Human Rights Practices: Bosnia and Herzegovina.

[27] U.S. Department of State (2020c) Country Reports on Human Rights Practices: Kosovo.

[28] U.S. Department of State (2020d) Country Reports on Human Rights Practices: Montenegro.

appropriate and timely restitution for property." "Private property rights in North Macedonia are mostly respected," found an international thinktank, stressing that the new post-nationalist government "created a reform momentum which alleviated some problems within judiciary."[29]

Property issues, government's policies, and the resulting sense of insecurity by individuals and institutions undermine economic freedoms in these countries. The judicial proceedings are another set of indicators in creating economic indices, but they will be addressed in more detail as part of the Rule of Law, Corruption and Human Rights Index. It serves to illustrate the state of play in the section on economic freedoms. Corruption is another element that might help to illustrate this index and will be addressed in more details in the next chapter.

There is a "pervasive corruption in all branches of government and municipal institutions"[30] in Albania and, added to impunity, it has created the situation where "officials, politicians, judges, and persons with powerful business interests often were able to avoid prosecution."[31] Another study found "insufficient struggle against corruption has been among major non-political and domestic obstacles"[32] for the progress of economic freedoms in Albania.

"Officials," in Bosnia-Herzegovina, "frequently engaged in corrupt practices with impunity, and corruption remained prevalent in many political and economic institutions."[33] "Corruption and nepotism are widespread among the civil service, and the judiciary is not immune to these problems,"[34] states a different report.

Authorities in Kosovo prosecuted and took some legal steps to root out corruption practices. "Many corrupt officials, however, continued to occupy public sector positions,"[35] the U.S. government report claims. Its section on Montenegro states that "officials often engaged in corrupt practices with impunity."[36] Corruption, both perceived and real, was one of the main issues in the parliamentary elections in Montenegro in 2020.

In Serbia, "corruption was prevalent in many areas and remained a problem of concern," the U.S. report stated and added that "police corruption and impunity remained problems."[37] Another report put the issue into the broader period context stating, "corruption is steadily re-gaining ground in Serbia after the anti-graft frenzy, unrealistic expectations and some real-life improvements as of the mid-2010s."[38]

---

[29] Despotović et al. (2019), p. 88.

[30] U.S. Department of State (2020a) Country Reports on Human Rights Practices: Albania.

[31] U.S. Department of State (2020a) Country Reports on Human Rights Practices: Albania.

[32] Despotović et al. (2019), p. 36.

[33] U.S. Department of State (2020b) Country Reports on Human Rights Practices: Bosnia and Herzegovina.

[34] Despotović et al. (2019), p. 55.

[35] U.S. Department of State (2020c) Country Reports on Human Rights Practices: Kosovo.

[36] U.S. Department of State (2020d) Country Reports on Human Rights Practices: Montenegro.

[37] U.S. Department of State (2020f) Country Reports on Human Rights Practices: Serbia.

[38] Despotović et al. (2019), p. 112.

North Macedonia is placed higher than the rest of the Western Balkans by indices on economic freedoms. "Regulatory environment in North Macedonia is mostly business friendly,"[39] a report found. However, another organisation reported "NGOs stated the government's dominant role in the economy created opportunities for corruption,"[40] but also provides details of several trials for corruption by former high-ranking officials.

Businesses in Albania are faced with "significant challenges and shortcomings, stemming from widespread corruption and favoritism [Sic!] among public officials in their dealings with business entities."[41] Business activities in Bosnia and Herzegovina are affected by "excessive red tape, high bureaucracy costs and high regulatory uncertainty," the report underlines. "Corruption thrives in this kind of environment," it adds, "both petty corruption and centralized high corruption that stems from [the] political influence of high officials."[42] "The biggest challenges," to businesses in Serbia, "stem from the low level of [the] rule of law, partial or biased regulatory implementation and corruption." The same report found that "Serbia exhibits some characteristics of a captured state."[43]

5.3 Western Balkans and "Malign Influences"

"US Secretary of State Mike Pompeo warned against the 'malign' influence of Russian trolls and Chinese investment during a brief tour through the Western Balkans."[44] The Western concern over such influences shows this area is a microcosm of a global contest between the leading powers.

The restructuring of the international system during the post-Cold War period has been moving from an attempted U.S. dominated unipolar system to the current new bipolar or multipolar system depending on the number of superpowers or ambitious powers to develop as one of the poles. While geopolitical zones of influence are in many global regions determined, there are few zones where the struggle for domination or an understanding of interests, at least, are an ongoing process. The Western Balkans is one such area.

Significant fields of contention could be found in subtle or open media campaigns, thus affecting the fields of freedom of expression, political and civil rights by inspiring the countries to follow specific political model, i.e., liberal democratic, hybrid or authoritarian, and the field of economic ties developed with the specific

---

[39] Despotović et al. (2019), p. 89.

[40] U.S. Department of State (2020e) Country Reports on Human Rights Practices: North Macedonia.

[41] Despotović et al. (2019), p. 38.

[42] Despotović et al. (2019), p. 57.

[43] Despotović et al. (2019), p. 115.

[44] Euractiv (7 October 2019).

globally or regionally dominating power. In addition to the Western influences that were dominant, if not entirely exclusive, throughout the 1990s and in the early twenty-first century, Russian and Chinese presence and some Muslim countries influence have become more apparent lately.

These powers use different methods and focus on different fields. The West has been showing concerns mainly with "Russian Malign Influence in the Western Balkans."[45] The Atlantic Council, meanwhile, asked: "How to push back against Kremlin's malign influence."[46] The US House Foreign Affairs Committee heard "how far-right and other destabilizing actors are using support from Moscow to advance their agendas" during the hearing titled "Undermining Democracy: Kremlin Tools of Malign Political Influence."[47]

Russian influence is focussed in political and media spheres, but the Chinese have engaged in economic projects. The Organized Crime and Corruption Reporting Project stated the "US Warns Balkans of Chinese Encroachment."[48] The Prague Security Studies Institute published the study "Western Balkans at the Crossroads: Assessing Influences of Non-Western External Actors." The study covers "engagement of all major non-Western actors actively present in the region – Russia, Turkey, China, the Gulf States and Iran – in Serbia, Bosnia and Herzegovina (BiH), North Macedonia, Montenegro and Kosovo."[49] The International Republican Institute offers a report "by experts from 12 vulnerable democracies," titled "Chinese Malign Influence and the Corrosion of Democracy."[50] The only two European countries studied in the report were Serbia and Hungary.

One analysis concludes: "The US National Defense [Sic!] Strategy articulates today's era of great power competition clearly," stressing the "competition is playing out in the Western Balkans."[51] Although Western influences dominate the region, the regimes in the Western Balkans are not liberal and therefore do not reflect the Western political model.

While not being a political model, Chinese state capitalism offers an economic model to rely on in the Western Balkans. Influences from various Muslim countries, primarily Turkey, are present, but reliance on religious alliances restrict them to dominantly Muslim states, and even then, it is its authoritarian character that is being modelled upon. Leaders see the Chinese economic model in the Western Balkans as a potential source of investments and their preservation of political power."

The 2008 financial crisis instilled a sense among Serbian leadership that the West is vulnerable, and that China is rising."[52] This argument is applicable throughout the

[45] Conley (2019).

[46] Wemer (21 May 2019).

[47] Carpenter (21 May 2019).

[48] Organized Crime and Corruption Reporting Project (OCCRP) (8 October 2019).

[49] Chrzová et al. (2019).

[50] Shullman (2019).

[51] Wilson (17 September 2019).

[52] The Diplomat (1 January 2019a).

Western Balkans. Serbian President Aleksandar Vučić underlined this view stating that "thirty years ago you had one, absolutely dominant military, political, and economic power,"[53] while the rise of China is changing everything. This is reflected in the levels of economic freedoms found in the region.

The 16+1 form of cooperation between China and sixteen, later seventeen, countries of CEE present a possible alternative to the conditioned western investment. "Since 2012, the 16+1 format has provided China with growing political influence in Central Europe," the argument states, "exacerbating tendencies toward greater fragmentation in Europe."[54] For many, "it is clear that the 'Chinese way,' which has been in full swing in Africa or South Asia, for example, is more suitable to less regulated, pluralistic countries."[55] The Western Balkans, therefore, is a perfect theatre for the "Chinese Way".

Examples of significant projects developed through Chinese involvement are motorways, railways, bridges, steelworks, thermoelectrical plants, copper mining and smelting complex. The key infrastructural projects have been won by Chinese companies throughout the Western Balkans, while Chinese financial institutions often provide loans for such projects, thus creating a cycle of money from China to China via the Western Balkans. "The EU's structural funds in the form of grants are larger and cheaper than Chinese loans," but it is the conditionality of the EU policies and politics in the Balkans that includes "poor governance on the part of some local politicians" that shift these countries towards deals with China.[56]

The relationship does not rely on the political model offered by China but on economic power expressed through "loans made by Beijing to CEE countries" that might "create potential for financial instability."[57] Experts warned that a "(different kind of) strings attached" to these loans that should not be underestimated.[58] The situations created by strings attached have led the Western Balkans to become "a top priority of China's Belt and Road Initiative, on which 16+1 meetings now center."[59] The EU has acknowledged the contest between the two poles of the developing international system by describing China as "an economic competitor in the pursuit of technological leadership, and a systemic rival promoting alternative models of governance."[60] The Index of Economic Freedoms found China in the 103rd place categorised as "mostly unfree.[61] Only Ukraine, of the European countries, is positioned worse. The Economic Freedom of the World Index placed China in the 113th place in its "III Quartile" below Greece and with only Ukraine of the European

[53] The Diplomat (1 January 2019a).

[54] The Diplomat (16 August 2018).

[55] The Diplomat (1 January 2019a).

[56] The Diplomat (1 January 2019a).

[57] Mercator Institute for China Studies (10 July 2018).

[58] Mercator Institute for China Studies (10 July 2018).

[59] The Diplomat (1 January 2019a).

[60] High Representative of the Union for Foreign Affairs and Security Policy (12 March 2019).

[61] The Heritage Foundation (2020), p. C2.

countries placed below China in the "least free" category.[62] Therefore the Chinese influence prevents faster progress of economic freedoms in the Western Balkans.

Geopolitics could be directly seen through the behaviour of Montenegro and the state's major infrastructural project. The highway Bar-Boljare in Montenegro is likely to increase the national debt to a level of unsustainability. After signing the loan with a Chinese company in 2014, 7 years later, "Montenegro has asked the EU for assistance with paying off a $1bn Chinese loan for an incomplete highway project that has imperilled the finances of the small western Balkan nation."[63] "This is the first time," an analyst was quoted by the Financial times, "that Montenegro or any other country from the western Balkans" has made this type of outreach towards Brussels to combat rising Chinese influence."[64] The EU, however, "rejected a call by Montenegro's government" and said they were going to "continue to stand by them, but we are not repaying the loans they are taking from third parties."[65] This might increase the Chinese influence and possibly enable the Chinese bank to take over control of assets owned by Montenegro eventually. Economic freedoms will undoubtedly be affected if this takes place.

In Bosnia-Herzegovina, the Banja Luka-Mlinište highway is also associated with the 16+1 initiative. A Chinese consortium has signed the contract for upgrading the Budapest-Belgrade railway link. A Chinese bank has provided the loan for at least one section of the line in Serbia. The nationalist government in North Macedonia selected "a Chinese State-owned Enterprise (SOE)," in 2012, "to build two highways . . . in a deal that went on to become one of the biggest corruption affairs in Macedonian history, bringing down the Prime Minister Nikola Gruevski and his Government."[66] Albania's "sole international airport, located nearby the capital, was transferred to a Chinese-led joint venture under a concession in 2016. Another large concession Chinese companies have been awarded in Albania is the "oil extraction concession in Patos-Marinza."[67]

Formerly considered a part of the Western Balkans, Croatia, while receiving the EU funds, has awarded a Chinese company with the project of building Pelješac bridge. This example puts the Chinese policies in a broader context. However, it is easier to implement their initiatives in non-EU countries where the rule of law is yet to be fully developed.

The relations are complex because "interlocutors can perform multiple and contradictory roles all at the same time," as "the evolution of China-CEE cooperation indicates."[68] The EU and China are contesting each other's means in the Western Balkans. Local countries attempt to play the models and their advocating

[62] Fraser Institute (2018), p. 9.
[63] The Financial Times (11 April 2021).
[64] The Financial Times (11 April 2021).
[65] Politico (12 April 2021).
[66] Krstinovska (6 November 2019).
[67] Madhi (19 May 2020).
[68] The Diplomat (29 March 2019b).

powers against each other to their advantage. The challenge from China is geopolitical and is based on increasing economic influence that would make the CEE space more dependable on them, but, unlike the illiberal model, there is no ambition of exporting the political model. The Chinese economic model, though, affects economic freedoms and dynamics in the Western Balkans, corrupts further the governing structures, and, in turn, makes conditions for investment from liberal markets more restrained.

References

Carpenter M (21 May 2019) Testimony before the House Foreign Affairs Committee. In: Wemer DA How to push back Kremlin's Malign influence. Atlantic Council: New Atlanticist, Washington, D.C . https://www.atlanticcouncil.org/blogs/new-atlanticist/how-to-push-back-against-kremlin-s-malign-influence/. Accessed 6 Oct 2021

Chrzová B, Grabovac A, Hála M, Lalić J (eds) (2019) Western Balkans at the crossroads: assessing influences of non-western external actors. The Prague Security Studies Institute, Prague. https://6e7a0e8d-d938-46ff-832d-a1d2166bc3a6.filesusr.com/ugd/2fb84c_0111856c88724a8cb0caac1dad0d762e.pdf. Accessed 6 Oct 2021

Conley HA (2019) Russian malign influence in Montenegro: the weaponization and exploitation of history, religion, and economics. CSIS Briefs. Center for Strategic and International Studies. https://www.csis.org/analysis/russian-malign-influence-montenegro. Accessed 6 Oct 2021

Despotović I, Gamser D, Gajić M (2019) Freedom barometer Europe. Friedrich Naumann Foundation for Liberty. http://freedombarometer.org/files/download/Freedom_Barometer_Europe_2019.pdf. Accessed 6 Oct 2021

Euractiv (7 October 2019) Pompeo warns of 'Russian bots' and 'Chinese bribes' in the Balkans. Euractiv.com with AFP. https://www.euractiv.com/section/enlargement/news/pompeo-warns-of-russian-bots-and-chinese-bribes-in-the-balkans/. Accessed 6 Oct 2021

Fraser Institute (2018) Economic Freedom Index. https://www.fraserinstitute.org/economic-freedom/dataset?geozone=world&year=2018&page=dataset&min-year=2&max-year=0&filter=0. Accessed 10 May 2021

Gwartney J, Lawson R, Hall J, Murphy R (2019) Economic Freedom of the World: 2019 Annual Report. Fraser Institute, Vancouver. https://www.fraserinstitute.org/studies/economic-freedom. Accessed 10 Apr 2021

High Representative of the Union for Foreign Affairs and Security Policy (12 March 2019) Joint Communication to the European Parliament, the European Council and the Council EU: China – A Strategic Outlook. Strasbourg

Krstinovska A (6 November 2019) exporting corruption? The case of a Chinese highway project in North Macedonia. China Observers in Central and Eastern Europe (CHOICE). https://chinaobservers.eu/exporting-corruption-the-case-of-a-chinese-highway-project-in-north-macedonia/. Accessed 6 Oct 2021

Madhi G (19 May 2020) Story of a Chinese Airport in Albania. China observers in Central and Eastern Europe (CHOICE). https://chinaobservers.eu/a-story-of-a-chinese-airport-in-albania/. Accessed 6 Oct 2021

Mercator Institute for China Studies (10 July 2018) Belt and road reality check: how to assess China's investment in Eastern Europe. https://www.merics.org/en/blog/belt-and-road-reality-check-how-assess-chinas-investment-eastern-europe. Accessed 6 Oct 2021

Organized Crime and Corruption Reporting Project (OCCRP) (8 October 2019) US Warns Balkans of Chinese encroachment. https://www.occrp.org/en/27-ccwatch/cc-watch-briefs/10840-us-warns-balkans-of-chinese-encroachment. Accessed 6 Oct 2021

Politico (12 April 2021) EU rebuffs Montenegro plea to help repay $1B Chinese highway loan. Politico. https://www.politico.eu/article/eu-montenegro-billion-dollar-china-unfinished-highway-loan/. Accessed 6 Oct 2021

Shullman D (2019) Chinese malign influence and the corrosion of democracy. International Republican Institute, Washington, DC. https://www.iri.org/sites/default/files/chinese_malign_influence_report.pdf. Accessed 6 Oct 2021

Thatcher M (8 April 2013) Margaret Thatcher: a life in quotes. The Guardian. https://www.theguardian.com/politics/2013/apr/08/margaret-thatcher-quotes. Accessed 6 Oct 2021

The Diplomat (16 August 2018) China's Europe policy poses a challenge to EU cohesion. https://thediplomat.com/2018/08/chinas-europe-policy-poses-a-challenge-to-eu-cohesion/. Accessed 20 Dec 2020

The Diplomat (1 January 2019a) Serbia: China's open door to the Balkans. https://thediplomat.com/2019/01/serbia-chinas-open-door-to-the-balkans/. Accessed 6 Oct 2021

The Diplomat (29 March 2019b) China's '16+1' Is Dead? Long live the '17+1'. https://thediplomat.com/2019/03/chinas-161-is-dead-long-live-the-171/. Accessed 6 Oct 2021

The Financial Times (11 April 2021) Montenegro calls for EU help over $1bn Chinese highway loan. The Financial Times. https://www.ft.com/content/3dd7a516-5352-4f48-bfac-236e43b2342d. Accessed 23 Apr 2021

The Heritage Foundation (2019) Index of Economic Freedom. https://www.heritage.org/index/download#. Accessed 10 April 2021

The Heritage Foundation (2020) Index of economic freedom. https://www.heritage.org/index/. Accessed 6 Oct 2021

The World Bank (2018) Index of economic freedom score. https://tcdata360.worldbank.org/indicators/idx.econ.free.scr?country=BRA&indicator=747&viz=line_chart&years=2013,2018. Accessed 6 Oct 2021

U.S. Department of State (2020a) Country reports on human rights practices: Albania. https://www.state.gov/reports/2020-country-reports-on-human-rights-practices/albania/. Accessed 6 Oct 2021

U.S. Department of State (2020b) Country Reports on Human Rights practices: Bosnia and Herzegovina. https://www.state.gov/reports/2020-country-reports-on-human-rights-practices/bosnia-and-herzegovina/. Accessed 6 Oct 2021

U.S. Department of State (2020c) Country reports on human rights practices: Kosovo. https://www.state.gov/reports/2020-country-reports-on-human-rights-practices/kosovo/. Accessed 6 Oct 2021

U.S. Department of State (2020d) Country Reports on Human Rights Practices: Montenegro. https://www.state.gov/reports/2020-country-reports-on-human-rights-practices/montenegro/. Accessed 6 Oct 2021

U.S. Department of State (2020e) Country Reports on Human Rights Practices: North Macedonia. https://www.state.gov/reports/2020-country-reports-on-human-rights-practices/north-macedonia/. Accessed 6 Oct 2021

U.S. Department of State (2020f) Country Reports on Human Rights Practices: Serbia. https://www.state.gov/reports/2020-country-reports-on-human-rights-practices/serbia/. Accessed 6 Oct 2021

Vásquez I, McMahon F (2020) Human freedom index. Cato Institute and Fraser Institute, Washington, D.C., Vancouver. https://www.cato.org/human-freedom-index/2020 Accessed 31 Mar 2021

Wemer D A (21 May 2019) How to push back Kremlin's Malign influence. Atlantic Council: New Atlanticist Washington, D.C. https://www.atlanticcouncil.org/blogs/new-atlanticist/how-to-push-back-against-kremlin-s-malign-influence/. Accessed 6 Oct 2021

Wilson D (17 September 2019) Great power competition in Southeast Europe. Atlantic Council: New Atlanticist Washington, D.C. https://www.atlanticcouncil.org/blogs/new-atlanticist/great-power-competition-in-southeast-europe/. Accessed 6 Oct 2021

World Economic Forum (2020) Social mobility index 2020. http://www3.weforum.org/docs/Global_Social_Mobility_Report.pdf. Accessed 1 May 2021

Chapter 6
Insufficient Human Rights, the Rule of Law, and Superfluity of Corruption

6.1 The Complexity of the Category

It is possible to develop a strong argument against this group of indices being put together. However, it is also feasible to keep the four indices together. Indeed, like many other indices, they overlap with some of the indicators used in other categories. Human rights are the all-inclusive category that personal and economic freedoms contribute to. Freedom of expression is undoubtedly part of human rights. Following the adoption of the Universal Declaration of Human Rights in 1948, they have become an obligatory part of state policies, and with the third wave of democratisation, human rights have become a *conditio sine qua non* of state recognition.

Nineteen new states in Europe have been created or recreated during the 1990s and the early 2000s. The recognition relied on the democratic character of the regimes, human rights protection by the newly developed states and other usual conditions of the international system, i.e., a clearly defined territory, permanent population, functioning government, and the capacity to enter into relations with other states. All the regimes claiming state sovereignty had to show compliance with human rights. The human rights norms, Lauren observed, "have inspired regional intergovernmental organizations and states acting on their own or in conjunction with others to use the observance or violation of human rights as criteria for their foreign policies."[1]

This might provide a case to include human rights into the category titled "Regimes", but this group is too narrow with concerns mainly with the issues of democracy. Human rights are individual rights as defined and understood since the 1948 declaration,[2] but some of them are enjoyed collectively, as seen in practice ever since. National minority rights and other group rights are part of this practice. Some

[1]Lauren (1998), p. 280.

[2]The Universal Declaration of Human Rights (9 December 1948).

N. Andjelic, *Covid-19, State-Power and Society in Europe*, European Union and its Neighbours in a Globalized World 5, https://doi.org/10.1007/978-3-030-91073-0_6

authors, like Lohmann, argue that "this interpretation of human rights contradicts traditional conceptions in which a community takes precedence over individual members."[3] The purpose of this work is not a discussion of different generations of human rights and their interpretations. Nevertheless, collective rights are certain rights, understood as individual rights, that are to be enjoyed and protected, for that matter, collectively. As the same author argued against the one-sidedness of such an understanding, he nevertheless acknowledged: "Said bluntly: human rights protect the individual, and not communities."[4] After all, of the thirty articles of the Universal Declaration of Human Rights, only two, "representing articles 27-28, focuses on the third generation of rights, those associated with communal and national solidarity."[5]

According to a "classical liberal view," as Forsythe presented, "the good society is based on respect for the equality and autonomy of individuals."[6] This project accepted the understanding that is looking into the character of a society, searching for the "open society" that would, in essence, correspond to the liberal view, as stated by Forsythe, of a good society. The liberal understanding of human rights as individual rights prevails in this project, but collective rights are acknowledged and investigated as case studies. Issues of societal solidarity are addressed. Therefore, while understanding different concepts of human rights, the indices and case studies provide the basis for developing elements of this index.

The "Human Rights Index"[7] has several indicators based on individual rights, like economic freedoms, but also collective rights, like gender equality. The four sub-indices used in the production of this index reconfirm this approach: Personal Safety, Access to Education, Tolerance & Inclusion, and Personal Rights.

The category of "Personal Freedoms", as a part of the overall "State-Power and Society Index" of this project, was formed around indices that focus on freedoms, human freedoms, electoral freedoms, and civic space. As stated, they are certainly part of human rights, but the focus of these indices is narrowed to some specific aspects of freedoms and civil liberties, and this justified the creation of the separate group.

The indices of economic freedoms have several indicators from the rule of law, government functioning, legal protection and other freedoms that are also parts of the indices in different categories. The corruption indices and the rule of law indices overlap. However, as the economic nature of the indices has primacy, they have been grouped in a specific category. This all leaves the rule of law, human rights and corruption indices in the separate category that focuses on the legal protection of citizens, rights, and liberties in the societies. The index, itself, might be difficult to be

[3] Lohmann (2015), p. 388.

[4] Lohmann (2015), p. 389.

[5] Ishay (2008), p. 4.

[6] Forsythe (2012), p. 3.

[7] Friedrich Naumann Foundation for Freedom. East and Southeast Europe (2020) Human Rights Index 2019.

named, but, perhaps, a rather complex name is the most telling sign of the content—"The Rule of Law, Human Rights and Corruption Index".

This method leaves several indices dealing with the freedom of expression out of this particular index. The right of expression is enshrined in the Universal Declaration of Human Rights[8] and is a cause of concern for many organisations, including governmental and non-governmental, at both international and national levels. Due to the particular focus on this set of rights by many actors a separate category on the freedom of expression, media, and press freedoms will be analysed in the next chapter.

The legal protection of human rights is closely linked with the rule of law. The Rule of Law Index, authors claim, "recognizes that a system of law that fails to respect core human rights guaranteed under international law is at best "rule by law" and does not deserve to be called a rule of law system."[9] The authors developed this index based on both the "minimalist conception of the rule of law that focuses on formal, procedural rules" and the broader understanding "that includes substantive characteristics, such as self-governance and various fundamental rights and freedoms."[10]

The absence of corruption is just one factor in creating the Index of the Rule of Law. There are separate indices on political corruption and the perceived corruption added to the group category of this project—"The Rule of Law, Human Rights and the Corruption". Both the corruption indices somewhat overlap with other indices, underlining the understanding that the broad input of the overall findings supports the general knowledge resulting in the final index of the project.

Transparency International's global index showed several regions. Europe is divided into the two: "Western Europe & European Union" with an average score of 66 out of 100, and "Eastern Europe and Central Asia" with 35.[11] Central Asian republics have a significantly lower score than Eastern Europe, and one could be cynical about this version of the regionalisation. With a score of 39, Serbia has far more similarities and commonalities with Bulgaria that scored 45 in this index, than with Turkmenistan with a score of 19. The different scores only reflect more profound differences that exist between the regions. Therefore, the average score for non-EU Eastern European countries is 38, which is still significantly lower than the EU member states and the four non-members from the West.

Countries in Eastern Europe, the report states, "experience limited separation of powers, abuse of state resources for electoral purposes, opaque political party financing and conflicts of interest." The same report adds "state capture and the concentration of power in private hands" as "a major stumbling block in the region."[12] This is further reflected in the Political Corruption Index derived from

[8] Universal Declaration of Human Rights (1948), Article XIX.

[9] World Justice Project (2020), p. 9.

[10] World Justice Project (2020), p. 9.

[11] Transparency International (2020), p. 8.

[12] Transparency International (2020), p. 16.

executive, legislative, judicial, and public sector corruption indices.[13] The index makes further distinctions of various types of political corruption, but the focus for this project is on their findings. Table 6.1 shows the indexing method.

6.2 A Pan-European View

Fourteen European countries have earned the highest, "very strong", status in the overall index in this category. Thirteen of them had an immaculate score in each of the four indices, while the United Kingdom had a slightly lower score in the Human Rights Index.[14] The highest-ranking countries are all in what is colloquially known as Western Europe, with the addition of Estonia. The distinction within these highest-scoring countries is based on the "Corruption Perception Index", where eight of them had a "very clean" score and the remaining six scored "clean".[15]

Eleven countries make up the second-best category, named "strong". The remaining western countries, including two small island countries in the Mediterranean, are joined by five formerly communist countries. The medium category of "moderately strong" consists, in addition to Greece, of six other former communist countries, four of them now in the European Union. Bulgaria is the lowest positioned EU country in the category "weak", where it is joined by Belarus and five countries of the Western Balkans. Bosnia-Herzegovina is in the lowest-scoring category of "very weak" together with "Ukraine, Turkey, Russia and Azerbaijan. Table 6.2 shows the findings in more detail.

There is consistency in countries' scores across the four indices, with most countries having all their scores within two out of five categories. However, there are eight exceptions where the scores are spread across three different ranks. All these countries are former communist countries that were supposed to end the transition processes some time ago, but the indices show that some did not develop, and reach equally and fully, all the EU standards yet. Czechia, Slovenia, Croatia, and Hungary scored better in the Human Rights Index than in the others. Serbia and Albania also have higher scores in this field, although their scores are generally lower than those of the four EU member states. Poland's and Armenia's scores in the Political Corruption Index are higher than in the other fields.

[13] V-Dem Institute. University of Gothenburg (2020) Political Corruption Index.

[14] Transparency International (2020) Global Corruption Perception Index 2019.

[15] Friedrich Naumann Foundation for Freedom. East and Southeast Europe (2020) Human Rights Index 2019.

Table 6.1 The Rule of Law, Human Rights and Corruption Indexing

Corruption perceptions index[a]		Political Corruption Annual Democracy Report 2019[b]		Rule of Law Index[c]		Human Rights Index[d]		Final		
Status	Index	Status	Index	Status	Ind-ex	Status	Index	Index	Status	Points 4-20
Clean/Very Clean 70–87	1	0.01–0.10	1	1.0–0.75 (strongest)	1	Highest	0–1 distance	1	Very strong	4–6
Fairly Clean 60–70	2	011-0.25	2	0.75–0.66 (strong)	2	Good	1–2 distance	2	Strong	7–10
Corrupt 50–60	3	0.26–0.50	3	0.66–060 (medium)	3	Moderate	2–3 distance	3	Mod. Strong	11–14
Very Corrupt 40–50	4	0.51–70	4	055–0.50 (weak)	4	Low	3–4 distance	4	Weak	15–17
Highly Corrupt 28–40	5	0.71–1	5	0.50–0.40 (weakest)	5	Lowest	4+ distance	5	Very Weak	18–20

[a]Transparency International (2020) Global Corruption Perception Index 2019
[b]V-Dem Institute. University of Gothenburg. (2020) Political Corruption Index
[c]World Justice Project (2020) The Rule of Law Index. World Justice Project
[d]Friedrich Naumann Foundation for Freedom. East and Southeast Europe (2020) Human Rights Index 2019

Table 6.2 The Rule of Law, Human Rights and Corruption Index

Position	Country	Index	Status	Points	Corruption Perceptions Index 2019[a]	Political Corruption 2019[b]	Rule of Law Index 2020[c]	Human Rights Index 2019[d]
1	Denmark	1	Very strong	4	One 87 very clean	One 0.01	One 0.90 strongest	One 8.86
1	Finland	1	Very strong	4	One 86 very clean	One 0.03	One 0.87 strongest	One 9.19
1	Germany	1	Very strong	4	One 80 very clean	One 0.03	One 0.84 strongest	One 8.64
1	Luxembourg	1	Very strong	4[e]	One 80 very clean	One 0.07	[e]	One 8.80
1	Netherlands	1	Very strong	4	One 82 very clean	One 0.02	One 0.84 strongest	One 8.86
1	Norway	1	Very strong	4	One 84 very clean	One 0.01	One 0.89 strongest	One 8.90
1	Sweden	1	Very strong	4	One 85 very clean	One 0.02	One 0.86 strongest	One 9.03
1	Switzerland	1	Very strong	4[e]	One 85 very clean	One 0.02	[e]	One 8.95
9	Austria	1	Very strong	4	One 77 clean	One 0.05	One 0.83 strongest	One 8.90
9	Belgium	1	Very strong	4	One 75 clean	One 0.03	One 0.79 strongest	One 8.43
9	Estonia	1	Very strong	4	One 74 clean	One 0.04	One 0.81 strongest	One 8.27
9	Iceland	1	Very strong	4[e]	One 78 clean	[e]	[e]	One 9.26
9	Ireland	1	Very strong	4[e]	One 74 clean	One 0.06	[e]	One 8.89
14	UK	1	Very strong	5	One 77 clean	One 0.07	One 0.79 strongest	Two 8.13
15	Lithuania	2	Strong	6.66[e]	Two 60 fairly clean	Two 0.14	[e]	One 8.27
16	France	2	Strong	7	Two 69 fairly clean	One 0.09	Two 0.73 strong	Two 7.79
16	Portugal	2	Strong	7	Two 62 fairly clean	Two 0.16	Two 0.70 strong	One 8.45
16	Spain	2	Strong	7	Two 62 fairly clean	One 0.04	Two 0.73 strong	Two 7.57
19	Czechia	2	Strong	8	Three 56 corrupt	Two 0.25	Two 0.73 strong	One 8.29
19	Poland	2	Strong	8	Three 58 corrupt	One 0.09	Two 0.66 strong	Two 7.60
19	Slovenia	2	Strong	8	Two 60 fairly clean	Three 0.26	Two 0.69 strong	One 8.83
22	Italy	2	Strong	9	Three 53 corrupt	Two 0.20	Two 0.66 strong	Two 7.28
23	Cyprus	2	Strong	9.33[e]	Three 58 corrupt	Two 0.18	[e]	Two 7.36
23	Latvia	2	Strong	9.33[e]	Three 56 corrupt	Two 0.15	[e]	Two 7.47

25	Malta	2	Strong	10[e]	Three 54 corrupt	[e]	[e]	Two 8.02
26	Slovakia	3	Mod. strong	10.66[e]	Three 50 corrupt	Three 0.27	[e]	Two 7.98
27	Georgia	3	Mod. strong	11	Three 56 corrupt	Two 0.14	Three 0.60 medium	Three 6.30
28	Croatia	3	Mod. strong	12	Four 47 very corrupt	Three 0.32	Three 0.61 medium	Two 7.69
29	Greece	3	Mod. strong	13	Four 48 very corrupt	Three 0.30	Three 0.61 medium	Three 7.04
29	Hungary	3	Mod. strong	13	Four 44 very corrupt	Three 0.49	Four 0.53 weak	Two 7.33
31	Armenia	3	Mod. strong	13.33[e]	Four 42 very corrupt	Two 0.22	[e]	Four 6.10
32	Romania	3	Mod. strong	14	Four 44 very corrupt	Four 0.56	Three 0.63 medium	Three 6.88
33	Belarus	4	Weak	14.66[e]	Four 48 very corrupt	Three 0.31	Four 0.51 weak	[e]
34	Bulgaria	4	Weak	15	Four 44 very corrupt	Four 0.66	Four 0.55 weak	Three 7.09
35	Albania	4	Weak	16	Five 35 highly corrupt	Four 0.65	Four 0.50 weak	Three 6.30
35	Montenegro	4	Weak	16[e]	Four 45 very corrupt	Four 0.67	[e]	Four 6.18
37	N. Macedonia	4	Weak	17	Five 35 highly corrupt	Four 0.70	Four 0.53 weak	Four 5.91
37	Moldova	4	Weak	17	Five 32 highly corrupt	Four 0.52	Four 0.50 weak	Four 6.23
37	Serbia	4	Weak	17	Five 39 highly corrupt	Five 0.71	Four 0.50 weak	Three 6.43
40	Kosovo	4	Weak	17.33[e]	Five 36 highly corrupt	Four 0.52	Four 0.54 weak	[e]
41	B & H	5	Very weak	18	Five 36 highly corrupt	Five 0.77	Four 0.52 weak	Four 5.47
41	Ukraine	5	Very weak	18	Five 30 highly corrupt	Five 0.73	Four 0.51 weak	Four 5.93
43	Russia	5	Very weak	20	Five 28 highly corrupt	Five 0.74	Five 0.47 weakest	Five 4.29
43	Turkey	5	Very weak	20	Five 39 highly corrupt	Five 0.73	Five 0.43 weakest	Five 3.77
45	Azerbaijan	5	Very weak	20[e]	Five 30 highly corrupt	Five 0.93	[e]	Five 4.56

[a]Transparency International (2019)
[b]V-Dem Institute. University of Gothenburg (2020)
[c]World Justice Project (2020)
[d]Friedrich Naumann Foundation for Freedom. East and Southeast Europe (2020)
[e]Some countries have been omitted from some indices. Therefore, the average score had to be calculated for the particular feature

6.3 A Surplus of Corruption and Shortages of the Rule of Law and Human Rights in the Western Balkans

Not unlike in the other indices, five Western Balkans countries are in the second-worst category (See Table 6.3). The only exception is Bosnia-Herzegovina that joined the "usual suspects", Ukraine, Russia, Turkey, and Azerbaijan, in the worst category. This reflects a longer tendency also noticed by analysts: "With a score of 36, Bosnia and Herzegovina significantly declined by six points on the CPI since 2012. The country also suffers from weak enforcement of campaign finance regulations." The same analysis reflected reported concerns of political parties and civil society "over voting irregularities, threats against voters, the misuse of public resources and unequal access to the media."[16]

Vetevendosje (Self-Determination) political party won the elections in Kosovo partly by promising to fight corruption that is widespread and where the previously dominant political forces had a "usual practice of political appointments in state-owned enterprises."[17] This element would fit with the economic freedoms where Kosovo is ranked 35th and in the medium category. The authors of the Human Freedom Index underline the importance of freedoms, arguing: "As such, economic freedom is not just inherently valuable; it empowers individuals to exercise other freedoms."[18] Therefore, the idea and the argument presented in this work that the freedoms, rights, and obligations overlap across several categories are reinforced and reconfirmed.

Vásquez and Porčnik recall Hayek's argument that "a complete monopoly of employment... would possess unlimited powers of coercion."[19] Hayek further quotes Trotsky, who offered his criticism of a totalitarian ideology. In the original work, Trotsky said: "In a country where the sole employer is the state, this means death by slow starvation. The old principle: who does not work shall not eat, has been replaced with a new one: who does not obey shall not eat."[20]

The state control over the resources, suppression of the society and ultimate denial of many aspects of freedoms created conditions in the post-communist states of the Western Balkans of the all-powerful elites that reflect Trotsky's description of the totalitarian state in the 1930s Soviet Union. While lives are not endangered, and citizens are free to subscribe to different ideologies, their dependence on the state to provide them with employment opportunities creates a relationship where citizens are powerless and dependant on the state while elites are utterly corrupt and all-powerful. All conditions are thus set for the rise of populist politics. In the 1990s, nationalism was the leading force in the local politics that had created

[16] Transparency International (2020), p. 10.

[17] Transparency International (2020), p. 17.

[18] Vásquez and Porčnik (2019), p. 16.

[19] Vásquez and Porčnik (2019), p. 16.

[20] Trotsky (1936), Ch. 11.

Table 6.3 Western Balkans: The Rule of Law, Human Rights, Corruption Index

Position	Country	Index	Status	Points	Corruption Perceptions Index 2019[a]	Political Corruption 2019[b]	Rule of Law Index 2020[c]	Human Rights Index 2019[d]
35	Albania	4	Weak	16	Five 35 highly corrupt	Four 0.65	Four 0.50 weak	Three 6.30
35	Montenegro	4	Weak	16[e]	Four 45 very corrupt	Four 0.67	[e]	Four 6.18
37	N. Macedonia	4	Weak	17	Five 35 highly corrupt	Four 0.70	Four 0.53 weak	Four 5.91
37	Serbia	4	Weak	17	Five 39 highly corrupt	Five 0.71	Five 0.50 weak	Three 6.43
40	Kosovo	4	Weak	17.33[e]	Five 36 highly corrupt	Four 0.52	Four 0.54 weak	[e]
41	B & H	5	Very weak	18	Five 36 highly corrupt	Five 0.77	Four 0.52 weak	Four 5.47

[a]Transparency International (2019)
[b]V-Dem Institute. University of Gothenburg (2020)
[c]World Justice Project (2020)
[d]Friedrich Naumann Foundation for Freedom. East and Southeast Europe (2020)
[e]Not included in this index

conditions for the rise of populist methods. During the post-conflict period, widespread dissatisfaction leads to dissent and the potential rise to populist forces that claim the anti-corruption struggle. This has been manifested in elections in several countries, most notably in Kosovo.

Another crucial element from the *Vetevendosje* party's programme is the request for self-determination, which would mean a possible unification of Kosovo and Albania. This makes the political party that has twice, in a short interval, won the right to form a government in Kosovo a potentially dangerous actor despite the promise and efforts to fight corruption. The findings show that a perceived corruption is worse in North Macedonia and Albania than in Kosovo and Bosnia-Herzegovina by just one point out of 100, with only Moldova, Azerbaijan, Russia, and Ukraine performing even worse.[21]

The potential for a rise of similar forces in these states is undoubtedly present and developed to some extent. After all, the change of government in North Macedonia and the former Prime Minister seeking political asylum in Hungary in 2018 after being sentenced on corruption charges show the shift. Albania and the electorate in Bosnia-Herzegovina stick with their elites in power despite the reports and apparent signs of widespread corruption. The U.S. government reported on the situation in Bosnia-Herzegovina that "corruption was especially prevalent in the health and education sectors, public procurement processes, local governance, and public administration employment procedures."[22] The same document reported "pervasive corruption in all branches of government and municipal institutions"[23] in Albania.

In Montenegro, a "wave of anti-government protests" in 2012 was "motivated by discontent over increasing energy prices, alleged mismanagement of the privatisation of public enterprises, corruption and lack of employment opportunities,"[24] Kenneth Morrison analysed. It was noticed that "large numbers in Podgorica" gathered "to vent their anger" but were not capable of "generating a strong enough momentum to seriously challenge the government."[25] However, Morrison argued, the masses and dissatisfaction "could be harnessed politically"[26] and this is precisely what happened in 2020.

Another proof of corruption practised by governing officials was captured on a video provided by a businessman who alleged to have handed over 97,000 euros as bribes to the Podgorica Mayor and brought masses to the streets in 2019. Nevertheless, again, the regime was not challenged seriously enough, but the elections in 2020, after all, brought a change. In addition to the perceived corruption, the Law on Religious Communities mobilised masses and, after 30 years, deprived the

[21] Transparency International (2020).

[22] U.S. Department of State (2020b), Country Reports on Human Rights Practices: Bosnia and Herzegovina.

[23] U.S. Department of State (2020a), Country Reports on Human Rights Practices: Albania.

[24] Morrison (2018), pp. 151–168.

[25] Morrison (2018), pp. 151–168.

[26] Morrison (2018), pp. 151–168.

governing party, with its partners, of the majority by just one parliamentary seat. Đukanović's party showed inclusive ethnic policies since Montenegrin independence and governing coalitions always included political parties of national minorities except for Serbs political parties. Thus, pro-Serb parties formed a broad coalition with the opponents of the regime from the main ethnic group and just about managed to produce the change.

North Macedonia might be a positive case from the region as 'the EC stated the country "has made good progress as reflected in its consolidated track record on investigating, prosecuting and trying high level corruption cases."'[27] The remaining five countries were described in a different tone.

The American administration's report on Serbia highlights "numerous acts of government corruption" and "reported 344 corruption-related convictions through trial and 783 convictions based on plea agreements" during the 2 years preceding the pandemic.[28] The reported cases of corruption in Montenegro "involved public administration, the private sector, and the judiciary."[29] Activists and international organisations in Kosovo reported "numerous failures by the judicial system to prosecute corruption, noting that very few cases brought against senior officials resulted in indictments."[30] "The multitude of state, entity, cantonal, and municipal administrations, each with the power to establish laws and regulations affecting business, created a system that lacked transparency and provided opportunities for corruption"[31] at all levels in Bosnia-Herzegovina. Low-level corruption cases have been pursued, making significant progress in Albania, the report states, but adds that "prosecution of higher-level suspects remained rare due to investigators' fear of retribution, a lack of resources, and corruption within the judiciary itself."[32]

After years of international involvement in the region and the proclaimed determination of political elites in the Western Balkans countries to join the EU, legal frameworks are generally satisfactory for preventing corruption at different levels of government in all the countries. It is the practice that keeps high ranking officials and closely connected party supporters out of prosecution or with lenient sentences after the trials that is problematic and keeps corruption levels higher than in the rest of Europe, with the notable exception of the four countries already mentioned. Another report states "a lack of political will and a decline in implementation of laws and regulations" as challenges.[33]

V-Dem's Political Corruption Index offers a view of more diversity among the states of the Western Balkans. According to the index, the worst situation is in

---

[27] U.S. Department of State (2020e), Country Reports on Human Rights Practices: North Macedonia.

[28] U.S. Department of State (2020f), Country Reports on Human Rights Practices: Serbia.

[29] U.S. Department of State (2020d), Country Reports on Human Rights Practices: Montenegro.

[30] U.S. Department of State (2020c), Country Reports on Human Rights Practices: Kosovo.

[31] U.S. Department of State (2020b), Country Reports on Human Rights Practices: Bosnia and Herzegovina.

[32] U.S. Department of State (2020a), Country Reports on Human Rights Practices: Albania.

[33] Transparency International (2020), p. 16.

Albania with an index of 75, closely followed by Bosnia-Herzegovina's 74. Kosovo's index of 35 is on the opposite end, leaving the remaining three on the scale in between the two extremes.[34]

Weak democratic institutions in the Western Balkans and ambition for authoritarian rule by political leaders might be compared to the Chinese "ideological tradition of Mass Line that directly connects the state with the public, often bypassing administrative regulations and the legal procedure, resulting in weak institutions and civic organisations."[35] This quasi-democratic decision-making process creates the impression of a participatory society and might seem similar to a mass society. It organises the relationship between elites and masses, as Mao Zedong said in 1967, communicates ideas "from the masses, to the masses."[36]

This kind of relationship makes elites accessible to the masses who commit themselves to the regime, which, in turn, might create the impression or ability to "correct unpopular policies and purge incompetent officials."[37] Nevertheless, "the Party leadership is central in Mao's conception of the mass line."[38] This form of "political socialisation in this populist authoritarian political tradition"[39] creates support for national government and dissatisfaction with lower-level leaderships, setting conditions for creating popular authoritarian leadership at the national level. A cult of personality is the extreme version of this kind of regime.

Serbia under Aleksandar Vučić might be an example of the successful application of the old Chinese concept of the mass line into the Serbian political model adapted to the current conditions. In addition to the control of media, strong influence over the judiciary, and fragmented opposition, alternatives to his rule are not visible if existent at all. Thus, periodical electoral exercise in quasi-democracy is destined for success. The rule receives legitimacy from the electorate, who, despite lacking many freedoms, seems to be satisfied after seeing the removal of some lower rank officials and the built-up perception of the regime dealing decisively with problems of corruption. Their removal reconfirms the regime's claims of the rule of law. Perhaps, because of being weaker than the Serbian president, authoritarian regimes in the other countries of the Western Balkans did not develop this strategy.

The West has successfully developed policies of conditionality towards the countries in transition in Central and Eastern Europe (CEE) in the past. Popular expectations, however, have not been fulfilled and helped develop a sense of disappointment. Expected economic improvements did not follow political and systemic reforms. The result is political disappointment in the western model and a rise of political apathy. Alternative models of democracy have gained support, and authoritarian leaders have emerged.

---

[34] V-Dem Institute. University of Gothenburg (2020) Political Corruption Index.

[35] Tang (2016), p. 1.

[36] Tang (2016), p. 6.

[37] Tang (2016), p. 1.

[38] Young (1980), p. 225.

[39] Tang (2016), pp. 11–12.

6.4 The Rule of Law

The Rule of Law Index positions all the countries of the Western Balkans in the second-lowest group, as seen in Table 6.4. Montenegro was not part of this index. The index has been based on the information provided by a considerable number of indicators and subfactors that come from the eight categories of factors measured individually for the index. The authors also noted a ninth factor of "informal justice", but they did not include the results of this factor in the aggregated results. It is unfortunate, especially when the reader focuses the analysis on the Western Balkans where elements of the informal justice are often prevalent and "play a large role in countries where formal legal institutions are weak, remote, or perceived as ineffective."[40]

While all the countries are placed closely within the same group of nations, Kosovo ended up the best placed in the overall category of the rule of law and came on top of the region's countries in five out of eight factors measured. Constraints on the government, absence of corruption, fundamental rights, order, and security, are the categories in which Kosovo performed better than the other countries in the region. The civil justice factor, though, placed it last in the region.

Bosnia-Herzegovina is the best-placed country according to two factors – regulatory enforcement and criminal justice, and the worst placed by the factor of order and security. North Macedonia's findings are the best according to the civil justice factor, while five factors placed the country in the second position, making it overall the second-best in the region. Serbia and Albania share similar results altogether, having the same score, but Serbia positioned 75th globally, and Albania was 78th. The regional comparisons placed both countries as worst in three categories each. Serbia's worst record was measured by constraints on government powers, fundamental rights, and criminal justice. Albania underperformed in factors measuring the absence of corruption, open government, and regulatory enforcement.[41]

Constraints on government powers measured institutional limitations and accountability of government. Six indicators were used for the findings that included institutional checks, like limits by the judiciary and legislative limits, and non-institutional, like freedom and independence of press as a vital feature of putting the government in check. Kosovo's performance was significantly better than the rest, with Serbia being found distant last in this category.

The worst factor for the whole region is the absence of corruption where the best-placed country, Kosovo, scores lower than in any other category, and the worst-performing country's score, Albania, is also lower than in any other factor. The factor measured "three forms of corruption: bribery, improper influence by public or private interests, and misappropriation of public funds or other resources."[42]

[40] World Justice Project (2020), p. 12.

[41] World Justice Project (2020), pp. 16–29.

[42] World Justice Project (2020), p. 12.

Table 6.4 The Rule of Law Index in the Western Balkans[a, b]

Constraints on government powers	Absence of corruption	Open government	Fundamental rights	Order and security	Regulatory enforcement	Civil justice	Criminal justice
Kosovo 0.52	Kosovo 0.46	Kosovo 0.56	Kosovo 0.60	Kosovo 0.84	B & H 0.49	N Mac 0.55	B & H 0.48
N. Mac 0.47	N Mac 0.44	N Mac 0.48	B & H 0.59	N Mac 0.79	N Mac 0.48	Serbia 0.51	Kosovo 0.47
Albania 0.45	Serbia 0.44	B & H 0.47	Albania 0.59	Albania 0.79	Serbia 0.48	B & H 0.48	N Mac 0.45
B & H 0.45	B & H 0.44	Serbia 0.47	N Mac 0.59	Serbia 0.77	Kosovo 0.44	Albania 0.48	Albania 0.43
Serbia 0.39	Albania 0.37	Albania 0.47	Serbia 0.57	B & H 0.76	Albania 0.44	Kosovo 0.46	Serbia 0.40

[a]World Justice Project (2020), pp. 22–29

[b]Montenegro was not measured by this index

The open government factor showed similar order of the countries with Kosovo performing the best, North Macedonia coming second, Serbia and Bosnia-Herzegovina sharing the same score, and Albania having the worst performance. The factor was based on how the government shares the information, the empowerment of citizens to hold government accountable, and their participation in public policy deliberations.

The factor of fundamental rights found all the countries close to each other. Kosovo has the best record and is closely followed by the three countries with just a point worse indicator, leaving Serbia only two points lower. The authors acknowledged other indices that focus on human rights and henceforth focused purely on a narrow set of rights that "are most closely related to rule of law concerns."[43]

Perhaps surprisingly, the factor of order and security produced the best performance for the whole region. With the worst score in this field, Bosnia-Herzegovina would come out on top of any other factor with this numerical result. Kosovo, again, was measured as the best, followed by North Macedonia and Albania. Serbia's score is slightly better than Bosnia-Herzegovina's. Three indicators used for this factor checked whether crimes are effectively controlled, if the civil conflict is effectively limited and if people redress personal grievances by resorting to violence.

The regulatory enforcement results put Bosnia-Herzegovina on top, but all the countries had similar scores in this factor. The worst-placed Albania shares the score with Kosovo and is only five points below the top-scoring country. Serbia and Macedonia also share the score in-between. This factor investigates the effectiveness of implementing measures and the timing and a way of administrative proceedings.

Civil justice is measured by indicators looking into accessibility and affordability of civil justice systems. Lack of discrimination, corruption and improper influence affects the score. The particular factor "also measures the accessibility, impartiality, and effectiveness of alternative dispute resolution mechanisms."[44] Kosovo performed the worst in this category, and North Macedonia is the best-placed state in the region.

When it comes to criminal justice, Serbia had the lowest score and Bosnia-Herzegovina the highest. The entire criminal justice system is assessed by the set of indicators of this factor, including "the police, lawyers, prosecutors, judges, and prison officers."[45]

---

[43] World Justice Project (2020), p. 13.

[44] World Justice Project (2020), p. 14.

[45] World Justice Project (2020), p. 14.

6.5 Human Rights in the Western Balkans

The findings for the broad subject of human rights are spread across several indices that partly address human rights issues. In this place, the focus is on the index that covers the subject in the broadest terms. Several organisations provide some forms of indices or annual reports but are not consistent with all the countries, or the form is as a report and not an index. Therefore, they are used to understand and know the state of human rights but could not have been used to add to the index itself. Even the "Human Rights Index" for Europe in 2019 did not include Kosovo and Belarus.

The five countries from the Western Balkans showed similar results in many aspects. Although there is plenty of room for criticism, the gradual improvement is noticeable when comparing findings between 2011 and 2018. They generally show progress, albeit limited, in the four sub-indices that the Human rights Index is based on. However, some tendencies show the opposite direction of changes.

Bosnia-Herzegovina improved in all sub-indices and is still measured last in Europe in the Access to Education Sub Index. Albania's improvement on the state of rights in 2011 is noticeable overall, but the last Personal Safety Sub Index is worse than any during the previous 4 years. North Macedonia is showing improvements in all the categories except for Personal Rights. The index overall has improved in Serbia since 2011. However, except for the Personal Safety Sub Index, the remaining three categories show a decline over the most recent period.

Furthermore, the Personal Rights Sub Index shows the overall regress of rights. Montenegro's overall index has declined, as did all four sub-indices. The difference is that Personal Safety and Personal Rights show a gradual decline over the 10 years since 2011, while the Access to Education and Tolerance and Inclusion indices are better in 2019 than in 2011. However, despite the overall improvement over the 10 years, both indices also show a decline over the more recent period.

Focusing only on the latest findings on the eve of the pandemic, the Personal Safety Sub-Index is topped by Portugal and Slovenia with a score of 9.20. Russia is at the other extreme with a score of just 1.36. Albania is the best positioned regional country in the 32nd place, while Montenegro's score is regionally the worst in 38th place. Although the countries of the Western Balkans are positioned closer to the bottom of the table, their actual scores are similarly distant from both the leading countries in this category and the worst-performing country, Russia, which probably tells more about Russia being distinctly the least secure country in this category.

"Societal violence persisted against Kosovo-Serb and other ethnic minority communities, all of which were also affected by social and employment discrimination," the U.S. government report on Kosovo stated.[46] "Human rights defenders," a report found in Serbia, "were threatened."[47] "Ethnic Albanians," in North

[46]U.S. Department of State (2020) Human Rights Reports. Custom Report Excerpts: Albania, Bosnia and Herzegovina, Kosovo, Montenegro, North Macedonia, Serbia.

[47]Amnesty International (2019), p. 66.

Macedonia, "were subject to discrimination and disproportionately unemployed."[48] The same document in the section on Montenegro reported "crimes involving violence or threats of violence targeting persons with disabilities, members of national/racial/ethnic minority groups, or indigenous people."[49]

"A series of attacks by youths on Roma in Leskovac," in southern Serbia, "were not investigated as hate crimes."[50] Further south, in North Macedonia, "inter-ethnic hate speech and hate crimes," the report found, "remained consistently high."[51] In Bosnia-Herzegovina, "minorities continued to face widespread discrimination and social exclusion."[52] "Impunity remained a serious problem" in Albania where "officials, politicians, judges, and persons with powerful business interests often were able to avoid prosecution."[53] This kind of findings are reflected in the Personal Safety Sub Index shown in Table 6.5.

The Access to Education Sub Index shows Germany on top with a 9.58 score, and Bosnia-Herzegovina is the last in the whole of Europe with a score of 5.63. Table 6.6 shows results for countries of the Western Balkans. This particular aspect affects a significant part of the population, but minorities and especially Roma, are discriminated against more than others. "The 2019 World Bank study examining Roma inclusion in the Western Balkans between 2011 and 2017 found only limited progress in improving access to education, employment, health, housing, and documentation for Roma in the country."[54] Amnesty International reported that in Bosnia-Herzegovina, "Roma continued to face systemic barriers to education, housing, health services and employment."[55] "Many Roma girls," in Serbia, "left school before completing their primary education; and are almost fully absent from the education system after the age of 18."[56]

"Most members of Roma and Egyptian communities," a report found in Albania, "continued to face barriers in their access to a range of rights, including housing, education, employment and health services."[57] "Housing remains precarious for an estimated 40% of Roma households" in Montenegro.[58] In Serbia, "Roma continued to be denied their social and economic rights, including education, health and housing."[59]

"Some schools," in Albania, "resisted accepting Romani and Balkan-Egyptian students," and many of those "schools that accepted Romani students marginalized

[48] U.S. Department of State (2020).
[49] U.S. Department of State (2020).
[50] Amnesty International (2019), p. 67.
[51] Amnesty International (2019), p. 56.
[52] Amnesty International (2019), p. 14.
[53] U.S. Department of State (2020a) Country Reports on Human Rights Practices: Albania.
[54] Human Rights Watch (2020), p. 77.
[55] Amnesty International (2019), p. 15.
[56] Amnesty International (2019), p. 67.
[57] Amnesty International (2019), p. 9.
[58] Amnesty International (2019), p. 52.
[59] Amnesty International (2019), p. 67.

Table 6.5 Personal Safety Sub Index[a]

Position	Country	Index
32	Albania	5.25
34	Serbia	5.25
35	N. Macedonia	5.09
37	B & H	5.01
38	Montenegro	4.99

[a]Friedrich Naumann Foundation for Freedom. East and Southeast Europe (2020), p. 24

Table 6.6 Access to Education Sub Index[a]

Position	Country	Index
33	Montenegro	7.60
34	Serbia	7.57
36	Albania	7.41
41	N. Macedonia	6.34
45	B & H	5.63

[a]Friedrich Naumann Foundation for Freedom. East and Southeast Europe (2020), p. 25

them in the classroom, sometimes by physically setting them apart from other students." In Bosnia-Herzegovina, the same report found, "Roma, and especially Romani women, continued to be the most vulnerable and experience the most discrimination of any group in the country." "The Romani, Ashkali, and Balkan-Egyptian communities," the same report's section on Kosovo states, "often lacked access to basic hygiene, medical care, and education and were heavily dependent on humanitarian aid for subsistence." In Montenegro, "Romani women often faced double discrimination based on their gender and ethnicity."[60]

State discrimination against minorities is evident in numerous international organisations' reports and is widespread across the Western Balkans. Thus, it was reported that in North Macedonia, "Roma continue to experience institutional discrimination in education, health, housing and employment." However, the discrimination by ordinary citizens becomes more pronounced when, in the same country, Roma are prevented from "access to bars, cafés and shops."[61] "Members of the Roma, Ashkali and Egyptians (RAE) communities," in Serbia, "experienced chronic discrimination in education, health, housing and employment, and many lacked personal documentation."[62]

The Tolerance & Inclusion Sub Index found the best-performing Iceland scoring 9.34, and Turkey at the opposite end, with a score of 2.71. Countries of the Western Balkans are somewhere in the middle with the scores found between the best protected and the most discriminated. (See Table 6.7) "Crimes involving violence or threats of

[60]U.S. Department of State (2020) Human Rights Reports. Custom Report Excerpts: Albania, Bosnia and Herzegovina, Kosovo, Montenegro, North Macedonia, Serbia.

[61]Amnesty International (2019), p. 56.

[62]Amnesty International (2019), p. 68.

Table 6.7 Tolerance & Inclusion Sub Index[a]

Position	Country	Index
29	N. Macedonia	5.63
31	Albania	5.47
33	B & H	5.11
34	Serbia	5.11
38	Montenegro	4.86

[a]Friedrich Naumann Foundation for Freedom. East and Southeast Europe (2020), p. 26

violence targeting lesbian, gay, bisexual, transgender, or intersex persons" were reported in Bosnia-Herzegovina, Montenegro, and Serbia. Some minor linguistic differences in the report distinguished Kosovo with "attacks against members of ethnic minorities or other marginalized communities," and "instances of violence and threats of violence" in North Macedonia.[63] In Albania, the report found that "despite the law and the government's formal support for lesbian, gay, bisexual, transgender, and intersex rights, public officials sometimes made homophobic statements."[64]

Finland, Ireland, Luxembourg, the Netherlands, Norway, and Sweden all scored the best, 10.00, on the Personal Rights Index. Azerbaijan comes last in this category with a score of 1.74. In this particular sub index, the Western Balkans countries, like in the others, are positioned closer to the worst-performing countries, but their numerical scores are closer to the top-performing countries in Europe, as scores in Table 6.8 show.

The Human Rights Index has just confirmed the tendency seen in other indices that all Western Balkans countries are below the average European standards and placed just above some of the post-Soviet republics and Turkey. Only the Tolerance & Inclusion Sub Index positioned North Macedonia in 29th place. All the countries are found by this sub index and all others in thirty-something positions, with just two exceptions in the Access to Education Sub Index in which North Macedonia is 41st and Bosnia-Herzegovina is 45th, the last in the whole of Europe. The overall results by the Human Rights Index show this by placing all five countries between the 32nd and 40th position. (See Table 6.9) This index did not measure Kosovo.

In the broader context, Iceland has the best index of 9.26 while Turkey is the worst positioned with 3.77. The results of the Western Balkans countries thus come in the middle, but they are still below the average because a far greater number of countries have scores closer to Iceland than to Turkey. Only Russia and Azerbaijan have the score within a point of Turkey, and the next closest is Bosnia-Herzegovina, with a score of 1.70 higher than Turkey. The best-positioned country from the region is Serbia, and yet, the Human Rights Watch reported: "There was little improvement in human rights protection in Serbia in 2019."[65]

[63]U.S. Department of State (2020) Human Rights Reports. Custom Report Excerpts: Albania, Bosnia and Herzegovina, Kosovo, Montenegro, North Macedonia, Serbia.

[64]U.S. Department of State (2020) Country Reports on Human Rights Practices: Albania.

[65]Human Rights Watch (2020), p. 495.

Table 6.8 Personal Rights Sub Index[a]

Position	Country	Index
31	Serbia	7.78
33	Montenegro	7.29
34	Albania	7.08
36	N. Macedonia	6.60
39	B & H	6.11

[a]Friedrich Naumann Foundation for Freedom. East and Southeast Europe (2020), p. 27

Table 6.9 Human Rights Index[a]

Position	Country	Index
32	Serbia	6.43
33	Albania	6.30
36	Montenegro	6.18
39	N. Macedonia	5.91
40	B & H	5.47

[a]Friedrich Naumann Foundation for Freedom. East and Southeast Europe (2020), p. 23

The U.S. Department of State Human Rights Report found common issues for the Western Balkan countries. The section with "significant human rights issues" included "problems with the independence of the judiciary" in Albania and Bosnia-Herzegovina, while in Montenegro it stated, "serious problems with the independence of the judiciary" in addition to "allegations of torture by the government; arbitrary arrest or detention."[66]

Levels of corruption are differently described in the report reflecting the diversity of the methods and spread of the practice. There is "pervasive corruption in all branches of government and municipal institutions" in Albania. Bosnia-Herzegovina has issues with "government corruption" and Kosovo with "government corruption and impunity". There are "serious acts of corruption" in Montenegro, a "high-level corruption" in North Macedonia, and "numerous acts of government corruption" in Serbia.[67]

"Domestic violence remained a problem in Kosovo," a report found, "with inadequate police response, few prosecutions and continued failure by judges to issue restraining orders against abusive partners."[68] In Bosnia-Herzegovina, "domestic violence was recognized as one of the most important problems involving gender equality."[69] Another report found the implementation of the protection "patchy and non-existent" despite being provided by the law and thus "leaving

[66]U.S. Department of State (2020) Human Rights Reports. Custom Report Excerpts: Albania, Bosnia and Herzegovina, Kosovo, Montenegro, North Macedonia, Serbia.

[67]U.S. Department of State (2020) Human Rights Reports. Custom Report Excerpts: Albania, Bosnia and Herzegovina, Kosovo, Montenegro, North Macedonia, Serbia.

[68]Human Rights Watch (2020), p. 337.

[69]U.S. Department of State (2020) Human Rights Reports. Custom Report Excerpts: Albania, Bosnia and Herzegovina, Kosovo, Montenegro, North Macedonia, Serbia.

women vulnerable to domestic violence and employment discrimination, and under-represented in political life."[70] In Albania, "violence against women and girls was widespread and protection measures were inadequately implemented."[71] Furthermore, "only 19% of women owned property," in Albania, "due to poor implementation of the property registration law and a patriarchal tradition that favours male inheritance."[72]

The practice was reported in Montenegro that "officers often [were] counselling women to "forgive" their attackers or to "not harm their (the attackers) job prospects." The same report stated that "according to the Center for Women's Rights, sexual harassment, including street harassment, of women occurred often, but few women reported it."[73] The law in North Macedonia "provides women the right to obtain a restraining order against abusers," but the report found that "the government did not enforce the law effectively."[74] "The UN Committee on the Elimination of Discrimination Against Women (CEDAW)," Human Rights Watch report on Serbia stated, "raised concerns about the lack of effective investigations of cases of gender-based violence against women, the discrepancy between the number of criminal charges and convictions, and that the majority of those convicted receive suspended sentences."[75]

The legislation in the field of human rights has been adopted and modified over the years since the establishment of independence or democratisation in all Western Balkans countries. The declaratory determination of all of them to proceed with European integrations has made these changes inevitable. However, like with the regimes, they produce a theoretical and legal framework for the protection of human rights and civil liberties, while at the same time, the practice and work of state institutions deny many of these rights and liberties. Furthermore, the nature of the regimes, that is less than democratic despite formal democratic procedures, creates conditions for society to suppress many of the freedoms and breach human rights. This is especially visible in the context of the rights of minority groups and vulnerable individuals. Despite the efforts by civil society and the support of international organisations, it is proven that it remains difficult to be different in the Western Balkans. The regimes are often considered corrupt, the rule of law is in the seemingly permanent phase of development, and human rights are more of a declaratory nature than protected in everyday practice.

[70] Human Rights Watch (2020), p. 79.

[71] Amnesty International (2019), p. 8.

[72] Amnesty International (2019), p. 9.

[73] U.S. Department of State (2020) Human Rights Reports. Custom Report Excerpts: Albania, Bosnia and Herzegovina, Kosovo, Montenegro, North Macedonia, Serbia.

[74] U.S. Department of State (2020) Human Rights Reports. Custom Report Excerpts: Albania, Bosnia and Herzegovina, Kosovo, Montenegro, North Macedonia, Serbia.

[75] Human Rights Watch (2020), p. 499.

References

Amnesty International (2019) Human Rights in Europe. https://www.amnesty.org/download/Documents/EUR0120982020ENGLISH.PDF. Accessed 1 May 2021

Friedrich Naumann Foundation for Freedom. East and Southeast Europe (2020) Human Rights Index 2019. Friedrich Naumann Foundation for Freedom. East and Southeast Europe. https://www.freiheit.org/sites/default/files/import/2020-02/21969-humanrightsindex2019.pdf. Accessed 1 May 2021

Forsythe DP (2012) Human Rights in international relations, 3rd edn. Cambridge University Press, Cambridge

Human Rights Watch (2020) World Report (Events of 2019). https://www.hrw.org/sites/default/files/world_report_download/hrw_world_report_2019.pdf. Accessed 6 Oct 2021

Ishay MR (2008) The history of human rights: from ancient times to the globalization era. University of California Press, Berkeley

Lauren PG (1998) The evolution of international human rights: visions seen. University of Pennsylvania Press, Philadelphia

Lohmann G (2015) Individual Human Rights and obligations towards communities. Fudan J Human Soc Sci 8:387–399

Morrison K (2018) Nationalism, identity and statehood in post-Yugoslav Montenegro. Bloomsbury Academic, London

Tang W (2016) Populist authoritarianism: Chinese political culture and regime sustainability. Oxford University Press, Oxford

The U.S. Department of State (2020) Human Rights Reports. Custom report excerpts: Albania, Bosnia and Herzegovina, Kosovo, Montenegro, North Macedonia, Serbia. https://www.state.gov/report/custom/2c3d0564b8/. Accessed 6 Oct 2021

The Universal Declaration of Human Rights (9 December 1948) General assembly of the United Nations

Transparency International (2019) Corruption perceptions index. https://images.transparencycdn.org/images/2019_CPI_Report_EN.pdf. Accessed 6 Oct 2021

Transparency International (2020) Global Corruption Perception Index 2019, p 8. https://images.transparencycdn.org/images/2019_CPI_Report_EN_200331_141425.pdf. Accessed 1 May 2021

Trotsky L (1936) The revolution betrayed. Marxists internet archive. https://www.marxists.org/archive/trotsky/1936/revbet/ch11.htm. Accessed 6 Oct 2021

U.S. Department of State (2020a) Country reports on human rights practices: Albania. https://www.state.gov/reports/2020-country-reports-on-human-rights-practices/albania/. Accessed 6 Oct 2021

U.S. Department of State (2020b) Country Reports on Human Rights practices: Bosnia and Herzegovina. https://www.state.gov/reports/2020-country-reports-on-human-rights-practices/bosnia-and-herzegovina/. Accessed 6 Oct 2021

U.S. Department of State (2020c) Country reports on human rights practices: Kosovo. https://www.state.gov/reports/2020-country-reports-on-human-rights-practices/kosovo/. Accessed 6 Oct 2021

U.S. Department of State (2020d) Country Reports on Human Rights Practices: Montenegro. https://www.state.gov/reports/2020-country-reports-on-human-rights-practices/montenegro/. Accessed 6 Oct 2021

U.S. Department of State (2020e) Country Reports on Human Rights Practices: North Macedonia. https://www.state.gov/reports/2020-country-reports-on-human-rights-practices/north-macedonia/. Accessed 6 Oct 2021

U.S. Department of State (2020f) Country Reports on Human Rights Practices: Serbia. https://www.state.gov/reports/2020-country-reports-on-human-rights-practices/serbia/. Accessed 6 Oct 2021

Vásquez I, Porčnik T (2019) Human freedom index. Cato Institute, Fraser Institute, Friedrich Naumann Foundation for Freedom, Washington, D.C., Vancouver, Potsdam. https://www.fraserinstitute.org/sites/default/files/human-freedom-index-2019-rev.pdf. Accessed 31 Mar 2021

V-Dem Institute. University of Gothenburg (2020) Political corruption 2019. https://www.v-dem.net/en/analysis/MapGraph/. Accessed 1 May 2021

World Justice Project (2020) Rule of law index. https://worldjusticeproject.org/our-work/research-and-data/wjp-rule-law-index-2020. Accessed 1 May 2021

Young G (1980) On the mass line. Modern China 6(2):225–240

Chapter 7
Freedom of Expression and Media Freedoms on the Eve of the Pandemic

7.1 State of Mind, State of Freedom, and the State of the State

International organisations, whether government-supported or being independent of state financial structures, often divide European space into its "liberal" and "illiberal" or "liberalising" part. In addition to differences based on historical developments, the particular set of freedoms in the field of media and expression reflects the nature of political regimes and underline political diversity in Europe. Thus, the majority of post-communist countries are repressive to various degrees towards media and the freedom of expression.

This project sums up four different indices created by reputable international institutions, V-Dem Institute, Freedom House, Reporters Without Borders and Article XIX. Their findings have many common features for the majority of the countries. However, some differences could be noticed, while they often collaborate like fourteen organisations jointly producing the Council of Europe's project,[1] they stipulate that the opinions are of individual organisations, and each of them "reserves the right to make its own assessment of any issue or case."[2] V-Dem Institute did not participate in this project, but Article XIX uses their set of indices to create Article XIX's own index.

The Council of Europe's report confirms the division in Europe on societal environments more open to media freedom, usually in the north and the west, and more repressive environments, mainly in the east of the continent. While their report does not produce a specific index, the authoring organisations describe it as "a loud wake-up call to Council of Europe member states to act quickly and resolutely to end the assault against press freedom."[3] A careful reading of the report shows which

[1]Council of Europe (2020) Annual Report by the partner organisations to the Council of Europe Platform to Promote the Protection of Journalism and Safety of Journalists.

[2]Council of Europe (2020), p. 10.

[3]Council of Europe (2020), p. 10.

N. Andjelic, *Covid-19, State-Power and Society in Europe*, European Union and its Neighbours in a Globalized World 5, https://doi.org/10.1007/978-3-030-91073-0_7

countries came under the scrutiny of organisations of concern for media freedoms. Titled as "countries and regions in focus" are Albania, Azerbaijan, Bulgaria, Hungary, Poland, Russia, Serbia, Turkey, Ukraine, and a Russian controlled Crimea and eastern Ukraine. The only "non-eastern" countries in focus are France for violence against journalists covering protests and Malta.

In addition to determining the scores for media freedoms to countries, Article XIX directs attention to countries where these freedoms are endangered over a more extended period. The five top falling scores for the previous 5 years consist of Poland, Croatia, Hungary, Bosnia-Herzegovina, and Serbia. The list covering the previous 10 years adds Ukraine and Turkey to Hungary, Serbia, and Poland. Countries from the east, Armenia, North Macedonia, Moldova, and Georgia, also dominate the rising scores list. According to Article XIX, the lowest scores on the eve of the pandemic were in Turkey and Azerbaijan, while the top five were made of Switzerland sharing the score with three Scandinavian countries, Sweden, Norway and Finland, and Denmark on top.[4]

Many post-communist countries have transitioned towards, or back to, an authoritarian form of government that inevitably demands control or at least a strong influence over the media. Except for Turkey, all the countries with the worst falling scores have a communist regime experience in the second half of the twentieth century. Among the 16 best-performing countries, based on the aggregated scores of the four indices, only Estonia and Lithuania, in addition to Cyprus, are not from what is usually referred to as Western Europe.

"State capture marches on in the East," warns Article XIX, "as Hungary and Poland continue down the path to autocracy."[5] The Council of Europe describes the process as "the conversion of the public service broadcasters into state media or state capture of the private sector, and harassment targeting journalists or other media actors."[6] Viktor Orbán's policies in Hungary and Aleksandar Vučić's in Serbia are judged to "have had great success in snuffing out critical journalism." The Freedom House's report states that "both leaders have consolidated media ownership in the hands of their cronies, ensuring that the outlets with the widest reach support the government and smear its perceived opponents."[7]

Instead of open political pressure that is nevertheless not abandoned, authoritarian regimes use an "invisible hand of the market" tactics. The economic manipulation of the media is based on directing where the advertising is bought by choosing "friendly" media. When the state is all-powerful, the public sector is often the largest employer. The resulting economy relies on state contracts regardless of whether they are private or state owned. Privately-owned companies are doing wisely to follow the direction of investing their marketing budgets in the media suitable to the regime, while the state-owned companies nevertheless invest in media supporting government. The result is that financial resources for media critical of government policies are restricted. In the

---

[4] Article XIX (2020), p. 87.

[5] Article XIX (2020), p. 90.

[6] Council of Europe (2020), p. 41.

[7] Repucci (2019), p. 2.

longer run, they are prone to be bought by business allies of the governing structures and consequently transfer the formerly critical media to the government-friendly media. The process is to be observed across the "new" Europe.

Pressure by economic means is not always sufficient, however. The political and legal methods are adding to the overall position of the media in such regimes. Legislations are developed in many countries that are supposed to ban "fake news", "spreading panic", or "providing a platform for terrorists". In practice, however, this often results in the government using legal means to suppress independent reporting and media freedoms. Russia, Turkey, and Albania are examples of such developed legislation. The difference between these regimes and liberal democracies is that when Boris Johnson's government attempted to regulate harmful online material, they were opposed by civil society and many media organisations. Some politicians' intent in different kinds of regimes might be the same or similar, but the result is different due to the developed institutions in liberal democracies that prevent such political actions from fruition. The question, though, is for how long the institutions can resist such political interference.

Authoritarian regimes often bring a series of strategic lawsuits against the media and journalists that investigate government actions and policies. Another method of creating conditions where media and journalists are preoccupied with legal and administrative activities instead of investigative journalism and independent reporting are frequent visits by tax inspectors and financial authorities. A combination of legal proceedings, tax inspections, and financial pressure is often enough to reduce the number of media independent of the regime.

A state of permanent crisis is often developed in such societies. It could be a state security issue, territorial integrity, economic crisis, or, lately, the national health issue that keeps the state of crisis when the legislation is invoked to deal with journalists and others that question the situation, policies, or the crisis itself. The imaginary rule of law principle is put in place to satisfy the needs of the regime.

Liberal regimes, though, are not immune to putting journalists under pressure. As the vital tool and value of investigative journalism, the protection of anonymous sources is endangered when governments, like in Spain, France, and the Netherlands, threaten journalists with legal suits unless the sources are revealed. It inevitably contrasts the issues of freedom of expression and independence of media with national security. Like in the debate about the suppression of hate speech and a consequent endangering of the freedom of expression, there are no definite answers, and many states struggle with the solution. Societies with developed institutions are in a stronger position to preserve freedoms and secure national interests. However, even traditional liberal democracies are not immune to repressive solutions. Hence the conclusion of the Council of Europe's report that "the condition of media freedom in Europe today is deeply unsatisfactory." The report describes "political attempts to "capture" the media and failures by many state authorities to maintain a credible framework of protections for media freedom [that] have become systemic."[8]

[8]Council of Europe (2020), Annual Report by the partner organisations to the Council of Europe Platform to Promote the Protection of Journalism and Safety of Journalists. p. 10.

7.2 The Democratisation of Media and the State

There are serious threats to media freedom across Europe that involve attempts to control mainstream and online media rigidly. Digital revolutions that generally coincided with the period after the end of the Cold War have democratised media. The internet revolution, followed by the mobile media and finally by social networks, created a democratised jungle where everything is allowed for the sake of pure survival, not unlike the situation described by Thomas Hobbes in seventeenth century England and the struggle of individuals for survival.[9] The old business model is dead, or at least significantly reformed. Traditional and established media had to adjust and develop new platforms, including opening up the direction of communication going two-ways. In addition to the direction from the information source towards the citizen, or towards the consumer, that a citizen has become in a neoliberal media model, the stream of information now also goes in the opposite direction: from the consumer, still regarded as citizen in some media models, towards the media platform. This is a process of democratisation providing citizens with the opportunity to address issues in public, often unmoderated.

The situation is described as "the profound change that came with the spread of online news and the collapse of the traditional advertising market [that] has sent outlets and owners scrambling for profits by prioritizing content that spurs outrage."[10] While it is not possible to have media, politics and the economy generally controlled by a large group of the elite in society, new attempts are made by the elite to preserve influence or develop new tools of influence. Situations of uncertainty have contributed to the rise of populist politics that has largely built its foundations on anti-elitism. The change in the media world not only reflects the political changes, but the media effectively pronounces the need for political change. Anti-elitism is being used in some countries by the ruling elite to cement their power by directing the anger towards others—other countries, the European Union, immigrants, minorities—and orchestrating support for domestic elites that result in illiberal regimes. In liberal societies, the struggle is ongoing, and societies are further polarised. "The growing prominence of fake news and disinformation has further fed into political polarization."[11]

Another issue is the rise of the new economic elite that uses its economic power and global dependence on their platforms to influence society. Article XIX noted: "Big Tech have too much power over the free flow of information and no accountability to balance this power."[12] They inevitably influence society and politics through their platforms used by media. States are yet to address this issue. Authoritarian regimes, like Turkey banning YouTube, unless the company's representative resides in the country, and Russia, conditioning android phone sales by having

[9] Hobbes (2020).

[10] Csaky (2019), p. 21.

[11] Csaky (2019), p. 21.

[12] Article XIX (2020), p. 34.

alternative search engines to Google, effectively forced the Big Tech companies to accommodate state demands. Turkey "tops the list for legal requests by the state to remove content."[13] In Russia, a new law has been signed by Vladimir Putin that criminalises "insult" of the state and the dissemination of "fake news".

Thus, authoritarian regimes have spread their activities and attempts to control the media, from traditional media to online platforms, and consequently developed legislation that makes the state's action legal. The legitimacy of such state activities is doubtful from the point of view of civil freedoms and human rights. While social media are increasingly becoming a crucial part of the contemporary media by radically expanding access to information, it is the regime's response in non-democratic countries that show the unchanged nature of the powerholders. The only immediate change is the regime's attempt to exercise control of the new media if possible. When Big Tech companies make deals with such regimes, they further undermine democratic gains achieved on social networks, as examples from Turkey and Russia proved.

Liberal democracies, meanwhile, struggle under market conditions because by vying the big companies to be present in their countries and thus providing jobs and some financial contributions, they are abandoning their instruments of directing media developments. The democracies undermine each other in this process, thus making Big Tech even bigger and less accountable. It is the Big Tech and not the state that conditions the relations. Some liberal democracies, meanwhile, controversially attempt to exercise control over the online content produced by individuals or organisations that are not their Big Tech partners. Thus, some citizens become even more alienated towards the regime, even though it could be a traditionally liberal and open society. A sense of injustice and inequality develops among some citizens over time.

Journalists are not arrested in liberal societies for their professional work, but it is doubtful whether this could be a reason for satisfaction. On the eve of the pandemic, there were 105 journalists in prisons: "91 journalists jailed in Turkey, seven in Azerbaijan, four in Russian-controlled Crimea, and three in the Russian Federation."[14] Belarus is not included in this number as the country is not part of the Council of Europe.

Hate speech is lacking a universally accepted definition. Its usual targets include, but are not restricted to, members of a minority, whether political, social, ethnic, religious or of some specific sexual orientation. The vagueness of the situation is further added by the lack of the universally accepted definition of a national minority, for example. Thus, the behaviour of the state in attempting to regulate hate speech is open to debate. Freedom of expression is challenged by the rules of protection against hate speech.

[13] Amnesty International (2020) Turkey: Stifling free expression during the COVID-19 pandemic.

[14] Council of Europe (2020) Annual Report by the partner organisations to the Council of Europe Platform to Promote the Protection of Journalism and Safety of Journalists. p. 11.

This is where different forms of power in the state come with their role to intervene. In their toolkit, Article XIX distinguishes three categories of the state's response. States are required by international law to prohibit severe forms of hate speech. States may prohibit discriminatory or bias-motivated threats or harassment. Finally, some lawful forms of hate speech enjoy the protection under the freedoms of expression but "nevertheless raises concerns in terms of intolerance and discrimination, meriting a critical response by the State."[15]

This legal openness for the interpretation provides governments with a tool to suppress some forms of free speech or justify repression of the free media by legal provisions against hate speech while taking measures against the media critical of the government. In Poland, "*Gazeta Wyborcza* alone reported that 50 criminal and civil cases have been brought against it by various state or state-controlled institutions."[16] This set of actions is not exclusive of increasingly authoritarian regimes only. Spain, Italy, Germany, and the United Kingdom were all referenced in Article XIX's report for some forms of over-regulating or regulating the issues of hate speech wrongly.[17]

Journalists and media are increasingly accused and prosecuted by some states for "hate speech", while the actual offence is determined and interpreted by the regime. At the same time, the state authorities often ignore actual expressions of hate and threats issued against journalists. The resulting impunity has become an increasing characteristic of the level of endangered media freedoms in several countries. The state failed to prosecute offenders against journalists, thus making reporting a more dangerous activity. Security forces' behaviour in some states comes as no surprise after numerous reports of the state of media freedoms. Attempts to report on demonstrations in south-eastern Turkey are met with arbitrary arrests. Activists in Belarus use live streaming on social networks to document the heavy-handed approach used by security forces during the protests, thus proving a new opportunity arising for the regime's opponents. However, the forced landing of a plane carrying a blogger critical of the regime proves the regime is untouched by material proofs of its violent nature.

Some other examples came from countries with a tradition of established media freedoms, such as Italy and France, where police forces used violence against journalists and media reporting on the protests against some government policies. Instances of such actions have been reported during the "*Gilets Jaunes*" (Yellow Vests) protests in France and, in Italy, when anti-riot police attacked reporters during the neo-fascist and far-right rallies. The leader of the far-right political party, Matteo Salvini was the then Minister of Interior.

---

[15] Article XIX (2015) 'Hate Speech' Explained: A Toolkit.

[16] Council of Europe (2020), p. 42.

[17] Article XIX (2020), p. 93.

7.3 Media in Public Service or the Service of Government

The position of public service media is questioned under circumstances of increased tensions, regardless of whether they are internal or external, thus creating a situation of crisis when the state takes an effective control over the service, which becomes a service tool of the state instead of the public. It often ends up being a service of the party in power under such circumstances. The examples are numerous, including Russia, Hungary, Poland, but also the United Kingdom, where the government accused the BBC and another public service broadcaster, Channel 4, of bias against their policies. The government's intentions were further revealed upon Johnson raising "the prospect of changing the law to decriminalise non-payment of the licence fee."[18]

While the governing party in the United Kingdom did not transform the BBC into the state or party service, they managed to influence some significant changes to the public service that included a ban on political expressions by BBC staff on their private social media accounts and the insistence on opening up the news to more radical views coming from the political right. The largest political party in Switzerland supported the referendum to cut taxpayer funding into public services that would endanger the broadcast in four state languages. The voters expressed their overwhelming support for the public service, but the irony is the fundamental duality of citizens' attitudes: while supporting the public service, they also in large numbers support the political party that opposes the public service.

Starving media of statements and appearances from the government undermines such media in the long run as the public is deprived of hearing from the powerholders. It is often not apparent to the public whether the lack of official appearances was the government's decision or the media being in firm opposition to the government. Thus, media independence gradually becomes understood as bias against the government and eventually described as opposition media, although the particular platform has no connection with the opposition parties and movements.

Ministers in the government of Boris Johnson are carefully avoiding public service media when contacted for interviews to clarify government policies. Viktor Orbán has not given an interview to a non-friendly media in Hungary for 5 years, Euronews reported in 2019.[19] "Nearly 80 percent of the media are owned by government allies"[20] in Orbán's Hungary, which is the result of a process of "forced closure or effective government takeover of independent media and assembling a vast pro-government media empire sharing the same editorial line and sharing source materials."[21] Aleksandar Vučić has developed similar policies, and when a critical mouthpiece is persistent, the Serbian President has found a friendly business person

---

[18] Council of Europe (2020), p. 31.

[19] Euronews (21 November 2019) What happened in the Hungarian media could happen in your country too.

[20] Repucci (2019), p. 2.

[21] Council of Europe (2020), p. 41.

to buy over *Kurir*, the high circulating tabloid previously critical of him. The businessman and the government denied any involvement in a deal that benefitted both. "The suspicions are strengthened by the fact that *Kurir* dramatically changed its editorial policy overnight, moving from the loudest critic to Vučić's private publication."[22]

The global geopolitical struggle to establish a new and lasting international system is reflected in the behaviour of different ideological regimes both domestically and internationally. Thus, the loudest proponent of illiberal democracy, Viktor Orbán, and his government have "mobilised massive state resources, including state advertising, to marginalise remaining independent outlets."[23] However, the mission is not restricted to internal affairs, but several government allies have set up an international news agency in London. The V4NA, in the name of the agency, stands for Visegrád Four News Agency, thus aiming at audiences in the four allied countries in Central Europe, although the service was initially being provided in two languages only—Hungarian and English.

The overlapping of state and private resources is proven by the involvement of a wealthy and close ally of Orbán, Árpád Habony, and the Hungarian Ambassador to London who registered the company. The new service provides information to the vast media empire that is in various ways connected or controlled by forces who look at the Hungarian regime sympathetically. Attempts to influence politics internationally are strengthened by Hungarian tycoons, close to the government, buying into media in neighbouring Slovenia. The newly acquired outlets tend to support Slovenian Prime Minister Janez Janša, who happens to be a close ideological ally of Orbán. Hungarian State Secretary, Zoltán Kovács, adds to this geopolitical strategy in his lengthy anti-liberal diatribes explaining the rightfulness of the Hungarian government when interviewed by western media. The titles of the agency's items like "Islam can take over Sweden in 50 years," and "Migrants unhappy with the free money they get" reflect the ideological background of the agency's output.[24]

Autocratic regimes from Turkey and Russia have their media output through global services of TRT in Turkish and English, and RT in Russian and English. Anadolu News Agency has a strong presence in post-Ottoman countries, but Western media also carry out its packages. Russia's Sputnik agency is focused on countries where Russian political interests are strong but is also developing its activities in the West alongside the RT.

However, the opposite direction is also present with western services targeting audiences in the east of Europe, primarily Russia, and increasingly developing activities for Turkish audiences. The EU has set up the East StratCom Task Force and disseminates their regular Disinformation Review. The fake news strategies are obviously polluting media space across Europe and within the European Union. This reaction by the European strategists reflects the seriousness of the issues affecting

[22] Jutarnji list (30 August 2020).

[23] Council of Europe (2020), p. 41.

[24] The Guardian (5 May 2019) London media agency carries Viktor Orbán's nativist message.

media in the contemporary world. Russian language services by various western media outlets are certainly part of the overall process.

Western democracies are also targeting Turkish audiences, but the tactics are different. Deutsche Welle, BBC, France24, and Voice of America (VOA), joined resources to address the media repression in Turkey and launched a YouTube channel in the Turkish language. "The stated goal of the channel, +90, is to "provide independent and accurate information that promotes free speech and a multitude of perspectives on current affairs," Freedom House stated in their report.[25] However, several foreign news providers are present with their Turkish language news, including Deutsche Welle Türkçe, BBC Türkçe and VOA Turkish already broadcasting for these audiences but, seemingly, their state owners realised the additional effort was needed. Two years after the launch of the channel, +90 has 477 thousand subscribers.[26] Turkish government service, TRT World, at the same time had around three times more, 1.3 million subscribers,[27] supporting the seeming conclusion of who is currently winning this media battle.

The private sector is also involved in the vast market as CNN Turk has been present there for decades. However, the whole new enterprise might not have polluted the planned results as Erdoğan's government forced YouTube to accept the newly developed laws affecting internet-based platforms. The presence of Sputnik Turkey adds other elements to this media war.

7.4 Findings by the Evaluators

Results of four indices have been aggregated to find the overall score for each of the 45 countries. All the indices showed similar results for the countries, except for eight states that experienced relatively recent significant political changes that could possibly explain a level of inconsistency between the evaluators. If they had slightly different timings for their evaluations, indices would have produced a more spread scale of results. A murder of an investigative journalist in Slovakia and a consequent change at the head of government and the state might have produced dissimilarity in reports. Greece, Armenia, and Kosovo also experienced a change of government. Romania and Georgia had three governments between 2018 and 2020, and Moldova even four during the same period. Bulgaria is the only of the eight countries that did not have a change of government but have experienced street protests because of the perceived government officials' corruption. "A country's media landscape can be affected by countless other factors, such as the election of a more tolerant government or improvement in the local economy," some political scientists observed.[28]

[25] Shahbaz (2019), p. 26.

[26] +90 (2021).

[27] TRT World (2021).

[28] Burgess (2010), p. 5.

If Greece is disregarded for being an "honorary member of the West", all these countries are in Europe's east. Additionally, the overall findings show that between the 24th positioned Slovakia and the worst positioned Azerbaijan, only Malta and, conditionally Greece are not eastern countries. Furthermore, they are all post-communist societies, except for Turkey. Some autocratic leaders from this region argue that criteria reflect western values and democratic practices that are not historically suited for different cultures and regions. "Claims of Western bias in the studies," John Burgess found, "have spurred the development of new rating systems that are meant to have universal acceptance or to be tailored to the conditions of particular regions."[29] There are some specialised reports and indices, like the Bertelsmann Transformation Index,[30] or the Media Sustainability Index,[31] looking exclusively at eastern Europe or post-communist countries. As this project is about the whole of Europe, regardless of how valuable their findings might be, they could not have been used for indexing. However, their reports are invaluable.

All the organisations attempting to mathematically measure media freedoms, from the longest producing indices, Freedom House, to the latest to develop sets of indices, V-Dem Institute, including the *Reporters sans frontières* and the Article XIX, use slightly different methods but produce very similar results in their "attempt to apply mathematical precision to a huge and, in many ways, subjective state of affairs: the entire media universe of individual countries."[32]

The four indices, if combined, should reconfirm the results found by each index, as shown in Table 7.1. As it has already been shown, only eight countries findings show an element of disagreement between the indices, often produced by recent political changes and depending on the specific timing of the index-taking. Thus, 37 out of 45 countries show very consistent findings by four different sets of indicators. Eleven countries making a group of states where all the indices have found full media freedoms are regarded as Western, except for Estonia. Further five countries, including Lithuania in the east, and southern Cyprus, were found second-best by just one of the four indices. This makes it that only three of the top 16 countries are not Western in this index.

The usual four countries led by autocratic leaders are at the bottom of the overall table: Azerbaijan, Turkey, Russia, and Belarus. Ukraine is usually in other indices just above these autocracies, but Ukraine's findings are significantly better in this index than the bottom four countries. Both Ukraine and Serbia, with the same score, are just behind a series of post-communist and Western Balkans countries. Only Malta is measured together with these countries in places between 26th Romania and 37th Moldova. The prolonged investigation into the brutal murder of an investigative journalist in Malta is obviously reflected in the indices.

[29]Burgess J (2010), p. 12.

[30]Bertelsmann Stiftung (2020) Bertelsmann Transformation Index.

[31]IREX, USAID (2019) Media Sustainability Index.

[32]Burgess (2010), p. 7.

Table 7.1 Expression and Media Freedoms Index

Position	Country	Index	Status	Points	Freedom of Expression Index 2019[a]	2020 World Press Freedom Index[b]	Freedom and the Media 2019[c]	Global Expression Index 2019–2020[d]
1	Norway	1	Good	4	One 0.96	One 7.84 good	One 4 on scale 0-4	One open
1	Finland	1	Good	4	One 0.96	One 7.93 good	One 4 0n scale 0-4	One open
1	Denmark	1	Good	4	One 0.97	One 8.13 good	One 4 on scale 0-4	One open
1	Sweden	1	Good	4[e]	[e]	One 9.25 good	One 4 on scale 0-4	One open
1	Netherlands	1	Good	4	One 0.93	One 9.96 good	One 4 on scale 0-4	One open
1	Switzerland	1	Good	4	One 0.97	One 10.62 good	One 4 on scale 0-4	One open
1	Portugal	1	Good	4	One 0.97	One 11.83 good	One 4 on scale 0-4	One open
1	Germany	1	Good	4	One 0.96	One 12.16 good	One 4 on scale 0-4	One open
1	Belgium	1	Good	4	One 0.97	One 12.57 good	One 4 on scale 0-4	One open
1	Ireland	1	Good	4	One 0.96	One 12.60 good	One 4 on scale 0-4	One open
1	Estonia	1	Good	4	One 0.95	One 12.61 good	One 4 on scale 0-4	One open
12	Cyprus	1	Good	5	One 0.91	Two 20.45 satisfactory	oNE 4 on scale 0-4	One open
12	Lithuania	1	Good	5	One 0.90	Two 21.19 satisfactory	One 4 on scale 0-4	One open
12	France	1	Good	5	One 0.96	Two 22.92 satisfactory	One 4 on scale 0-4	One open
12	UK	1	Good	5	One 0.96	Two 22.93 satisfactory	One 4 on scale 0-4	One open
16	Luxembourg	1	Good	5.33[e]	One 0.95	Two 15.46 satisfactory	One 4 on scale 0-4	[e]
17	Austria	2	Satisfactory	6	One 0.93	Two 15.78 satisfactory	Two 3 on scale 0-4	One open
17	Latvia	2	Satisfactory	6	One 0.96	Two 18.56 satisfactory	Two 3 on scale 0-4	One open
17	Spain	2	Satisfactory	6	One 0.92	Two 22.16 satisfactory	Two 3 0n scale 0-4	One open
17	Italy	2	Satisfactory	6	One 0.94	Two 23.69satisfactory	Two 3 on scale 0-4	One open
17	Czechia	2	Satisfactory	6	One 0.92	Two 23.57 satisfactory	Two 3 on scale 0-4	One open
17	Slovenia	2	Satisfactory	6	One 0.88	Two 22.64 satisfactory	Two 3 0n scale 0-4	One open
23	Iceland	2	Satisfactory	6.66[e]	[e]	Two 15.12 satisfactory	Two 3 on scale 0-4	One open
24	Slovakia	2	Satisfactory	7	One 0.90	Two 22.67 satisfactory	Three 2 on scale 0-4	One open

(continued)

Table 7.1 (continued)

Position	Country	Index	Status	Points	Freedom of Expression Index 2019[a]	2020 World Press Freedom Index[b]	Freedom and the Media 2019[c]	Global Expression Index 2019–2020[d]
24	Greece	2	Satisfactory	7	One 0.92	Three 28.80 problematic	Two 3 on scale 0-4	One open
26	Romania	2	Satisfactory	8	One 0.85	Three 25.91 problematic	Two 3 on scale 0-4	Two less restrict.
26	Georgia	2	Satisfactory	8	One 0.91	Three 28.59 problematic	Three 2 on scale 0-4	One open
26	Armenia	2	Satisfactory	8	One 0.85	Three 28.60 problematic	Three 2 on scale 0-4	One open
29	Poland	3	Problematic	9	Two 0.72	Three 28.65 problematic	Two 3 on scale 0-4	Two less restrict.
29	Croatia	3	Problematic	9	Two 0.71	Three 28.51 problematic	Two 3 on scale 0-4	Two less restrict.
29	Kosovo	3	Problematic	9	One 0.86	Three 29.33 problematic	Three 2 on scale 0-4	Two less restrict.
32	Malta	3	Problematic	9.33[e]	[e]	Three 30.16 problematic	Two 3 on scale 0-4	Two less restrict.
33	Bulgaria	3	Problematic	10	Two 0.77	Four 35.06 difficult	Two 3 on scale 0-4	Two less restrict.
33	N. Macedonia	3	Problematic	10	Two 0.75	Three 31.28 problematic	Three 2 on scale 0-4	Two less restrict.
33	B & H	3	Problematic	10	Two 0.67	Three 28.51 problematic	Three 2 on scale 0-4	Two less restrict.
33	Albania	3	Problematic	10	Two 0.69	Three 30.25 problematic	Three 2 on scale 0-4	Two less restrict.
37	Hungary	3	Problematic	11	Two 0.69	Three 30.84 problematic	Three 2 0n scale 0-4	Three restricted
37	Montenegro	3	Problematic	11	Two 0.62	Three 33.83 problematic	Three 2 on scale 0-4	Three restricted
37	Moldova	3	Problematic	11	Two 0.79	Three 31.16 problematic	Four 1 on scale 0-4	Two less restrict.
40	Serbia	4	Difficult	12	Three 0.50	Three 31.62 problematic	Three 2 on scale 0-4	Three restricted
40	Ukraine	4	Difficult	12	Three 0.58	Three 32.52 problematic	Three 2 on scale 0-4	Three restricted
42	Belarus	5	Repressed	17	Four 0.36	Four 49.75 difficult	Five 0 on scale 0-4	Four highly rest.
43	Russia	5	Repressed	18	Four 0.33	Four 48.92 difficult	Five 0 on scale 0-4	Five in crisis
44	Turkey	5	Repressed	18	Five 0.14	Four 50.02 difficult	Four 1 on scale 0-4	Five in crisis
45	Azerbaijan	5	Repressed	19	Four 0.30	Five 58.48 very serious	Five 0 on scale 0-4	Five in crisis

[a]V-Dem Institute. University of Gothenburg (2020)
[b]Reporters Without Borders (2020)
[c]Freedom House (2019)
[d]Article 19 (2020)
[e]: Some countries have been omitted from some indices. Therefore, the average score had to be calculated for the particular feature.

7.5 Media Freedoms in the Western Balkans

Press freedoms are under a severe threat in the region. The U.S. government's report found "restrictions on free expression and the press" in Albania. The situation in Kosovo is characterised by "undue restrictions on the press, including violence or threats of violence against journalists." At the same time, it is even more difficult in Bosnia-Herzegovina with "restrictions of free expression, the press, and the internet, including violence and threats of violence against journalists." "Violence and threats of violence against journalists" were also reported in North Macedonia. Montenegro is described as having similar issues of "serious restrictions on free expression; substantial interference with the freedom of peaceful assembly and freedom of association." "Serious restrictions on free expression and the press" were reported in Serbia, "including violence, threats of violence, and unjustified arrests and prosecutions against journalists.[33]

"The authorities," another report on Serbia stated, "actively eroded media freedom."[34] Freedom House stated that "in Montenegro and Serbia, independent journalists, opposition figures, and other perceived foes of the government faced ongoing harassment, intimidation, and sometimes violence."[35] The Friedrich Naumann Foundation reported that journalists were under "the verbal and physical attacks in Serbia and Montenegro."[36] A convicted war Criminal made sexual threats against Serbia's Commissioner for the Protection of Equality because the Commissioner previously condemned his abusive statements about a journalist who had written about the Srebrenica commemoration.[37]

Of the countries and regions in the focus of the Council of Europe's report on the safety of journalists, only two Western Balkans countries are included. The report underlined in Albania "harassment and intimidation of journalists, including physical violence." The same report warns of the situation in Serbia where "the number of attacks on media, including death threats, is on the rise, and inflammatory rhetoric often comes from public officials." Ordinary people also pose threats to journalists. Thus, reporters of the N1 television were threatened when a group of people shouted ""spies", "thieves" and "American mercenaries" at the journalists and tried to break their camera and microphone."[38]

While focusing on post-communist countries only, the Media Sustainability Index covers all six states from the Western Balkans. The overall index consists of five sub-indices: Free Speech, Professional Journalism, Plurality of News Sources,

[33] U.S. Department of State (2020) Human Rights Reports. Custom Report Excerpts: Albania, Bosnia and Herzegovina, Kosovo, Montenegro, North Macedonia, Serbia.

[34] Amnesty International (2019), p. 66.

[35] Freedom House (2020) Freedom in the World 2020. p. 24.

[36] Friedrich Naumann Foundation (2019), p. 5.

[37] Amnesty International (2019), p. 67.

[38] Council of Europe (2021) Platform to promote protection of journalism and safety of journalists.

Business Management and Supporting Institutions.[39] Each of these sub-indices is based on several indicators that are based on thorough research within the country. A table was created for this project based on this series of indices and the overall Media Sustainability Index. The index in the range of 0-1 is categorised as "Unsustainable, Anti-Free Press" and the index ranging between 1 and 2 is categorised as "Unsustainable Mixed System". According to the authoring organisations, the range of indices between 2 and 3 is marked "Near Sustainability", and the index between 3 and 4 is "Sustainable".

As shown in Table 7.2, the overall index found Serbia and Bosnia-Herzegovina have an "unsustainable mixed system". Serbia is the lowest-ranked country in this category, leaving only Azerbaijan below it, of the European countries, in the unsustainable category. All the Western Balkans countries in all the categories are either within the "Unsustainable Mixed System" or marked "Near Sustainability". The highest status of "Sustainable" was achieved in just one category: Supporting Institutions, by just one country, Kosovo. On a positive note, not a single category has shown any of these countries having an "unsustainable" mark.

Therefore, a general description of the media situation in Serbia and Bosnia-Herzegovina is that they "minimally meet objectives." Some elements of the government and legal system are "opposed to a free media system." However, there is "evident progress in free speech advocacy" and an "increased professionalism".[40]

The remaining four, North Macedonia, Montenegro, Albania, and the best-placed Kosovo, are generally described within their category as having "progressed in meeting multiple objectives, with legal norms, professionalism, and the business environment supportive of independent media." Changes in government did not undermine the achievements of the previous powerholders. "However," the description states, "more time may be needed to ensure that change is enduring."[41]

This specialised index reflects in many ways the aggregated findings of the four indices used for the project. Table 7.3 shows Kosovo in the best-placed position, slightly distinguished from the rest of the region, tightly ordered just above the problematic countries suppressing media freedoms. Serbia is the worst positioned of the Western Balkans' countries with some features in common with autocratic regimes at the bottom of the overall, pan-European table and sharing some features with neighbouring countries.

The diversity of media is present across the states in the region. However, the existence of diverse media does not mean that they are reaching the audience. The media in Albania is "diverse but polarised" and influenced by the owners' political affiliations and interests. Pluralism of media in Kosovo "improved, with fewer physical attacks on journalists." In Albania, based on an NGO report, "one in three journalists reported being physically or verbally assaulted because of their

[39] IREX, and USAID (2019) Europe & Eurasia Media Sustainability Index 2019.

[40] IREX, and USAID (2019), p. 15.

[41] IREX, and USAID (2019), p. 15.

Table 7.2 Media Sustainability Index[a]

Country	Overall		Free Speech		Professional Journalism		Plurality of News Sources		Business Management		Supporting Institutions	
	Index	Sustainability	Index	Sustainability	Index	Sustainability	Index	Sustainability	Index	Sustainability	Index	Sustainability
Serbia	1.45	2	1.47	2	1.07	2	1.51	2	1.10	2	2.12	3
B & H	1.72	2	2.24	3	1.36	2	1.80	2	1.33	2	1.95	2
N. Macedonia	2.26	3	2.44	3	1.97	2	2.46	3	1.76	2	2.68	3
Montenegro	2.45	3	2.61	3	2.30	3	2.67	3	1.96	2	2.46	3
Albania	2.49	3	2.71	3	2.33	3	2.69	3	1.98	2	2.75	3
Kosovo	2.53	3	2.52	3	2.41	3	2.72	3	2.19	3	3.02	4

[a]IREX, and USAID (2019), pp. 15–16

Table 7.3 Expression & Media Freedoms in the Western Balkans

Position	Country	Index	Status	Points	Freedom of Expression Index 2019[a]	2020 World Press Freedom Index[b]	Freedom and the Media 2019[c]	Global Expression Index 2019–2020[d]
29	Kosovo	3	Problematic	9	One 0.86	Three 29.33 problematic	Three 2 on scale 0–4	Two less restrict.
33	N. Macedonia	3	Problematic	10	Two 0.75	Three 31.28 problematic	Three 2 on scale 0–4	Two less restrict.
33	B & H	3	Problematic	10	Two 0.67	Three 28.51 problematic	Three 2 on scale 0–4	Two less restrict.
33	Albania	3	Problematic	10	Two 0.69	Three 30.25 problematic	Three 2 on scale 0–4	Two less restrict.
37	Montenegro	3	Problematic	11	Two 0.62	Three 33.83 problematic	Three 2 on scale 0–4	Three restricted
40	Serbia	4	Difficult	12	Three 0.50	Three 31.62 problematic	Three 2 on scale 0–4	Three restricted

[a]V-Dem Institute. University of Gothenburg (2020)
[b]Reporters Without Borders (2020)
[c]Freedom House (2019)
[d]Article 19 (2020)

work." Investigative journalists in Montenegro came under pressure from the state that prosecuted journalists and organised criminal groups that shot a journalist. In Serbia, the report states, "the President and ministers conducted a smear campaign against independent journalists. Threats were commonplace." "The pattern of threats, political pressure and attacks against journalists continued," states a section on Bosnia-Herzegovina in Amnesty International's report.[42] Another organisation reported an increase in "direct intimidation of journalists," as the Association of Journalists in Bosnia-Herzegovina "registered 12 physical attacks on and 13 death threats received by journalists" in 2018.[43]

The media situation in Albania is described as diverse where "all the big parties have their own mouthpieces," and stating, "the intimate links between politics, business and media."[44] These links are common in the states of the region. In Serbia, the government actively eroded media freedom by rewarding supportive media with advertising and funding and harassing critical media through taxation or legal proceedings."[45] A similar situation was present in Kosovo, where "selective advertising by the government was used to influence newspapers." However, "new amendments to the law on public procurement banned this practice."[46]

Media freedoms in Bosnia-Herzegovina are affected by "political pressure" that adds to "self-censorship; nontransparent media ownership; a corrupt relationship between media and advertisers in a shrinking advertisement market with an increasing share of government and public companies; nontransparent government funding for media; and regular civil libel suits against critical media outlets and journalists."[47]

A close relationship between media and political actors is omnipresent in all countries. However, the media interprets and reports differently on the same event as a result of political influence. "The media generally work hand-in-hand with particular political parties," it has been reported for Montenegro, where "certain media outlets are closely tied to influential political actors, which causes significant differences in media reporting about the same events."[48]

The change from the nationalist government in North Macedonia has decreased the pressure from the government on journalists, but "the media landscape remains polarized." Both the government and the opposition supported the law "that would allow for the development of a clientelistic relationship between the government and the media."[49]

---

[42] Amnesty International (2019), p. 15.

[43] Bertelsmann Stiftung (2020) Bertelsmann Transformation Index.

[44] Bertelsmann Stiftung (2020).

[45] Amnesty International (2019), p. 67.

[46] Bertelsmann Stiftung (2020).

[47] Bertelsmann Stiftung (2020).

[48] Bertelsmann Stiftung (2020).

[49] Bertelsmann Stiftung (2020).

The state legally guarantees freedom of expression and media freedoms across Europe. Despite the theoretical and legal provisions, however, when observed and checked by international organisations and independent researchers, significant obstacles are found in achieving these freedoms and rights in practice. The developed democracies with a long tradition of civil liberties and human rights are faced with the new media and the necessity to regulate new platforms. However, they are, in some cases, simultaneously endangering civil freedoms in these attempts.

The developing democracies, on the other hand, like the countries of the Western Balkans, are faced with more complex issues. In addition to the need to develop and protect freedoms, local powerholders frequently act intending to control the media and suppress freedom of expression and media freedoms. Unlike in the past, they generally do not use legislation to influence and control the media but are creating a business environment unfriendly to independent or government non-friendly media. In addition to the "invisible hand of market", the practice also shows frequent use of administrative measures to control health and safety in offices of such media or tax inspections. Numerous judicial processes against journalists and media organisation further contribute to the suppression of freedoms. Finally, some criminal groups that could not be directly connected to governing parties use violence and intimidation in suppressing dissent with governing and dominant views.

References

+90 (2021). https://www.youtube.com/c/plus90/about. Accessed 6 Oct 2021

Amnesty International (2019) Human Rights in Europe. https://www.amnesty.org/download/Documents/EUR0120982020ENGLISH.PDF. Accessed 1 May 2021

Amnesty International (2020) Turkey: Stifling free expression during the COVID-19 pandemic. https://www.amnesty.org/en/latest/campaigns/2020/06/turkey-stifling-free-expression-during-the-covid19-pandemic/. Accessed 5 Oct 2021

Article XIX (2015) 'Hate Speech' explained: a toolkit. https://www.article19.org/data/!les/medialibrary/38231/'Hate-Speech'-Explained%2D%2D-A-Toolkit-(2015-Edition).pdf

Article XIX (2020) The global expression Report. https://www.ecoi.net/en/file/local/2039407/GxR2019-20report.pdf. Accessed 5 Oct 2021

Bertelsmann Stiftung (2020) Bertelsmann transformation index. https://www.bti-project.org/en/index/political-transformation.html. Accessed 6 Oct 2021

Burgess J (2010) Evaluating the evaluators: media freedom indexes and what they measure. Monitoring and evaluation. http://repository.upenn.edu/cgcs_monitoringandeval_videos/1. Accessed 6 Oct 2021

Council of Europe (2020) Annual Report by the partner organisations to the Council of Europe Platform to Promote the Protection of Journalism and Safety of Journalists. https://rm.coe.int/annual-report-final-en/16809f03a9. Accessed 1 May 2021

Council of Europe (2021) Platform to promote protection of journalism and safety of journalists. https://www.coe.int/en/web/media-freedom/issues-and-countries-in-focus. Accessed 20 May 2021

Csaky Z (2019) A new toolbox for co-opting the media. In: Freedom and the media 2019. Freedom House. https://freedomhouse.org/report/freedom-and-media/2019/media-freedom-downward-spiral. Accessed 1 May 2021. pp 16–23

Euronews (21 November 2019) What happened in the Hungarian media could happen in your country too. https://www.euronews.com/2019/11/21/a-free-press-no-more-the-media-in-hungary-has-become-nothing-more-orban-s-mouthpiece-view. Accessed 6 Oct 2021

Freedom House (2019) Freedom and the Media 2019. https://freedomhouse.org/report/freedom-and-media/2019/media-freedom-downward-spiral. Accessed 1 May 2021

Freedom House (2020) Freedom in the World 2020. https://freedomhouse.org/report/freedom-world/2020/leaderless-struggle-democracy. Accessed 1 May 2021

Friedrich Naumann Foundation (2019) Freedom Barometer: Europe Edition 2019. http://freedombarometer.org/files/download/Freedom_Barometer_Europe_2019.pdf. Accessed 1 May 2021

Hobbes T (2020) Leviathan. Independently published

IREX, USAID (2019) Media sustainability index. https://www.mediasustainabilityindex.org/. Accessed 1 May 2021

Jutarnji List (30 August 2020) Kako je Vučić novcem Telekoma Srbije kupio kritičare i pouzdanicima dao dio medija u Hrvatskoj. https://www.jutarnji.hr/vijesti/svijet/kako-je-vucic-novcem-telekoma-srbije-kupio-kriticare-i-pouzdanicima-dao-dio-medija-u-hrvatskoj-15016284. Accessed 6 Oct 2021

Reporters Without Borders (2020) World Press Freedom Index 2020. https://rsf.org/en/ranking/2020. Accessed 6 Oct 2021

Repucci S (2019) Freedom and the media: a downward spiral. In: Freedom and the Media 2019. Freedom House. pp 1–7. https://freedomhouse.org/report/freedom-and-media/2019/media-freedom-downward-spiral. Accessed 6 Oct 2021

Shahbaz A (2019) Why social media are still worth saving. In: Freedom and the media 2019. Freedom house. pp 24–30. https://freedomhouse.org/report/freedom-and-media/2019/media-freedom-downward-spiral. Accessed 6 Oct 2021

The Guardian (5 May 2019) London media agency carries Viktor Orbán's nativist message. https://www.theguardian.com/world/2019/may/05/london-based-media-agency-channels-victor-orban-nativist-message-hungary. Accessed 6 Oct 2021

The U.S. Department of State (2020) Human Rights Reports. Custom report excerpts: Albania, Bosnia and Herzegovina, Kosovo, Montenegro, North Macedonia, Serbia. https://www.state.gov/report/custom/2c3d0564b8/. Accessed 6 Oct 2021

TRT World (2021). https://www.youtube.com/channel/UC7fWeaHhqgM4Ry-RMpM2YYw. Accessed 5 June 2021

V-Dem Institute. University of Gothenburg (2020) Freedom of Expression Index 2019. https://www.v-dem.net/en/analysis/MapGraph/. Accessed 1 May 2021

Chapter 8
Democracy, Liberties and Rights Under the Threat of State Fighting the Pandemic

8.1 Societies Under Pressure from State Measures

State interventionism during the pandemic is a difficult task that several organisations made attempts to study and produce reports for. Probably the most ambitious project was set up by the Oxford University Blavatnik School of Government.[1] The International Centre for Not-for-Profit Law and the activist website Pandemic Big Brother have also produced data on state actions caused by the pandemic. Their findings are used as raw data supporting the research and findings of this study. Contributions by several human rights organisations and academic institutions were also consulted for this work.

European states responded to the global pandemic in 2020 by introducing generally stringent measures that have affected citizens' lives and some standard democratic procedures, civil liberties, and human rights. Human Rights Watch (HRW) found "at least 83 governments worldwide have used the Covid-19 pandemic to justify violating the exercise of free speech and peaceful assembly."[2] The European Center for Not-For-Profit Law (ECNL), while monitoring "the deployment of emergency powers across the globe," found that "at least 103 countries have declared a state of emergency in response to the current crisis."[3] In Europe, the Institute for Democracy and Electoral Assistance (IDEA) found that "more than a quarter of countries (12) have implemented measures that are deemed concerning for democracy."[4]

The ECNL, in another report, states that governments "directly restricted the possibility for individuals to exercise their civic freedoms of association, assembly,

---

[1] Oxford University's Blavatnik School of Government (13 April 2020) Oxford Covid-19 Government Response Tracker.

[2] Human Rights Watch (2021).

[3] European Center for-not-for Profit Law (2021), p. 7.

[4] Institute for Democracy and Electoral Assistance (2021), p. 7.

N. Andjelic, *Covid-19, State-Power and Society in Europe*, European Union and its Neighbours in a Globalized World 5, https://doi.org/10.1007/978-3-030-91073-0_8

and participation among others."[5] The IDEA reported similar concerns naming "the aspects of democracy most affected by the pandemic are Freedom of Movement and Freedom of Association and Assembly," and adding "Freedom of Expression and Media Integrity, as well as Personal Integrity and Security."[6] Amnesty International reported that across Europe, "the police enforcement of lockdowns disproportionately impacted poorer areas, which often have a higher proportion of residents from minority ethnic groups."[7]

The practice is not country-specific or spread across one region, but it is endemic across the continent. The same report states examples from France wherein the most impoverished mainland area, Seine-Saint-Denis, "where the majority of inhabitants are Black or of North African origin, the number of fines for breaching the lockdown was three times higher than in the rest of the country." "In the UK," the report continues, "the proportion of Black people who were searched rose by nearly a third" while, in London, the practice of stop and search increased by 22%. The report evidenced Spanish policemen violently pushing a young North African man in Bilbao "despite posing no threat to them." Governments in Bulgaria and Slovakia "brought in mandatory quarantines on Roma settlements. In Slovakia they also tasked the military with enforcing them." Refugees, asylum-seekers, and migrants were faced with "selective quarantines in Germany, Cyprus and Serbia, and with forced evictions in France and Greece." The military was tasked in Serbia with monitoring the curfew in "a strict 24-hour mandatory quarantine" explicitly designed for centres housing refugees and migrants.[8]

While 45 countries in Europe had some form of legislative responses to the COVID-19 pandemic that affected civic freedoms, 38 states extensively used the state of emergency regimes and in most cases without a "proper notification of the derogation from international commitments," as obliged by the European Convention on Human Rights. The ECNL's report further states that "declarations of the state of emergency were followed by adoption of unprecedented restrictions to human rights and civic freedoms."[9] Freedom of movement in various forms, like curfews, international travel bans or bans for travel within the country, was affected in 40 countries. "Public gathering were [Sic!] somehow restricted in all countries throughout Europe." Many governments adopted measures to allow disproportionate surveillance, thus intruding into the right to privacy. Freedom of association was also affected while state authorities monopolised the right to information and expression, the report states.[10] The issues of concern were public health, that the government has a duty and obligation to protect, and the restrictions, proportionality,

[5]European Center for Not-For-Profit Law (2020), p. 1.

[6]Institute for Democracy and Electoral Assistance (2021), p. 7.

[7]Amnesty International (2020a).

[8]Amnesty International (2020a).

[9]European Center for Not-For-Profit Law (2020), p. 1.

[10]European Center for Not-For-Profit Law (2020), p. 2.

and time-limitation necessity. Another institute, however, names only Belarus, Sweden, and Iceland as exceptions to restrictions on the freedom of movement.[11]

Democracies in Europe are distinguished, in the IDEA analysis, from authoritarian regimes of Azerbaijan and Belarus, and hybrid regimes of Russia and Turkey that "implemented measures to curb the pandemic that presented concerns from a democracy and human rights perspective." Still, "8 of the 40 democracies (or 20 per cent of them)" implemented the same or similar measures. "Bulgaria, Hungary and Serbia stand out in this regard, but also to a lesser extent Poland, Slovenia and Ukraine." Slovakia is the remaining country, alongside Israel, that IDEA considers in Europe, with similar measures but, unlike other mentioned democracies, did not experience democratic backsliding during the 5 years prior to the pandemic.[12]

The HRW's global report highlights two European countries, Ukraine and Serbia, out of 18 such states globally, where security or government officials "have physically assaulted journalists or bloggers for reporting on COVID-19 policies as well as protesters, political opponents, or lawyers."[13] Amnesty International reacted to "images of Serbian police firing tear gas and stun grenades indiscriminately into the crowd, and of protesters and bystanders being charged by mounted police and beaten by police in riot gear."[14] Protesters were detained in Ukraine for attempting to "protest against a far-right violence." Their complaints of having a constitutional right to assemble peacefully were reportedly silenced, as the HRW carries a report, by the police response of "the Constitution is not working now."[15] The IDEA report found cause for the concern "in some countries—for example, Azerbaijan and Serbia—where authorities have arrested or used excessive force on protesters."[16]

Another organisation has "identified several cases when public authorities misused the coronavirus restrictions for cracking down on their critiques."[17] Belarus stripped several foreign journalists of their accreditation, while the report is also critical of Turkey and Azerbaijan. Access to information was limited in several countries. The use of facial recognition technologies became more widespread, providing a possibility for hybrid or authoritarian regimes, even for democracies under special measures, to monitor citizens and breach their right to privacy. Bulgarian authorities reportedly passed the legislation that "enabled police to monitor everyone's mobile phone traffic metadata and internet contacts without a court order."[18] Operators are obliged in Armenia "to provide state bodies with information

[11] Institute for Democracy and Electoral Assistance (2021), p. 13.

[12] Institute for Democracy and Electoral Assistance (2021), p. 7.

[13] Human Rights Watch (2021).

[14] Amnesty International (2020b).

[15] Human Rights Watch (2021).

[16] Institute for Democracy and Electoral Assistance (2021), p. 13.

[17] European Center for Not-For-Profit Law (2020), p. 4.

[18] European Center for Not-For-Profit Law (2020), p. 3.

on the customers' location and phone numbers the customers' have contacted, including dates and duration of phone calls."[19]

Criticising government policies in some cases resulted in arbitrary arrests, detention, or prosecution in countries like Poland, Belarus, Hungary, Serbia, Montenegro, Greece, Azerbaijan, Russia, and Turkey.[20] It is interesting to recall that Hungary and Poland are frequently criticised for the state of their democracies by fellow European countries. Political turmoil following the culmination of the economic crisis in Greece and the refugee crisis all further polarised the society, and security forces and state institutions increasingly used severe measures to achieve their aims, which were not always democratic. Other countries on this list are either authoritarian or hybrid regimes.

The IDEA has found 16 countries that "have passed laws or taken actions that restrict freedom of expression or curtail media integrity. There are five countries—Bosnia and Herzegovina, Hungary, Russia, Serbia and Turkey—that have passed new disinformation laws during the pandemic."[21] These tendencies endangered the state of democracy and individual human rights in these states, already marked by authoritarian tendencies and nationalist, almost totalitarian, ideologies.

A group of countries, including Hungary, Romania, Turkey, and Kosovo, and some post-Soviet states like Russia, Armenia, Azerbaijan and Moldova, used censorship through laws after adopting legislature that criminalised certain behaviours critical of government policies and measures in response to the pandemic, or by blocking reporting.[22] The government's order in Moldova stated: "Journalists will unilaterally renounce formulating their own opinion or other arbitrary opinions in reflecting on topics concerning the COVID-19 pandemic."[23]

New legislation was adopted quickly in Russia following Vladimir Putin's speech "about the need to counter "provocations, stupid gossip and malicious lies" about the outbreak."[24] Three journalists have been arrested in Azerbaijan, and "at least two more journalists have been harassed or assaulted by unidentified plainclothes men while interviewing opposition politicians and citizens."[25] Azerbaijani authorities, Human Rights Watch reported, "have sentenced at least six activists and a pro-opposition journalist to detention for between 10 and 30 days on spurious charges including breaking lockdown rules or disobeying police orders."[26] Article XIX reported "the arrests of journalists and critics reporting on the pandemic in Azerbaijan, Belarus, Russia and Turkey."[27]

---

[19] European Center for Not-For-Profit Law (2020), p. 3.

[20] Human rights Watch (2021).

[21] Institute for Democracy and Electoral Assistance (2021), p. 13.

[22] Human rights Watch (2021).

[23] Balkan Insight (2020b).

[24] Associated Press (1 April 2020).

[25] International Press Institute (23 April 2020b).

[26] Human Rights Watch (16 April 2020).

[27] Institute for Democracy and Electoral Assistance (2021), p. 13.

In Turkey, during the just over 2 months of the initial period of the pandemic, "the Cyber Crimes Unit of the Interior Ministry alleged that 1,105 social media users had made propaganda for a terrorist organization, including by 'sharing provocative Coronavirus posts'. Of these, 510 were reportedly detained for questioning," Amnesty International noted.[28] Protests have been banned or disbanded using the new COVID-19 legislation in Russia, Ukraine, and Turkey. Belarus and Hungary are among the countries that restricted access to public health information.[29]

A more sophisticated derogation from rights and freedoms included a contact tracing app that was put in service in 28 countries regardless of their democratic development, including liberal democracies with open societies.

Based on the reports by leading human rights organisations and media, this overview of some incidents shows the division in Europe. The Oxford University's Blavatnik School of Government's project on measuring stringency measures worldwide showed no particular correlation between the type of the regime and stringency measures, at least in Europe. Therefore, the difference is not in the levels of stringency imposed by governments under extraordinary circumstances but the misuse of the measures or the justification of the state's non-democratic practices and activities that restrict individual freedoms and rights.

8.2 Messages from the Indices on Stringency

While Sweden has the second-lowest stringency index, and Finland, Denmark, Switzerland, Germany, and the United Kingdom are just slightly above, these "Open Societies" are mixed with Belarus, a closed society with the lowest stringency index, "Fairly Open Societies" of Iceland and Latvia, and "Opening Society" of Bulgaria. However, open societies tend to have lower stringency indices and are all positioned below the 25th position, except for Ireland in the 9th position. Nevertheless, there is a mixture of responses, and instead of a trend, one could observe a tendency only, as seen from Table 8.1.

However, when studying reports by the human rights organisations, another view is reinforced, a view of divided Europe where liberal Europe has gone into lockdowns and where governments have introduced various levels of stringency, but where, despite occasional misuse, the measures have been under some scrutiny. With authoritarian or hybrid regimes and shorter democratic experience, the other Europe has disproportionately applied measures for political gains. Human Rights Watch provided an overview of countries that committed breaches in one or more of the five spheres. See Table 8.2.

Six post-Soviet countries committed violations, as did four EU member-states, three Western Balkans states, and Turkey. Hungary is reported with similar

[28] Amnesty International (2020c).

[29] Human rights Watch (2021).

Table 8.1 Stringency Index According to the Oxford University's Blavatnik School of Government[a]

Position	Country	Society	Stringency index at its peak	Period of the highest stringency
1	Serbia	Suppressed	100	21/03–20/04
1	Georgia	Opening	100	31/03–26/04
3	Azerbaijan	Closed	96.30	21/06–17/07
3	Croatia	Opening	96.30	23/03–26/04
5	Cyprus	Fairly open	94.44	16/04–03/05
6	Italy	Fairly open	93.52	12/04–03/05
7	Kosovo	Opening	92.59	24/03–17/05
7	Bosnia-Herzegovina	Suppressed	92.59	10/04–23/04
9	France	Fairly open	90.74	17/03–10/05
9	Ireland	Open	90.74	06/04–17/05
11	Albania	Opening	89.81	18/04–17/05
11	Slovenia	Fairly open	89.81	30/03–19/04
13	Portugal	Fairly open	89.74	09/04–13/04 & 01/05–03/05
14	Malta	Opening	87.04	08/04–21/05
14	Romania	Opening	87.04	31/03–10/05
14	Moldova	Suppressed	87.04	24/03–17/04
14	Russia	Closed	87.04	30/03–05/04
14	Slovakia	Opening	87.04	08/04–13/04
14	Lithuania	Fairly Open	87.04	10/04–13/04
20	Spain	Fairly Open	85.19	30/03–03/05
20	Austria	Open	85.19	16/03–13/04
22	Greece	Opening	84.26	23/03–03/05
23	Poland	Fairly Open	83.33	09/04–24/05
24	Czechia	Fairly Open	82.41	23/03–01/04
25	Belgium	Fairly Open	81.48	20/03–04/05
26	Netherlands	Open	79.63	31/03–10/05
26	Luxembourg	Open	79.63	17/03–19/04
26	Norway	Open	79.63	24/03–19/04
29	Estonia	Fairly Open	77.78	29/03–26/04
29	Turkey	Closed	77.78	11/04–12/04 and 18/04–19/04
31	Hungary	Opening	76.85	28/03–03/05
32	Ukraine	Closed	75.93	03/04–21/05
32	United Kingdom	Open	75.93	26/03–11/05
34	Germany	Open	73.15	22/03–03/05
34	Switzerland	Open	73.15	17/03–26/04
34	Bulgaria	Opening	73.15	21/03–30/03 & 15/04–15/05
37	Denmark	Open	72.22	18/03–14/04
38	Latvia	Fairly Open	65.74	27/03–10/05
39	Finland	Open	60.19	28/03–14/04
40	Iceland	Fairly Open	53.70	20/03–03/05

(continued)

Table 8.1 (continued)

Position	Country	Society	Stringency index at its peak	Period of the highest stringency
41	Sweden	Open	40.74	04/04–12/06
42	Belarus	Closed	19.44	04/04–19/04
No Data	Armenia	Opening	No data	No data
No Data	Montenegro	Suppressed	No data	No data
No Data	North Macedonia	Opening	No data	No data

[a]Hale et al. (2021) and Our World in Data (2021a, b)

Table 8.2 Countries that violated Human Rights according to HRW report[a]

Country	Violence	Arbitrary arrest, detention, prosecution	Censorship through laws, threats, and blocking reporting	Restricting access to public health information	Banning protests and other public assemblies
Hungary		X	X	X	
Russia		X	X		X
Turkey		X	X		X
Azerbaijan		X	X		
Belarus		X		X	
Serbia	X	X			
Ukraine	X				X
Armenia			X		
Greece		X			
Kosovo			X		
Moldova			X		
Montenegro		X			
Poland		X			
Romania			X		

[a]Human rights Watch (2021) Covid-19 triggers wave of free speech abuse

frequency as Russia and Turkey in three out of five categories of violations. Of the European Union countries, Poland, Romania, and Greece are noted in one category each, like the non-EU countries Armenia, Kosovo, Moldova, and Montenegro. Violations in two categories are reported in Azerbaijan, Belarus, Serbia, and Ukraine. All these countries are post-communist countries, except for Greece and Turkey. This might incline towards concluding that the communist past might be a factor in the behaviour of the state. However, another twelve post-communist countries are not reported by the HRW index for violation of the human rights of their citizens during the pandemic.

Other practices in some of these countries have shown the functioning rule of law, checks and balances in practice, thus undermining attempts to generalize observations on mispractice in countries. The Constitutional Court in Romania "ruled that isolation at home, quarantine and hospitalisation cannot be imposed based on ministerial order," but when derogating from human rights is necessary measures "can only be established by a law, and clearly regulated."[30] "The preventive measures adopted during the coronavirus pandemic, the Constitutional Court in Kosovo deemed "unconstitutional, because they were too extensive to be adopted without Assembly's authorization."[31]

A look at another set of stringency details that researchers have found enables a more studious conclusion about stringency during the pandemic. Instead of looking at the measures when they peaked, which was not at the same time in each country, the last day of the year 2020 offers the state of play across Europe. Table 8.3 shows that Georgia still has the most stringent measures, but Serbia, the only other country with the stringency index at 100 when it peaked, was 25th on 31 December 2020 with an index of 60.19. Belarus consistently had the lowest index, but Bosnia-Herzegovina shared the lowest index with Belarus at the end of the year. Though the index for Bosnia-Herzegovina in April, when it peaked, was the seventh highest at 92.59.

Countries generally adopted less different approaches. Thus, their positions might have fluctuated between the time of the peaking measures and the end of the year, but the index itself was not radically different. The Netherlands was 26th with the index of 76.93 when measures were most stringent but were 12th on 31 December with an almost similar index of 78.70. The United Kingdom was 11th with an index of 76.93 at the end of the year. The difference between the most and the least stringent measures was 80.56 when the most stringent periods are compared. The difference on 31 December 2020 between the two extremes was 41.67.[32]

The most stringent measures at the end of the year were, among other states, in the most closed society, Azerbaijan, and in one of the most open societies, Ireland. Belarus, another autocratic state, had the least stringent measures adopted and shared the index with a heavily decentralised and hardly functioning state of Bosnia-Herzegovina. Open societies of Denmark and Finland are just three positions above. The two most autocratic, perhaps even dictatorial, states in Europe, Azerbaijan, and Belarus, have the radically opposite approaches to introducing government policies dealing with the pandemic. The issue, therefore, should not be policies generally, although there are rather few cases where these policies were either adopted against the procedural rules or breached constitutions and international agreements.

The state policies have necessarily been stringent. The levels of stringency were diverse and, in some cases, responded to national philosophy, like in Scandinavia, where states are historically reluctant to impose control over the society. However, this was not the rule and, depending on the infection levels, even the Scandinavian states strengthened the measures. The use of the policies for political or economic

[30] European Center for Not-For-Profit Law (2020), p. 7.

[31] European Center for Not-For-Profit Law (2020), p. 7.

[32] Haleet al. (2021) and Our World in Data (2021a, b).

Table 8.3 Stringency on 31 December 2020[a]

Position	Country	Index	Society
1	Azerbaijan	84.26	Closed
1	Georgia	84.26	Opening
1	Greece	84.26	Opening
1	Ireland	84.26	Open
1	Italy	84.26	Fairly open
6	Austria	82.41	Open
6	Germany	82.41	Open
8	Slovenia	81.48	Fairly open
9	Poland	80.56	Fairly open
10	Turkey	80.09	Closed
11	UK	79.63	Open
12	Netherlands	78.70	Open
12	Spain	78.70	Fairly open
14	Lithuania	76.85	Fairly open
14	Romania	76.85	Opening
16	Portugal	75.00	Fairly open
17	Cyprus	74.07	Fairly open
18	Czechia	73.15	Fairly open
19	Hungary	72.22	Opening
20	Kosovo	71.30	Opening
21	Sweden	69.44	Open
22	Luxembourg	67.59	Open
23	France	63.89	Fairly open
23	Latvia	63.89	Fairly open
25	Belgium	60.19	Fairly Open
25	Serbia	60.19	Suppressed
25	Switzerland	60.19	Open
28	Slovakia	58.33	Opening
29	Moldova	57.41	Suppressed
30	Albania	56.48	Opening
31	Norway	56.02	Open
32	Estonia	55.56	Fairly open
33	Ukraine	54.63	Closed
34	Bulgaria	53.70	Opening
35	Iceland	52.78	Fairly open
35	Malta	52.78	Opening
37	Finland	52.31	Open
38	Denmark	51.85	Open
39	Croatia	50.93	Opening
40	Russia	47.69	Closed
41	Belarus	42.59	Closed
41	B & H	42.59	Suppressed

(continued)

Table 8.3 (continued)

Position	Country	Index	Society
No Data	Armenia	XXXX	Opening
No Data	Montenegro	XXXX	Suppressed
No Data	N. Macedonia	XXXX	Opening

[a]Hale et al. (2021) and Our World in Data (2021a, b)

gains is of concern in some countries. The Western Balkans provided a fair share of abuses.

8.3 Western Balkans in the Time of Pandemic

Governments of Western Balkan states carried policies not dissimilar from the rest of Europe. The measures were most stringent around mid-April 2020 in all the countries, between Serbia's index of 100 and Albania's 89.81.[33] Montenegro and North Macedonia were not included in the data but reports of their policies reconfirm an almost uniformed reaction to the pandemic in the region.

All six countries introduced curfews at some point during the pandemic with varying length, but generally, any outdoor activities were banned during the night hours. The elderly were banned altogether from leaving their homes in some countries like Serbia and Bosnia-Herzegovina. While citizens aged over 65 were banned altogether from leaving their homes, policies for the under-18s were more liberal in the Bosnian entity Republika Srpska where they have not been banned from leaving homes like the children in the Federation have been. Authorities in Livno Canton banned citizens of the country, i.e., fellow citizens of Bosnia-Herzegovina not living in the canton, from entering the territory under their local authority.

Restrictions imposed by social distancing might be interpreted as affecting freedom to assembly, as some organisations argue.[34]

In a different way, the case of Bosnia-Herzegovina is telling. Firstly, one must look into the state structure, as it has already been described, where two entities can execute different policies. The country is not unique in this as the devolved United Kingdom, while remaining officially a unitary state, has the government's decisions applied in England only, while separate executive bodies implement their own policies in Scotland, Northern Ireland, and Wales.

Complex states in Europe largely suspended elements of their national or (con)-federal order. "In cases of 'extraordinary situations' in Switzerland, "the Cantons must abide by the Confederation's legal prescriptions." While subnational units in these states retained many powers and used them to act, new laws have been adopted

[33]Hale et al. (2021) and Our World in Data (2021a, b).

[34]The International Center for Not-for-Profit Law (2020).

at the state, (con)federal level. "Several Federal Acts on Covid-19 were adopted" in Austria, "authorizing federal ministers to adopt regulations to deal with the pandemic." In Belgium, "the legal basis for the special powers at the federal level was promulgated by two laws that entered into force on 30 March, with a retroactive effect from 1 March." "The 2001 Protection against Infectious Diseases Act," in Germany, "was amended in March 2020 to confer additional competencies to the Federal Ministry of Health. Russian "Federal law No. 98-FZ dated 1 April 2020" clarified the powers of the Regions by "amendments to several federal laws."[35]

"The reason for the lack of coordination" in Bosnia-Herzegovina, states the Konrad Adenauer Stiftung's report, "is an especially complicated state structure. The two entities are responsible for majority of the measures against the pandemic." However, Goran Čerkez, Assistant Minister of Health in the Federation of Bosnia-Herzegovina, explained that the authorities of the two entities coordinated their activities in most of the cases. The country's borders are under the national jurisdiction, and the state authorities introduced measures restricting entry to Bosnia-Herzegovina from countries with high infection levels. The exceptions were neighbouring countries whose citizens were allowed entry even without specific tests. When Serbia, Croatia and Montenegro experienced higher infection levels, experts from federal institutions proposed restriction of entry for citizens of the neighbouring countries. However, the Council of Ministers of Bosnia-Herzegovina did not even consider these measures at the insistence of Republika Srpska's representatives.[36]

This example shows that even when there is coordinated activity between structures of governance, ethnopolitical decisions still take priority and prevent a full coordinated action. Sub-national governments are effectively free to impose their policies and undermine the state. Even during the pandemic's extraordinary situation, national efforts are a rarity and not coordinated well. With the high level of autonomy, governments of both entities saw the opportunity to reward their party supporters and activists with contracts to import protection equipment and deals with sub-national health systems.

While their policies, in the beginning, might have been of a more controlling character, the Western Balkans' states ended the year with a significantly more relaxed attitude as the index shows Bosnia-Herzegovina having the lowest index of 42.59, together with Belarus, while the most stringent measures in the region indexed at 71.30 were in Kosovo.[37] What differentiates this region from most of Europe are some government practices that reflected attempts of extending further state-capture and use the anti-pandemic measures to silence the opponents of the regime and non-controlled media. The accusations have appeared from opposition members in all the countries.

---

[35] OSCE Office for Democratic Institutions and Human Rights (ODIHR) (2020).

[36] Čerkez (5 October 2021).

[37] Hale et al. (2021) and Our World in Data (2021a, b).

Human Rights Watch has named 14 European countries, including Serbia, Kosovo, and Montenegro, in its report on human rights abuses. Serbia's security forces violently dealt with protesters against the curfew measures planned over the weekend. Amnesty International reported, "dozens of protesters, including some bystanders and several accredited journalists, were injured in the violence."[38]

In Tirana, the all-powerful Albanian Prime Minister Edi Rama was the first European powerholder to bring security forces onto the streets during the pandemic in Europe. The police "clashed with opposition supporters and activists, protesting against the long-disputed demolition of the National Theatre." The state's president sided with protesters describing the demolition as "a moral crime that cannot be granted amnesty." The institutionally weak president "also criticized the violence used against protesting artists and journalists by police."[39]

During opposition protests, Montenegrin police "used tear gas to disperse protesters, after which civil activists and opposition parties accused them of using excessive force." The protests were later recalled by the supposedly politically neutral National Coordination Body for Infectious Diseases "by blaming a recent rise in COVID-19 cases on the activities of the opposition Democratic Front,"[40] the party that was behind the protests.

No government violence during the crisis was reported in Kosovo and North Macedonia. However, Kosovo was criticised in the speech by the UN High Commissioner for Human Rights. "In the Russian Federation, China, Kosovo, Nicaragua and many other countries," Michelle Bachelet noted, "reports of threats and intimidation against journalists, bloggers and civic activists, particularly at the local level, with the apparent aim of discouraging criticism of the authorities' responses to COVID-19."[41]

In her critical analysis of the Western Balkans, former German Ambassador to Montenegro and North Macedonia, Gudrun Stainaker, argued that "in Serbia and the region, hybrid democracies, kleptocracies and mafia states are established. There will be little change as long as such "elites" suit the European Union."[42]

The protests in Bosnia-Herzegovina did not draw security forces' reaction, nor any substantial government response. Protesters in Sarajevo demanded "resignations of top government officials over their handling of the coronavirus pandemic and failure to launch a nationwide vaccination programme."[43] This came only after a full year of governments at different levels in the country proved their incompetence, corruption, and ignorance.

Following the imposition of restrictive measures, the nationalist leaders opted for party cronies lacking the competence to import personal protection and testing

[38] Amnesty International (2020b).

[39] Balkan Insight (17 May 2020d).

[40] Balkan Insight (17 May 2020c).

[41] Bachelet M (30 June 2020).

[42] Stainaker (25 July 2020).

[43] Reuters (6 April 2021).

equipment, the task in which they ultimately failed. The most notorious case is undoubtedly a contract to locate and import ventilators for COVID-19 patients awarded to an agricultural company. The company imported the ventilators for the inflated price with no knowledge that the ventilators were inadequate for hospitals' use. The contract was worth 10.5 million Bosnian Marks (around 6 million Euros). The ventilators have not been used, even with restricted purposes, because no company was willing to service them and put in the work following media discoveries. When the company installing the equipment was finally found 6 months later, some of the ventilators were faulty.

Among the temporarily arrested suspects in this deal was even the Prime Minister of the Federation. The lengthy court case proceeded. Ethnic divisions came yet again to the fore, following the arrest when the prominent hospital general director and wife of the Bosniaks nationalist leader asked: "Why Bosniaks only?"[44] Her husband, the Bosniak nationalist leader Bakir Izetbegović argued, "this is a continuation of attacks on Bosniak leaders."[45] The arrested Prime Minister was a member of his party. The suspects were released soon after these statements. Therefore, one might question, if not even dismiss, the independence of the judiciary and separation of powers.

While the producer of raspberries has imported the ventilators for the federal part of Bosnia-Herzegovina,[46] coronavirus tests have been imported by the furniture producer contracted by the federal government.[47] One importer of corona tests in Republika Srpska was an automobile manufacturer.[48] "Bosnia-Herzegovina is a country impossible to govern," argues former German diplomat, "where everything worth is divided between elites headed by kleptocrats like Milorad Dodik and Bakir Izetbegović."[49]

Despite the apparent signs of misrule by many political elites in all the countries, the electorate shows minimal signs of dissent with such regimes. Various forms of elections, either general or local, took place in all six countries. Serbian President Vučić enlarged his party's already large majority in the Serbian parliament with only his junior partner parties and minority representatives having seats. It was described in an analysis that "the election was marred by the opposition's boycott and the use of state institutions by the ruling party." The same report found that "the opposition received mainly negative coverage by most media outlets, whereas the coverage of the government was mostly neutral."[50]

Albanian Prime Minister Rama got his party's majority confirmed once more. In Kosovo, the populist *Vetëvendosje* party won the majority largely in support of their

[44] Oslobodjenje (3 June 2020).

[45] Radio Slobodna Evropa (29 May 2020c).

[46] Radio Slobodna evropa (28 May 2020b).

[47] Žurnal (15 April 2020).

[48] Dnevni Avaz (19 July 2020).

[49] Stainaker (25 July 2020).

[50] Institute for Democracy and Electoral Assistance (2021) p. 12.

anti-corruption rhetoric. Promises of anti-corruption policies seemingly helped the coalition in North Macedonia to retain power and the opposition in Montenegro to defeat the governing party for the first time in 30 years.

A pattern when an authoritarian leader has been in power for a prolonged period and is challenged by a diverse group of ideologically disparate groups has been established in the Western Balkans. The examples include elections and post-electoral manoeuvrings in Serbia in 2000, Sarajevo Canton in 2018, Macedonia general elections in 2016, or elections in Montenegro in August 2020. Disparate opposition parties united against the dominant political force – an autocratic leader or totalitarian political party that dominates local politics, often for decades. The democratic result is electoral victory, but the realpolitik is that these coalitions are frequently short-lived because of their ideological diversity, contradicting final aims, and questionable methods of rule. Newly formed governments are faced with the previous regime's control of the judiciary and legislative process with the media primarily in the hands and control of those closest to the defeated political forces.

The current victors in Montenegro celebrate with different flags, i.e. Serbian and Montenegrin, and are fond of the opposing sides in the Second World War, i.e. antifascist communist-led Partisans and royalist Serbian nationalists who often collaborated with Nazis. This kind of division among the electoral victors often leads to a short-lived victory and ultimately invites autocrats or totalitarians back to power on the democratic ticket.

The anti-DPS majority in Montenegro is only one seat in the Parliament—41 seats for the disparate victorious coalition and 40 seats for the parties that support Đukanović's Democratic Party of Socialists that remains the largest parliamentary party. Ratko Knežević, a former close confidant to Đukanović and best man who fell out of favour, summed up the reasons of the political defeat "because of the prolonged unchallenged power," before adding it was "a private state" with the deep "state capture."[51] The European Commission has used this term in their report on the Western Balkans in 2018, where the ruling party leadership controls the state resources for illicit purposes.[52]

The voters' turnout might be a telling sign of the electoral results. The turnout was lower than in previous elections in Serbia, Albania and North Macedonia, and the governing parties retained their positions. The change occurred in Montenegro where the turnout increased. In Kosovo, the turnout was higher in 2020, and the political party *Vetëvendosje* that briefly governed following the elections in 2019, doubled their seats in the parliament. This was also a confirmation of the change as previously this party had no control over the parliament and was in power by forming a coalition that included one of the old establishment parties. Thus, the increase of the voters' turnout enabled the rise of the new political forces to power on their terms. The decrease in voters turnout kept old forces in power in Serbia,

[51] Knežević R (7 October 2020).

[52] Bieber (2020), p. 110.

Albania, and North Macedonia, while the increase in turnout enabled new political powers to be established in Montenegro and Kosovo.

8.4 News, Fake News and Anti-Government Propaganda in the Western Balkans

Governments' attempts to control the media and information in the Western Balkans should be put into context of the pandemic when derogations from freedoms of expression and opinion were applied across Europe. The curtailment of such freedoms and rights has to be temporary, but when applied in societies where regimes already control major media, the consequences for future political life and democracy in the society might be severe. The electoral results during the pandemic might very well show this tendency.

A journalist was detained in Novi Sad "for "spreading panic and unrest" in an article she published about the lack of personal protective COVID-19 equipment available to medical staff at a health center."[53] The government in Serbia passed a decree, albeit reversed later, in which the pandemic information process had been centralised, and journalists were made "liable for prosecution for the 'use of unofficial sources.'"[54] Penalties were strengthened by detention or imprisonment of those who "spread panic and misinformation". Rules of criminal law have been applied to the indicted citizens. Several people have been arrested for telling jokes about the virus on streets in Novi Pazar, Serbia, while others have been accused of publishing wrong information on Facebook and other social networks.[55] The RFE reported, "three people in Serbia have been sentenced to jail for violating a self-isolation order aimed at slowing the spread of the coronavirus."[56] Thus, instead of financial punishment, breaking a self-isolation rule has become a criminal offence punishable by a jail sentence. This is when the state proves not to be exposed to checks and balances.

One person was detained in Montenegro for publishing on Facebook that 13 citizens of Montenegro were infected at the time when there was no reported infection in the state.[57] The arrests in Montenegro have been made even before the pandemic reached the country. "Citizens were arrested for spreading fake news about the COVID-19 pandemic on social networks. An opposition activist was arrested and kept in custody for 72 hours for spreading panic by "posting fake news about the health of President Milo Đukanović, claiming he had the coronavirus."[58]

[53] International Press Institute (3 April 2020a).

[54] Institute for Democracy and Electoral Assistance (2021), p. 13.

[55] Media Centar (27 March 2020).

[56] Radio Free Europe/Radio Liberty (27 March 2020b).

[57] Media Centar (27 March 2020).

[58] Balkan Insight (10 July 2020e).

Bosnian entity Republika Srpska "issued a decree that forbids causing 'panic and disorder' by publishing or transmitting false news during a state of emergency."[59] Activists saw this decree as a violation of free speech and put it under the category of censorship.[60] The entity's Minister of Internal Affairs reportedly said that "during an emergency, it is forbidden to publish false news and allegations that cause panic and severely disrupt public order and peace or prevent the implementation of measures by institutions exercising public authority." He further added that "[wrongdoers] will not be able to hide, even on social networks; we will find them."[61] Individuals found in violation of the decree faced a significant financial penalty between 1000 and 3000 Bosnian marks (500–1500 Euros). Organizations faced fines that were three times bigger.

There were reported cases of penalties issued to those "for spreading disinformation and panic" on Instagram, by stating that authorities do not report positive tests, and on Facebook, for criticism of the authorities. Media reported a doctor was also penalised for her criticism of the policies and a blogger for the text titled "Corona Madness: Another Opportunity for Robbery".[62] The Republika Srpska's government made such statements illegal by the decision adopted on 19th March. The other entity, the Federation of Bosnia-Herzegovina, did not adopt a similar decision, and yet, two persons have been penalised "for disturbances to public order" by their posts on Facebook.

The new situation and the lack of knowledge and expertise made it challenging to distinguish between fake news and real news critical of the authorities because of authorities' work, lack of competence, and capacity. This was inviting activists and independent media to report on the potential dangers of a lethal combination of the pandemic and incompetent authorities. The regimes, largely illiberal, acted disproportionately, sensing the potential for opposition to undermine the regime's authority and the grip on power.

The regimes that exercised paranoid features acted harshly to some fake news that were not always fake but just reasonably critical of the authorities. At the same time, these regimes contribute heavily to spreading fake news in the form of conspiracy theories. Radio Free Europe reported at the beginning of the pandemic that "Serbia's president and foreign minister offered an uncorroborated conspiracy theory that the virus... is part of an economic "war" on China, and jokingly implied that drinking alcohol could prevent its spread."[63] President Vučić was followed by the Foreign Minister Dačić, who "twice went on Serbian television to suggest that the coronavirus was a foreign plot targeting the Chinese economy."[64] A member of the Serbian Crisis Team, a medical doctor, went a step further by dismissing the dangers of the

[59] The International Center for Not-for-Profit Law (2020).

[60] Pandemic Big Brother (8April 2020).

[61] Balkan Insight (19 March 2020a).

[62] Media Centar (27 March 2020).

[63] Radio Free Europe/Radio Liberty (5 March 2020a).

[64] Radio Free Europe/Radio Liberty (5 March 2020a).

virus and claiming "women have very mild forms and practically do not die from the virus. Therefore go to shopping trip. Go to Italy. I am hearing mass reductions and sales will take place there because nobody is going there now."[65]

Media in Bosnia-Herzegovina showed the opposite attitude towards the Chinese. They reported in January 2020 a danger presented by Chinese tourists spreading the virus. The series of articles, often racist in their tone, followed the tour of the country by this group of tourists urging authorities to expel them.

Conspiracy theories are not a speciality of just one nation or region. The danger, nevertheless, is when the political elite that is in almost total control of media transmits such messages. Even when they reach a wider public, the opposition, often using social networks, proves to be subject to equally dangerous theories. An opposition member of Montenegrin parliament "posted on his Twitter account that COVID-19 is artificial biological weapon." Nebojša Medojević "claimed an alleged global deep state used the coronavirus to influence the result of the recent US presidential election."[66]

"5G Conspiracy Theories Shared via Chat Groups in Serbia," informs the independent website. President of a minor political party in Serbia, the Republican Party, "published information that 5G base stations had been installed in Novi Pazar, one of the Serbian cities most affected by the COVID-19 pandemic. It was reported that "5G Rumours on Social Media Cause Hysteria in North Macedonia." In Bosnia-Herzegovina, a "Facebook Page Urges Destruction of '5G Antennas' in Tuzla." By claiming it is a military weapon, "Bosnian Website Spreads Conspiratorial Claims About 5G." The website states the "connection between tests on COVID-19 and 5G networks, claiming that when testing for the virus is done, human DNA is taken and the samples transferred to a "super computer"."[67]

A research paper produced by the Balkan in Europe Policy Advisory Group focused on conspiracy theories and found the Western Balkans population more inclined to believe these theories than the rest of Europe. The population in Serbia were least likely, and Albanian citizens most likely to believe in COVID-19 conspiracy theories.[68] The same paper offers some shocking findings: "While in most of Europe COVID conspiracies are supported by a quarter to a third of the population, more than 75% of WB citizens surveyed believe in one or several of six COVID theories."[69]

In Albania, the "counter-terrorism police force is seeking penal charges for about ten people for allegedly using Facebook to spread fake news." It was alleged, "that one social media user said there is a plot to impoverish people in Europe, to cause social uproar and suggesting coronavirus was a biological weapon."[70]

---

[65] 24 Minuta sa Zoranom Kesićem (4 March 2020).

[66] BIRN Investigative Resource Desk (2021).

[67] BIRN Investigative Resource Desk (2021).

[68] Bieber et al. (2020), p. 4.

[69] Bieber et al. (2020), p. 1.

[70] BIRN Investigative Resource Desk (2021).

The significant difference between the region and the rest of Europe is in the responsibility of political elites in most of Europe and often irresponsible statements by some members of political elites in the Western Balkans. This inevitably leads towards widespread beliefs among the population that ultimately undermine state actions, like mass vaccination, technological development or even support for some geopolitical decisions. Fifteen EU states, including Croatia, have sought some collective action to deal with the spreading of conspiracy theories. YouTube has banned "all conspiracy theory videos falsely linking coronavirus symptoms to 5G networks."[71]

IDEA reported that "dangerous disinformation has spread in the form of hoaxes, misleading healthcare information or claims, conspiracy theories, illegal hate speech, consumer fraud, cybercrime, and undue foreign influence," that the European Commission has named as the COVID-19 'infodemic'."[72]

Like conspiracy theories that are often firmly connected, fake news influence public behaviour. Politicians, even when forced to deny some of the fake news, unwittingly recognise their potential. The Bosnian Social Democratic Party issued an apology after publicly criticising alleged behaviour in an anonymous video posted online of citizens of Mostar applauding from their balconies to nationalist chants at the football game in Croatia. The video was proved to be edited by using footage of Mostar citizens supporting medical workers and unrelated nationalist incidents at a football game.[73]

A politician of the ruling party in North Macedonia had to deny that an infected patient attended his wedding because of the fake news. The country's president said, "that the authorities detected and prevented several organised attempts at spreading false news regarding the coronavirus situation." One Twitter account claimed, "that part of the capital, Skopje, had become the main infected area of the city and had a large number of infected citizens." Fake news often reflects problems already present in society and accentuates them. Ethnic division of Slavs and Albanians in North Macedonia was addressed in the false claim by a Macedonian web portal that "claimed the country was faced a wheat shortage, and that large amounts of wheat were being exported to [dominantly Albanian] Kosovo."[74]

Serbian police have detained a person who published a photo of soldiers on his Facebook page claiming, "the army and police have been deployed in his town," and "that bread vouchers have been distributed." There is no research published that investigated people who post such fake news. Did they believe what they were posting, or there was a more profound plan to cause, for whatever ideological or other reasons, panic and disturb public order?

Sometimes, analysts fail to see a humorous or satirical posting and mistake it for fake news. Kosovo news portal Jeta Online "reported that a scientific laboratory in

[71] BIRN Investigative Resource Desk (2021).

[72] Institute for Democracy and Electoral Assistance (2021), p. 14.

[73] BIRN Investigative Resource Desk (2021).

[74] BIRN Investigative Resource Desk (2021).

the village of Komoran . . . was working to find a vaccine against COVID-19." The report stressed that "a fierce race is underway to uncover coronavirus among the world's capitals. Recently, Komoran has seriously entered the race through its scientists."[75] The irony of this news was not recognised by otherwise an excellent repository of sources, Balkan Investigative Reporting Network (BIRN), who failed to notice that the alleged village of Komorane/Komoran has a population of less than five thousand, whose main activity is agriculture, and the only reference to fame came as a checkpoint during the war in Kosovo.

Further to the south, in a town in North Macedonia, Veles, local youth have developed fake news enterprises. They are alleged to have influenced American presidential elections in 2016. All major American media consequently published reportages of the town and its teenagers and slightly older entrepreneurs. The titles included "Inside the Macedonian Fake-News Complex",[76] "A Crisis of Conscience in Fake News",[77] "The Fake News Machine: Inside the Town Gearing Up for 2020".[78] The BBC titled one of several of their items "The city getting rich from fake news".[79] Nevertheless, when fake news has been posted frequently during the pandemic, fake news factories in Veles remained unproductive.

Even more scandalous than political elites participating in spreading fake news is a set of cases when state institutions in several countries have breached citizens' rights to privacy. The identities of the first two cases of infection in Montenegro were published by some social media users, followed by insults of those infected and their ethnic and religious beliefs by other social media users. The government may not have been involved in this publication, but the state agency published names of persons required to self-isolate.[80] Although the Constitutional Court has revoked the Government's decision, 4 months later, some citizens sued the state of Montenegro. There were officially 10,000 citizens ordered to self-isolate or into a quarantine between 15 March and 22 April 2021, but it is unknown how many names were put on the list published on the government website.[81]

This practice was widespread in the region. Despite the Personal Data Protection Agency in Bosnia-Herzegovina issuing "a ban for all levels of authorities to publicly reveal personal data of individual infected with coronavirus, as well as those violating mandatory quarantine," the authorities in Republika Srpska initially published the list of 30 people "who did not adhere to Republika Srpska's self-isolation rules." The government of the other Bosnian entity urged its agency to "consider issuing an order which would allow local authorities to publish personal

[75] BIRN Investigative Resource Desk (2021).

[76] Wired (15 February 2017).

[77] The Atlantic (30 November 2018).

[78] CNN (2017).

[79] BBC (5 December 2016).

[80] Služba za odnose s javnošću Vlade Crne Gore (22 March 2020).

[81] Radio Slobodna Evropa (15 September 2020d).

data of those affected by COVID-19." However, they eventually opted to publish the names "of those who violate isolation measures."[82]

At a lower level, however, the authorities in the Canton 10, the same authorities that banned citizens from the rest of the country entering their territory, "published the personal data of 238 people who had been isolated or had self-isolated, most of whom had not violated isolation orders." It was reported that authorities in several municipalities "also published lists of people who tested positive for COVID-19."[83] Another type of reaction was self-initiative by citizens. A citizen testing positive, and her family, received threats from neighbours and on Facebook from real and fake accounts.[84]

States breached privacy in several countries. Serbian Ministry of Health published health records of two people, identified by initials and a year of birth, who died from complications caused by the coronavirus. In Kosovo, the Mayor of Gnjilane/Gjilan "published personal information on a citizen who had died of complications linked to COVID-19." Another Kosovo politician, a member of the parliament, shared personal information of activists of another political party, "claiming they had been allowed to leave state-run quarantine."[85] Personal information was shared in another Kosovo town of Orahovac/Rahovec. Exposing personal data was even used across the ethnic divide in Kosovo. Thus, municipalities of Prizren and Kosovo Polje/Fushe Kosove published ethnic backgrounds of citizens from minority communities who have been infected with COVID-19.[86]

The authorities in a small Serbian town of Šid published on the municipal website the personal data of a citizen confirmed as infected with COVID-19. In North Macedonia and Montenegro, criminal charges were filed against persons who collected and published personal data of patients infected by the virus.[87]

All these countries have legislation protecting personal data information and privacy laws in accordance with the European Convention on Human Rights; yet frequent breaches have been recorded in all the countries of the Western Balkans by authorities at all levels of governance. Furthermore, media played its role in spreading the information that was supposed to remain private. Social networks have been used when the media proved to be unavailable for this kind of "sensationalism". Individual citizens also found good use of social networks in their attempts to spread the information.

The role of the state has been challenged. In some cases, the state behaviour was corrected after the civil society reaction. However, the breach of state regulation by the state itself proves either lack of competence, ill-judgement, or bad intentions of state officials or possibly, in some cases, all three. The unelected officials in state

---

[82] BIRN Investigative Resource Desk (2021).

[83] BIRN Investigative Resource Desk (2021).

[84] Radio Kameleon (29 March 2020).

[85] BIRN Investigative Resource Desk (2021).

[86] BIRN Investigative Resource Desk (2021).

[87] BIRN Investigative Resource Desk (2021).

agencies provided wrong advice to executives which proves possible failures of recruitment policies by state institutions, or this reflects the behaviour of civil servants who aim their advice to suit the wishes of the state executives. The extraordinary circumstances of the pandemic provided additional opportunities for authoritarian forms of government to expand their control or suppression of the society. However, in some cases, the civil society proved its resilience and forced correction of some policies. Nevertheless, civil society in the Western Balkans relies heavily on Western support.

8.5 Covid Diplomacy and the State in the Western Balkans

Not dissimilar to the civil society, the states of the region looked towards the West in anticipation of support, firstly in testing equipment and later in vaccines. Bosnian authorities were the most flagrant in seeking donations, aid, or support that they utterly failed to secure to protect their citizens' health. Furthermore, like in the Sarajevo Canton, they contributed to further endangering public health. The Minister of Foreign Affairs, Bisera Turković, organised donations of dates from Saudi Arabia and humanitarian aid in rice and other food during Ramadan when the primary mission was to organise the delivery of vaccines. When the Astra Zeneca vaccines were delivered as a donation from Serbia to Bosnia-Herzegovina, the Bosnian foreign minister was dismissive about the quality because the vaccines were produced in India.

Serbian president Vučić made headlines with the Serbian policy of vaccination. His coquetry foreign policy with the European Union, Russia and China, and Donald Trump when he was still in power enabled Serbia to be at the forefront of the vaccination process. Vučić used a surplus of vaccines delivered from various sources for covid diplomacy by delivering donations to the Western Balkans countries and opening borders to any foreign nationals who wanted to get vaccinated in Serbia. Thousands of Bosnians used this opportunity at the time when their authorities failed them.

Patron states reconfirmed their status among the clients in the Balkans. Turkish President Erdoğan promised aid and held talks with the Bosniak leader and not the state president as diplomatic protocol would suggest. Serbia's president behaved in a similar fashion underlining Serbia's connection with the entity of Republika Srpska. Inevitable disappointment in the EU, after its lack of support in the crisis and a long-awaited and delayed next step in integrations, was rallied by the Serbian President Aleksandar Vučić, who "declared that "European solidarity was non-existent" and appealed to China for help, calling Chinese President Xi Jinping "a friend and brother" to Serbia."[88]

[88] Balkan Insight (6 August 2020f).

Probably the most outrageous state behaviour during this period is to be found in the decision by Croatian authorities to allow citizens of Bosnia-Herzegovina with dual Croatian citizenship into the country without negative testing while those with Bosnian only citizenship had to test negative and submit at the border their whereabouts in Croatia. It is not a question of citizens' rights to return or arrival to their country of citizenship but of risking the nation's health to underscore the benefits of having Croatian citizenship and show the state care for their citizens in "diaspora". Of course, there is always a possibility that Croatian state officials have discovered secret benefits of a Croatian passport in preventing the spread and cure of Covid-19, but nobody ever alleged such a daring invention.

Authorship on political behaviour that could only attract wry comments is not exclusive in the Western Balkans and is being kept by some states even upon entering the liberal club of the European Union. Harald Schenker wryly observed developments in North Macedonia where "the municipality of Skopje Centre and the Russian embassy jointly unveil a monument to the Soviet Army, which liberated the world from fascism. No doubt it did, at least temporarily; but in doing so it didn't even come close to Macedonian territory. So, one is compelled to ask: *cui bono*? What bothers me even more is the lack of any reaction by any political party or civil society."[89] "The internal weaknesses of the democratisation process in the Western Balkans, as the ruling elites create frameworks that are favourable to them and fail to foster fair political competition," Giorgio Fruscione offered an observation, "while deepening differences and divisions in societies if it helps them survive in power, negatively affect the will of citizens in trying to effect change from within."[90]

The state functioning and regime behaviour in the Western Balkans countries during the pandemic dramatically emphasised that "the European Union's disengagement is playing in favour of third countries interested in edging into the region."[91] Prelec and Tzifakis found that "Chinese-Serbian business progressed during the pandemic." Russia "sent assistance to Serbia and Bosnia and Herzegovina (BiH), while it disregarded the problems (e.g. evacuation of citizens) of the two Western Balkan countries that have recently joined NATO." The analysis adds that Russia "exploited any given opportunity to increase popular dissatisfaction with the West."[92]

In addition to material aid, Russia sent their team of experts for decontamination to Serbia. When the same team was invited to Bosnia-Herzegovina by the Bosnian Croat nationalist leader, Dragan Čović, the problem that arose was that the Russian team of experts were part of the Russian military forces. Bosnian Defence Minister, followed by the state Presidency, refused to approve the entrance to the country by the foreign military without the official request coming from Russia. This incident accentuates many of the problems of Bosnian sovereignty.

---

[89] Schenker (21 May 2020).

[90] Fruscione (2021), p. 118.

[91] Giffoni (2021), p. 101.

[92] Prelec and Tzifakis (2021), pp. 34–53.

The Russian military expert team had already visited Bosnia-Herzegovina earlier in April 2020, when Bosnian Serb nationalist leader, Milorad Dodik, "welcomed the Russians at the Banja Luka Airport and warmly thanked Moscow for the aid."[93] The Deputy Defence Minister, a Bosnian Serb from the strongest party of Bosnian Serbs, welcomed the Russians alongside Dodik in Banja Luka. His superior, a Bosniak from a civic party, passed the advice to the state Presidency where two members, a Bosnian Croat from the same civic party as the Defence Minister and a Bosniak nationalist member, outnumbered Dodik, a Bosnian Serb nationalist leader, who supported the deployment of Russians to Mostar hospital at the request of Bosnian Croat nationalist leader.

If the electoral law were different, although it already strongly favours established nationalist political groups, it would prevent in practice a possibility of non-nationalist political parties having elected a member of the state presidency and influencing major political decisions. Nationalist Croats complain of this situation, as they cannot ignore the state institutions, like Bosnian Serbs, and lead their policies regardless of procedures, law, and order. In their view, when interests of a civic, non-nationalist political party and Bosniak nationalists coincide, this alliance can block initiatives of the alleged "vital national interest" for Bosnian Croats.

The nationalists' argument is in favour of strengthening sub-national autocracies in Bosnia-Herzegovina. Bosnian Serbs are open in this process of the attempted dismembering of the state and ignoring, as much as they are allowed, the state institutions. Bosnian Croats frequently expressed the desire for similar behaviour and frustration for being prevented, either constitutionally or by some electoral results. Nevertheless, the nationalist Croat Democratic Union are in firm control of several cantons where, regardless of a decentralised structure of the Federation, the rule of the nationalist clique is secured and led by the all-influential Croat nationalist leader. While cantons with the majority Croat population are *de jure*, not mutually connected and dependant region, they are *de facto* an unofficially marked territory where an autocratic Croat nationalist leader is in almost complete control. Bosniak nationalists offer the rhetoric of *etatism* (statism) and patriotism, but in practice, behave similarly by undermining state institutions when it is in the interest of their nationalist leaders.

A statement by the UN High Commissioner for Human Rights, Michelle Bachelet, shows all the dangers that are yet to be overcome across the world: "I am profoundly concerned by certain countries' adoption of emergency powers that are unlimited and not subject to review. In a few cases, the epidemic is being used to justify repressive changes to regular legislation, which will remain in force long after the emergency is over."[94] Europe and, in particular, the Western Balkans are not exceptions. As shown, the states of the Western Balkans might even have proper legislation in place, but they lack the implementation. The power, in times of the pandemic, became even more concentrated.

[93] Radio Slobodna Evropa (4 May 2020a).

[94] Bachelet (2021).

References

24 Minuta sa Zoranom Kesićem (4 March 2020) Zaraznim smehom protiv Korona virusa. https://www.youtube.com/watch?v=wqvA9Krci3E. Accessed 6 Oct 2021

Amnesty International (2020a) Europe: COVID-19 lockdowns expose racial bias and discrimination within police. https://www.amnesty.org/en/latest/news/2020/06/europe-covid19-lockdowns-expose-racial-bias-and-discrimination-within-police/. Accessed 6 Oct 2021

Amnesty International (2020b) Serbia: Violent police crackdown against COVID-19 lockdown protesters must stop. https://www.amnesty.org/en/latest/news/2020/07/serbia-violent-police-crackdown-against-covid-19-lockdown-protesters-must-stop/. Accessed 5 Oct 2021

Amnesty International (2020c) Turkey: Stifling free expression during the COVID-19 pandemic. https://www.amnesty.org/en/latest/campaigns/2020/06/turkey-stifling-free-expression-during-the-covid19-pandemic/. Accessed 5 Oct 2021

Associated Press (1 April 2020) Fake news or the truth? Russia cracks down on virus postings. https://apnews.com/article/health-ap-top-news-international-news-moscow-virus-outbreak-dbbf02a747b11d8ffe3b07d5e33ff129. Accessed 6 Oct 2021

Bachelet M (30 June 2020) Global update on human rights and the impact of the COVID-19 pandemic. 44th session of the Human Rights Council. https://www.ohchr.org/EN/NewsEvents/Pages/DisplayNews.aspx?NewsID=26015&LangID=E#_ftn1. Accessed 6 Oct 2021

Bachelet M (2021) States' use of digital technology to combat the pandemic must respect human rights. Pandemic Big Brother. https://pandemicbigbrother.online/en/our-principles/. Accessed 6 Oct 2021

Balkan Insight (19 March 2020a) Bosnia's Republika Srpska imposes fines for corona virus 'Fake News'. https://balkaninsight.com/2020/03/19/bosnias-republika-srpska-imposes-fines-for-coronavirus-fake-news/. Accessed 6 Oct 2021

Balkan Insight (31 March 2020b) Battling Coronavirus, Moldova targets unwanted media 'Opinion'. https://balkaninsight.com/2020/03/31/battling-coronavirus-moldova-targets-unwanted-media-opinion/. Accessed 6 Oct 2021

Balkan Insight (17 May 2020c) Montenegro health body criticised for blaming COVID spike on opposition. https://balkaninsight.com/2020/07/06/montenegro-health-body-criticised-for-blaming-covid-spike-on-opposition/. Accessed 6 Oct 2021

Balkan Insight (17 May 2020d) Protesters, Police Clash over Theatre Demolition in Tirana. https://balkaninsight.com/2020/05/17/albania-premier-edi-rama-destroys-national-theatre/. Accessed 6 Oct 2021

Balkan Insight (10 July 2020e) Montenegro activist grilled for facebook post on Serbian Protests. https://balkaninsight.com/2020/07/10/montenegro-activist-grilled-for-facebook-post-on-serbian-protests/. Accessed 6 Oct 2021

Balkan Insight (6 August 2020f) Balkan infodemic – how the virus became a geopolitical weapon. https://balkaninsight.com/2020/08/06/balkan-infodemic-how-the-virus-became-a-geopolitical-weapon/?__cf_chl_captcha_tk__=486f5a6d0e80b8a61b9e5623f7eb26f7c52a40ca-1600076543-0-ASgA7xioUpi39TrRfdyAXBN2K9DrQYswRLttZiAWGuTv8HjYzYgadowgTKi3A9OoB20PPOO-sc9AGv66G3WUfbj3FyDmUyKl4-89Da-ZTmpCEhguVgpBHjye_w4bSvXO2syWqu0uMM8DYaxgJP0I3HCI_81F2PjnjtdATZ4CTmCuFlNhUrL2wa0vcH6KZEKiHHEyQou1zalAg37rs7i2y0CqjBVky0RwrL1M1zNu3bSBkd_QGV1YcZqh3gp_Skj2QBixNfeL-4T05J55F5iuFb79mPGEnqgW3jk1UMyQ8xoEu2YZAqMS1I-Tt8Zd6zqk-B6oa84vwI1XEHtOFu1-B5ncPAbS0e09HjMseAS37lCbkBe2Ov9atRxN-mGsDwK2AY7UFWZ6i7g1rsVdNztyYKsX5pYKUpRXJDcj2l4gWE9dJ-TJif0JVctF9QOwyoS_EveUOtCVp9uzwbd_gZAGjHvnZSiBztTGHoslbKZ-zBWJTjU3Z3R8RR-70bK8N1m7Ug97cILsiUvG0wSJUxMokHgXZxVKtIGFqVnbtbdfVPY0GWqfVZRCoCWdLxCg2H2P9i36JFJfsVxXUMe6Q5qTGfM. Accessed 6 Oct 2021

BBC (5 December 2016) The city getting rich from fake news. https://www.bbc.co.uk/news/magazine-38168281. Accessed 6 Oct 2021

Bieber F (2020) The rise of authoritarianism in the Western Balkans. Palgrave Macmillan, London

Bieber F, Prelec T, Jović D, Nechev Z (2020) The suspicious virus: conspiracies and COVID19 in the Balkans. Balkans in Europe Policy Advisory Group. https://biepag.eu/wp-content/uploads/2020/12/Conspiracies-and-COVID19-in-the-Balkan-English.pdf?fbclid=IwAR3qLIFRnCATCi2j8aSijDABkxg7gKFDdlCGI5kpyCI8G_fGv3GnG5iVqkE. Accessed 20 May 2021
BIRN Investigative Resource Desk (2021) digital rights in the time of COVID-19. https://bird.tools/mapping-digital-rights-during-coronavirus-outbreak/. Accessed 6 Oct 2021
Čerkez G (2021) Research interview. 5 October 2021
CNN (2017) The fake news machine: inside the town gearing up for 2020. https://money.cnn.com/interactive/media/the-macedonia-story/. Accessed 6 Oct 2021
Dnevni Avaz (19 July 2020) Podaci zvaničnih institucija otkrivaju: Uvoz testova za koronu postaje unosan biznis. https://avaz.ba/vijesti/bih/582690/podaci-zvanicnih-institucija-otkrivaju-uvoz-testova-za-koronu-postaje-unosan-biznis. Accessed 6 Oct 2021
European Center for Not-For-Profit Law (2020) Covid-19 and civic freedoms in Europe in 2020. https://ecnl.org/sites/default/files/2021-02/Europe%20Trends%20Overview%20Tracker%20%28Final%29-for%20publishing_1.pdf. Accessed 20 May 2021
European Center for Not-For-Profit Law (2021) Civic space in the era of securitised Covid-19 reponses. https://ecnl.org/sites/default/files/2021-02/ECNL%20Securitised%20Covid%20Responses%20and%20Civic%20Space%20final%202.pdf. Accessed 6 Oct 2021
Fruscione G (ed) (2021) The pandemic in the Balkans: geopolitics and democracy at stake. Italian Institute for International Political Studies, Milano
Giffoni ML (2021) Belgrade and Pristina: a dialogue between the deaf mediated by the blind? In: Fruscione G (ed) The pandemic in the Balkans: geopolitics and democracy at stake. Italian Institute for International Political Studies, Milano, pp 102–116
Hale T, Angrist N, Goldszmidt R, Kira B, Petherick A, Phillips T, Webster S, Cameron-Blake E, Hallas L, Majumdar S, Tatlow H (2021) A global panel database of pandemic policies (Oxford COVID-19 Government Response Tracker). Nat Human Behav. https://doi.org/10.1038/s41562-021-01079-8. Accessed 1 May 2021
Human Rights Watch (16 April 2020) Azerbaijan: crackdown on critics amid pandemic. https://www.hrw.org/news/2020/04/16/azerbaijan-crackdown-critics-amid-pandemic. Accessed 6 Oct 2021
Human Rights Watch (2021) Covid-19 triggers wave of free speech abuse. https://features.hrw.org/features/features/covid/index.html. Accessed 6 Oct 2021
Institute for Democracy and Electoral Assistance (2021) Taking stock of regional democratic trends in Europe before and during the COVID-19 pandemic. https://www.idea.int/sites/default/files/publications/regional-democratic-trends-europe-before-and-during-COVID-19.pdf. Accessed 6 Oct 2021
International Press Institute (3 April 2020a) Three Serbian journalists reporting on COVID-19 issues arrested in one week. https://ipi.media/three-serbian-journalists-reporting-on-covid-19-issues-arrested-in-one-week/. Accessed 6 Oct 2021
International Press Institute (23 April 2020b) Azerbaijan abuses quarantine rules to jail critical journalists and bloggers. https://ipi.media/azerbaijan-abuses-quarantine-rules-to-jail-critical-journalists-and-bloggers/. Accessed 6 Oct 2021
Knežević R (7 October 2020) HRT, 1 na 1. https://www.youtube.com/watch?v=oRVTeB1LG5Y. Accessed 6 Oct 2021
Media Centar (27 March 2020) Novčane kazne i hapšenja zbog širenja dezinformacija i panike o koronavirusu. https://www.media.ba/bs/vijesti-i-dogadaji-vijesti/novcane-kazne-i-hapsenja-zbog-sirenja-dezinformacija-i-panike-o. Accessed 6 Oct 2021
OSCE Office for Democratic Institutions and Human Rights (ODIHR) (2020) OSCE human dimension commitments and state responses to the Covid-19 pandemic. https://www.osce.org/odihr/human-rights-states-of-emergency-covid19. Accessed 6 Oct 2021

Oslobodjenje (3 June 2020) Sebija Izetbegović: *Zašto samo Novalić, zašto samo Bošnjaci?!*https://www.oslobodjenje.ba/vijesti/bih/sebija-izetbegovic-zasto-samo-novalic-zasto-samo-bosnjaci-hajde-svi-da-odgovaramo-561880. Accessed 1 May 2021

Our World in Data (2021a). https://ourworldindata.org/grapher/covid-stringency-index?time=2020-12-31&region=Europe&country=MLT~AFG. Accessed 6 Oct 2021

Our World in Data (2021b) Covid-19: Government stringency index. https://ourworldindata.org/grapher/covid-stringency-index?tab=chart&stackMode=absolute&time=2020-01-22..2020-09-05&country=ALB~AUT~AZE~BLR~BEL~BIH~BGR~HRV~CYP~CZE~DNK~EST~FIN~FRA~GEO~DEU~GRC~HUN~ISL~IRL~ITA~OWID_KOS~LVA~LTU~LUX~MDA~NLD~NOR~POL~PRT~ROU~RUS~SRB~SVK~SVN~ESP~SWE~CHE~TUR~UKR~GBR&region=Europe. Accessed 6 Oct 2021

Oxford University's Blavatnik School of Government (13th April 2020) Oxford Covid-19 Government response tracker. https://www.bsg.ox.ac.uk/research/research-projects/coronavirus-government-response-tracker. Accessed 6 Oct 2021

Pandemic Big Brother (8 April 2020). https://pandemicbigbrother.online/en/. Accessed 6 Oct 2021

Prelec T, Tzifakis N (2021) From mask to vaccine diplomacy: geopolitical competition in the Western Balkans. In: Fruscione G (ed) The Pandemic in the Balkans: geopolitics and democracy at stake. Italian Institute for International Political Studies, Milano, pp 34–53

Radio Free Europe/Radio Liberty (5 March 2020a) No Joke! Serbian president makes light of coronavirus as one more reason to hit the bottle. https://www.rferl.org/a/serbian-president-makes-light-of-coronavirus-as-one-more-reason-to-hit-the-bottle/30468925.html. Accessed 6 Oct 2021

Radio Free Europe/Radio Liberty (27 March 2020b) COVID-19: serbs jailed for breaking quarantine; member of Putin's staff infected. https://www.rferl.org/a/covid-19-roundup-coronavirus/30512526.html. Accessed 6 Oct 2021

Radio Kameleon (29 March 2020) Prvooboljela djevojka iz Lukavca Sandra Šahat: ''Dobijam prijetnje zato što imam COVID-19". https://radiokameleon.ba/2020/03/29/prvooboljela-djevojka-iz-luvca-sandra-sahat-dobijam-prijetnje-zato-sto-imam-covid-19/. Accessed 6 Oct 2021

Radio Slobodna Evropa (4 May 2020a) Šta je radio ruski vojno-medicinski tim u RS i Srbiji? https://www.slobodnaevropa.org/a/%C5%A1ta-je-radio-ruski-vojno-medicinski-tim-u-rs-i-srbiji/30592383.html. Accessed 6 Oct 2021

Radio Slobodna Evropa (28 May 2020b) Afera 'Respiratori': Premijer FBiH Fadil Novalić zadržan u SIPA-i. https://www.slobodnaevropa.org/a/respiratori-bih-afera-srebrena-malina/30639946.html. Accessed 6 Oct 2021

Radio Slobodna Evropa (29 May 2020c) Izetbegović i Džaferović: Hapšenje Novalića udar na Bošnjake. https://www.slobodnaevropa.org/a/30641641.html. Accessed 6 Oct 2021

Radio Slobodna Evropa (15 Septemeber 2020d) Zbog kršenja privatnosti građani Crne Gore tuže državu. https://www.slobodnaevropa.org/a/zbog-krsenja-privatnosti-gradjani-tuze-drzavu-/30840363.html. Accessed 6 Oct 2021

Reuters (6 April 2021) Bosnians protest, telling government to resign over lack of COVID vaccines. https://www.reuters.com/article/us-health-coronavirus-bosnia-protests-idUSKBN2BT1WH. Accessed 6 Oct 2021

Schenker H (21 May 2020) North Macedonia flounders in pandemic's political limbo. https://balkaninsight.com/2020/05/21/north-macedonia-flounders-in-pandemics-political-limbo/. Accessed 6 Oct 2021

Služba za odnose s javnošću Vlade Crne Gore (22 March 2020) NKT za zarazne bolesti počinje objavljivanje identiteta lica u samoizolaciji: zaštita zdravlja i životâ građana naš najviši prioritet. https://www.gov.me/clanak/223143%2D%2Dnkt-za-zarazne-bolesti-pocinje-objavljivanje-identiteta-lica-u-samoizolaciji-zastita-zdravlja-i-zivot-gradana-nas-najvisi-priori. Accessed 6 Oct 2021

Stainaker G (25 July 2020) Balkanom vladaju kleptokrate – uz blagoslov EU. DW – Deutche Welle. https://www.dw.com/sr/balkanom-vladaju-kleptokrate-uz-blagoslov-eu/a-54315153. Accessed 6 Oct 2021

The Atlantic (30 November 2018) The crisis of conscience in fake news. https://www.theatlantic.com/video/index/577033/fake-news-fairytale/. Accessed 6 Oct 2021

The International Centre for Not-for-Profit Law (2020) Covid-19 civic freedom tracker. https://www.icnl.org/covid19tracker/. Accessed 22 Sept 2020

Wired (15 February 2017) Inside Macedonian fake-news complex. https://www.wired.com/2017/02/veles-macedonia-fake-news/. Accessed 6 Oct 2021

Žurnal (15 April 2020) Dvadeset hiljada testova isporučio proizvođač namještaja! https://zurnal.info/novost/22966/dvadeset-hiljada-testova-isporucio-proizvodac-namjestaja. Accessed 6 Oct 2021

Chapter 9
Instead of the Conclusion

9.1 Divisions in Europe Confirmed

When in June 2021, Hungary's Parliament passed a law that banned gay people featuring in educational materials for schools and television shows for under-eighteens, reactions showed deep cultural divisions across Europe. Viktor Orbán's Fidesz party comfortably control the Parliament and was supported by the second largest political group in the Parliament, another far-right party, Jobbik, resulting in 157 votes supporting the bill and only one parliamentarian opposing it with some opposition members boycotting the process in the 199 seats assembly.[1]

The reaction of some EU member states reflected the values that liberal societies developed and preserved in their largely open societies. During a meeting in Luxembourg on June 22, 13 EU member states condemned the legislation and practices that the latest Hungarian legislation allows. The number of countries increased a day later to 16 as some countries were either hesitant or had a change of mind. Thus, the numbers shifted from 13 to 14, later to 16 and eventually to 17. However, some of the media and some politicians reported different signatories because of these changes. Belgium's foreign minister mentions Lithuania as a signatory but misses Malta.[2] Euronews reported on consecutive days that the "statement was also signed off by Lithuania, which also opted out from the new letter."[3] "Italy waited until the end of the meeting to add its name to the list, while Austria and Greece did so the following day."[4] Portugal was understood to support the action, but it had to remain officially neutral as the presiding country.

[1]The Guardian (15 June 2021a).

[2]Wilmès (22 June 2021).

[3]Euronews (24 June 2021b).

[4]Euronews (23 June 2021a).

N. Andjelic, *Covid-19, State-Power and Society in Europe*, European Union and its Neighbours in a Globalized World 5, https://doi.org/10.1007/978-3-030-91073-0_9

Although the Belgian Prime Minister Alexander de Croo said that signatories are "seventeen countries in the whole of Europe—east, west, north and south,"[5] the fact is that the final list contained only two eastern European countries, Estonia and Latvia. Besides Lithuania, which had a change of mind, Poland, Czechia, Slovakia, Hungary, Romania, Bulgaria, Croatia, and Slovenia did not support such a statement against discrimination. Together with perhaps calculated lateness by Austria and some southern European states, it becomes clear that geography shows a clear division of liberal and less liberal Europe. Western Europe with the north of the continent and some southern countries expressed a solid attachment to values of equality, non-discrimination, civil liberties, and human rights, while many countries in central and eastern Europe and some in the south are committed to a different set of values that often lead towards a dictatorship of the majority and the majority's cultural, social, and political values.

The seventeen signatories wrote, "in the light of threats against fundamental rights and in particular the principle of non-discrimination on grounds of sexual orientation," while not addressing Hungary in particular, they condemned the policies that target minorities and undermine rights. The list of signatories consists of Austria, Belgium, Cyprus, Denmark, Estonia, Finland, France, Germany, Greece, Ireland, Italy, Latvia, Luxembourg, Malta, the Netherlands, Spain, and Sweden.[6] When transferred to the map, it looks like a divided continent (Map 9.1).

The EU summit further proved the divisions in place, although the majority strongly supported the values of open societies. Dutch Foreign Minister Sigrid Kaag said, "respect for our European values is not optional," adding that "discriminating LGBTI persons under the pretext of protecting children is unacceptable in the EU."[7]

"Only Poland and Slovenia – the latter "a little bit" – had offered Hungary support,"[8] Belgian Prime Minister Alexander De Croo later said. This does not mean the map showing different understanding and interpretations of societal, cultural, and political values is wrong. Politico reported that "Orbán received support from Poland, which has also clashed with Brussels over rule of law, and to some extent also from Slovenia, while a few countries — such as Slovakia — did not take a clear position."[9] This confirms the map and differences of understanding democracy, the rule of law, civil liberties and human rights, even when these issues are discussed among the supposedly exclusive club of liberal nations that the EU is supposed to be.

The Council of Europe however, as a more inclusive organisation of 47 European states, might show even deeper divisions as many nations that did not fulfil the conditions to join the EU, including specific sets of values, show more similarities in

[5] Reuters (24 June 2021).

[6] Politico (24 June 2021b).

[7] Politico (23 June 2021a).

[8] The Guardian (25 June 2021b).

[9] Politico (25 June 2021c).

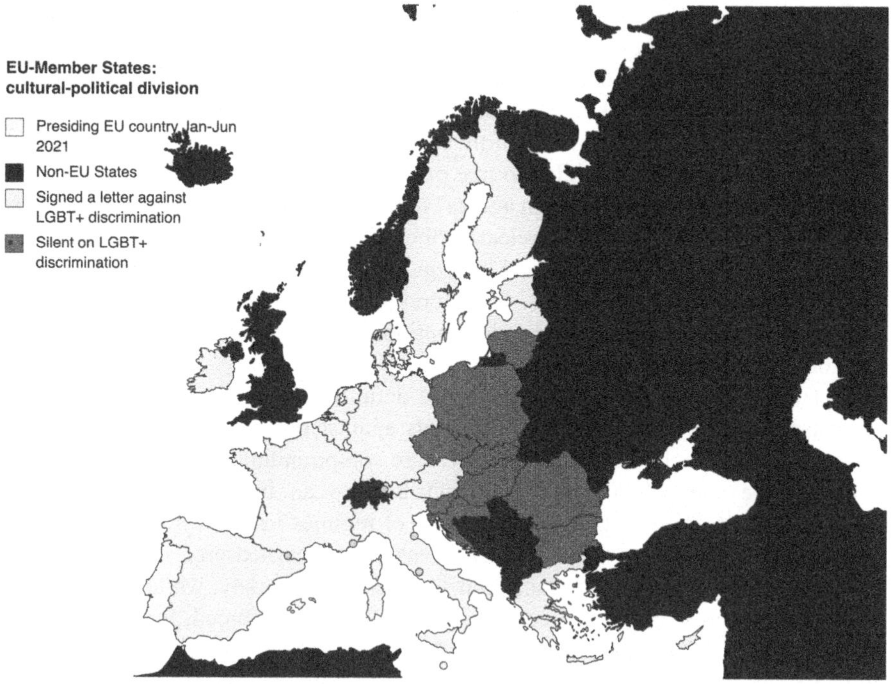

Map 9.1 EU member states: cultural-political division on LGBTQ+ discrimination

their policies and practices with the increasingly illiberal nations that are members of the EU. Although the possible stage for further debates over the values of the rule of law, human rights and democracy, the Council of Europe opposes the new Hungarian legislation on LGBTQ+ persons. The Human Rights Commissioner, Dunja Mijatović, said on the eve of the Hungarian legal amendments' adoption: "The proposed legislative amendments run counter to international and European human rights standards. It is misleading and false to claim that they are being introduced to protect children."[10]

9.2 Civic Space Endangered

Whatever kind of check on the state of play in European societies, the results are similar. Furthermore, if we take public documents and talks given by leading officials of international organisations as a lead towards results of studious research, the same countries are repeatedly mentioned. Civic space is endangered generally by political movements and developments globally, and COVID-19 has only

[10] Mijatović (14 June 2021).

accelerated the need to react and protect civic space. Europe is not spared of these developments. The UN High Commissioner for Human Rights Michelle Bachelet referred to few European countries in her talk at the beginning of 2021.

When talking about Russia, she stated her regret for "the entry into force late last year of new legal provisions which further limit fundamental freedoms, including the constitutionally guaranteed rights to free expression, peaceful assembly and association."[11] The definition of "foreign agents" in Russia is used to silence some of those critical of the regime. In a press release, "the OSCE Representative on Freedom of the Media, Harlem Désir, expressed his concerns today regarding the enactment of the law which extends the status of a "foreign agent" to private individuals, and introduces new restrictions on the distribution of information from media outlets categorized as "foreign agents"."[12]

In Turkey, the state's increasingly broad definition of "terrorism" is being used against opponents of the regime. "Reprisals against people who seek justice and accountability," Bachelet said for Turkey, "are compounding the erosion of judicial independence and rule of law, and contribute to an increasingly unsafe civic environment."[13] The similarity of the nature of regimes in Turkey and Russia does not end there. The report stated, "crackdowns on student-led protests underline the need for greater dialogue with many constituencies," in Turkey; while in Russia, the "existing restrictive laws have continued to be harshly enforced, including during recent demonstrations across the country."[14] The OSCE Parliamentary Assembly's human rights and democracy committee, while acknowledging that Turkey "continues today to face grave security concerns including terrorism" and refugee crisis, "stressed however that its response to challenges requires consolidation of democratic norms and full respect for human rights."[15]

By addressing the situation in Nagorno-Karabakh, Michelle Bachelet referenced two more European countries, Azerbaijan and Armenia, and called "for investigations into all alleged serious violations of international law that occurred in and around Nagorno-Karabakh."[16]

Even some EU countries, Germany, Greece, Italy, Malta, the Netherlands and Spain, have been criticised in her report for measures that "are restricting the work of organisations that protect migrants' rights, and deliver them life-saving assistance."[17] Hungary and Croatia were noted for their treatment of migrants including pushbacks to neighbouring countries, criminalising migrants in Hungary, lack of assistance to migrants, and, in Croatia, denying access to areas with migrants to European parliamentarians, Croatian ombudswoman and human rights organisations. Together

---

[11] Bachelet (26 February 2021a).

[12] Désir (3 December 2019).

[13] Bachelet (26 February 2021a).

[14] Bachelet (26 February 2021a).

[15] OSCEPA (13 April 2021).

[16] Bachelet (26 February 2021a).

[17] Bachelet (26 February 2021a).

with other organisations, Amnesty International "have documented numerous violations, including beatings and torture of migrants and asylum-seekers by Croatian police."[18]

Michelle Bachelet criticised both Hungary and Croatia again 4 months later in another address, expressing her "concerns on action taken against organisations that protect migrants' rights in several European countries, notably Hungary and Croatia." The pandemic, her report stated, affected more groups that have already been in a vulnerable position, like "mainly Roma residents of sub-standard informal settlements across the country," and "the poorest and socially excluded" in Ukraine. Of the European countries and regions, Bachelet has repeated her concerns over the Nagorno-Karabakh conflict zone, the Russian Federation, and Turkey. Restrictions on civic space in Belarus affect "the rights to freedoms of expression, peaceful assembly and association". Russia, the country with dedicated paragraphs in both addresses, was noted in June for "measures that further undermine people's right to express critical views".[19]

The UN Secretary-General, António Guterres, warned of "many mutually reinforcing strands and layers of inequality," that need to be addressed "before they destroy our economies and societies."[20] The statements by heads of leading human rights institutions show a need for a significant change in social relations between the states and within the states. While countries with closed and suppressed societies are restrictive in applying international standards, the countries with open societies show hesitance or even denial of measures when the proposed international agreements possibly endanger some elements of their elites. The illicit financial flows could only be dealt with by the agreement of the most powerful, most of them based in Western Europe. The taxation policies in many of these countries favour economic elites, thus further dividing societies. "Inequality defines our time," António Guterres said. When political elites do not combat rising inequality in contemporary societies, citizens' social protection becomes endangered. The resulting insecurity felt by many in the society opens up political space to alternatives to the current established political elites and the system. "A human rights economy requires transparency, accountability and a broad space for social dialogue, scrutiny and participation,"[21] said Michelle Bachelet.

Education and health services frequently come under both political and financial pressure, thus further restricting opportunities and possibilities for ordinary citizens even in prosperous countries. Citizens deprived of some rights that the previous generation enjoyed often find themselves without social protection under the new circumstances leaving them with only one option: democratic expression of dissent by voting for anti-establishment political groups. They build up their support from the situation that was accentuated by the pandemic and are "revealing fractures in the

[18] Amnesty International (10 November 2020).

[19] Bachelet (21 June 2021b).

[20] Guterres (18 July 2020).

[21] Bachelet (21 June 2021b).

fragile skeleton of the societies we have built," as the UN Secretary-General described it. "It is exposing fallacies and falsehoods everywhere: The lie that free markets can deliver healthcare for all; The fiction that unpaid care work is not work; The delusion that we live in a post-racist world; The myth that we are all in the same boat."[22]

Under such circumstances, some citizens are directed by populist rhetoric to look at their own elites as enemies that have created such a situation by aligning the nation with international forces that benefited from globalisation. The international forces are understood to be foreign, as workers provide competition for jobs in the opened up and globalised economies. Calls for a re-institutionalised nation-state, return of national sovereignty and "taking back control" are increasingly supported by citizens calling for a more closed society. Once in power, the formally "anti-elitist" governments deliver some of the promises, notably restricting some civil freedoms and human rights. The example from Hungary might be an outstanding one, but countries that hesitated to support the protesting note are ideologically on a similar path.

In the form closer to the beginning of the Cold War period than to the post-Cold War era, the return of the state also results in the rise of identity politics. Under such conditions, national minorities, and all kinds of minorities in society, are discriminated against. In some cases, minorities perceive their open existence even seriously challenged. The situation with migrants in Europe shows a more widespread attitude that is not only preserved for central and eastern European countries.

Viktor Orbán's Hungary and Jaroslaw Kaczyński's Poland might be the most prominent examples of identity politics and the rise of illiberal democracies within the EU. However, political parties of similar ideology are prominent in Austria, Denmark, Italy, France and generally across the EU. The difference is that the liberal position in these countries is strong enough to resist the illiberal challenges. However, to preserve and secure their majority and hold to power, the same political elites also accommodate some of the illiberal demands, especially in immigration policies which results in a less open society. Societies are therefore changed, and civic space becomes increasingly endangered. The inequalities in the society enable political forces that promise to address the issue to galvanise support and set off on a road of changes. "Addressing inequality," as António Guterres argued, "has therefore been a driving force throughout history for social justice, labour rights and gender equality.[23]

The problems arise when a new majority imposes new rules that do not tolerate and do not accommodate minority views. Instead of the road towards the end of history, as it looked likely in the 1990s, the new path is towards the more controlled society, a strong national leader, and the alleged anti-elite in power, where the society becomes a platform for identity politics. The new state of play offers a perception of increased opportunities for the underprivileged and socially excluded

[22] Guterres (18 July 2020).

[23] Guterres (18 July 2020).

that belong to the new majority. The reality of no tangible new opportunities is obscured by few examples of success and upward social mobility.

The east of the continent provides a series of such leaders in Azerbaijan, Belarus, Russia, Turkey, and even in Ukraine, where there was a recent change in leadership, but the whole concept of the closed society is still in place. A mixture of different ideologies, most commonly nationalistic, and characteristics of the regimes, most often hybrid, is to be found in most of the remaining countries of eastern and south-eastern Europe. Some leaders in these countries, like Aleksandar Vučić in Serbia, Edi Rama in Albania, or a nationalist set of three different leaders in Bosnia-Herzegovina, incline towards liberalising some of their policies while authoritarianising their regimes and suppressing societies. Thus, by paying lip service to some Western proclaimed values, like equality of minorities, civil freedoms, and human rights, they adopt more patterns from the regimes of Vladimir Putin in Russia and Recep Tayyip Erdoğan in Turkey. The resulting values in the society are somewhere in between Hungary or Poland and Russia or Turkey.

9.3 Callous Cunning Shysters

Western Europe manages to preserve the values inherited and developed further during the processes of integrating economies, societies and generally politics during the second half of the twentieth century. The institutions developed during this period proved to be too strong to allow for a significant change of values in the society. However, Brexit shows that change is possible even in a liberal democracy and an open society. According to the twenty indices consulted, the United Kingdom is still an "Open Society", but it is at the bottom of the top group with a realistic possibility of degrading some of the freedoms and rights and joining France and Italy with a "Fairly Open" societies.

The ruling class of the British Conservative Party was dominated in the Parliament for years by a pro-European snivelling faction that had a perception and belief of winning the referendum on Brexit. However, by overintellectualizing politics, they certainly did not have a touch strong enough with voters, many of whom felt the competition from global markets, competed on the domestic labour market with EU citizens and other foreigners, suffered consequences from the global financial crisis, observed the European migrant crisis of 2015, and witnessed rising inequality in the society. Part of the elite arguing for Brexit realised the importance of shaping perceptions. It was "others" that undermined positions of the "true Brits", and the cause of the problem was membership in the EU. Voters were given a perception of a return of the traditional sovereignty and a hope of improving their position.

The cosmopolitan elite produced stupefying policies and could not address the popular desire for autarkic economic nationalism. Culture also played an important factor, as it is a salient element of all identity politics, regardless of the country. As their vote actually decided the outcome of the referendum and therefore has to be in the focus of consideration, the English have lost their cultural capital. London is a city of foreigners and the perceived cosmopolitanised elite. Almost nine million people live in the city "where 40.2% of residents identified with either the Asian, Black, Mixed or Other ethnic group." The census of 2011 also showed that "London had the smallest percentage of White British people, at 44.9%."[24] Smaller communities won a democratic competition and unleashed new forces, often nationalistic, that target "others".

The examples of the British government under Boris Johnson and Brexit are just a more radical expression of the problem found across European societies. An increasing number of citizens in developed liberal democracies felt alienated, insecure, and unfairly rewarded for their work and their sacrifice during the economic turbulence caused by the global financial crisis. Essentially the crisis increased the potential for political alternatives that were not necessarily liberal and democratic. The economic turbulence was followed by the political rise of non-establishment political groups. *Syriza* came to power in Greece in 2015. Marine Le Pen, the National Front leader, reformed in 2018 as *Rassemblement National* (National Rally) and became the primary challenger of President Emmanuel Macron in France. *Alternative für Deutschland* (Alternative for Germany) became the largest opposition group in German Parliament in 2017. *Freiheitliche Partei Österreichs* (Freedom Party) established itself as the third-largest in the Austrian Parliament and the occasional junior partner in government. In the Netherlands, the minority government in 2010 relied on support by *Partijvoor de Vrijheid* (Party for Freedom). The party remained second or third largest over the several elections since the global financial crisis, albeit out of the government coalitions.

This brief overview of selected countries and parties in the liberal democracies could be added by the rise of two new movements in Spain, *Podemos* and *Ciudadanos*. Some radical parties, already present but not influential in society, achieved success in Sweden, where *Sverigedemokraterna* (Sweden Democrats) entered the Parliament for the first time in 2010. Another Scandinavian populist, *Perussuomalaiset* (Finns, formerly known as True Finns), entered the Finnish Parliament in 2011. The *M5S -Movimento 5 Stelle* (Five Star Movement) formed the coalition government in Italy in 2018. Previously, the *M5S* were the third largest political group and the second-largest party in the Italian Parliament following the elections in 2013. *Lega*, another anti-establishment party, was part of the coalition government with the *M5S*. Similar nationalist movements, albeit a part of the establishment, could be found in other countries like Switzerland and Norway.

Thus, the vote for Brexit in the United Kingdom is not an isolated development or historical incident. Instead, it is an expression, perhaps a more radical one, of the popular dissent with processes in advanced Western economies and developed liberal democracies. Globalisation has had diverse effects on the population, threatening the low skilled workforce and also white-collar workers with cheaper labour competition, while economic elites continued to prosper with increased profits and participation in profit-sharing processes. This situation resulted in widespread

[24] Gov.uk: Ethnicity facts and figures (7 August 2020).

demand for economic protection, something that the political, economic, and cultural elites are either refusing to pledge or failing to provide.

The electorate is, therefore, moving towards alternatives that might offer some sense of security through policies of economic nationalism. Economic and political nationalism enabled elements of the elite to further their profits but, simultaneously, interferes in society's perceptions of them as the elite. Temporary, at least, the masses perceive them as not being part of the "corrupt elite". These elites formed most of the governments in the Western world since the end of the Second World War. As a body, the elite is not unified; ideologically, they tend to incline towards the right-of-centre or left-of-centre, although some elite members are of more radical views. The overwhelming majority, however, are ideologically situated around the centre. Most Western governments in the second half of the twentieth century have been close to the centre.

The rich debate on the possible post-ideological world is not a subject of this work, but it is essential to consider some views. Regardless of one's position regarding the chimaera of post-ideology, as some authors argued of the post-Cold War era, it is imperative to investigate, analyse and search for conclusions why the socially and economically liberal left is finding itself sharing essential values with the socially liberal right-of-centre. Francis Fukuyama noticed "deterministic materialism that discounts the importance of ideology and culture and sees man as essentially a rational, profit-maximizing individual."[25] Splinters of the traditional, economically conservative left, with their opposition to globalisation, are increasingly finding commonalities with the far right.

One academic study of social democratic parties in 31 European countries between 1918 and 2017 found that "parties that once commanded over 40 per cent of votes have collapsed to the low twenties, teens or lower."[26] The same report found that "left-wing populist parties have stagnated and have a considerable influence only in southern Europe. The median support for left-wing populist in Europe is 1.3 per cent."[27] The data collected by the Timbro project offers insights into the results of the 25 most popular populist parties in Europe. There are only four left-wing parties in this group, although the report's authors have somehow included a fifth one—*Movimento Cinque Stelle* (Five Star Movement)—among left-wing populists.[28] The Greek *Syriza*, as well as the Cypriot AKEL (*Anorthotiko Komma Ergazomenou Laou*), the Spanish *Podemos,* and the Portuguese *Bloco de Esquerda* all stand for a different ideology than the *Movimento Cinque Stelle,* which can only be described as non-ideological.

Meanwhile, the rise of far-right politics has pulled mainstream right-wing political parties further to the right in their attempts to retain potential voters. Cas Mudde found that "far-right parties now average some 15% of the national vote in Europe,

---

[25] Fukuyama (1989), p. 6.

[26] Benedetto et al. (1 July 2019), p. 2.

[27] Timbro (February 2019), p. 20.

[28] Timbro (February 2019), p. 2.

they are considered *Koalitionsfähig* (acceptable coalition partners) in many countries, at least at local or regional levels."[29] The far-right—either in government as junior partners or outside the government as a conceivable threat to the right-of-centre and right-wing mainstream political parties—has pulled society significantly to the right. When the left had not moved towards the centre, a polarization of the political space has resulted in a loss of democratic contest and potentially catastrophic results for the polarised society. After all, this has already happened in the past.

9.4 Democracy, Sovereignty or Globalisation, That Is the Question

"The other major "contradiction" potentially unresolvable by liberalism is the one posed by nationalism and other forms of racial and ethnic consciousness," Fukuyama argued but was almost immediately dismissive of this threat stating that "it is not clear that nationalism represents an irreconcilable contradiction in the heart of liberalism."[30] Globalisation has had diverse effects on the population, threatening the low skilled workforce with cheaper labour competition, while economic elites continued to prosper with increased profits and participation in globalised profit-sharing processes. This situation resulted in widespread demand for economic protection, something that the political, economic, and cultural elites are either refusing to pledge or failing to provide. Internal movements within the society were caused by the actions and reactions of new political movements, often populist, against the financial elites, saved by the political elites' decisions during the global financial crisis and policies executed by bureaucratic elites running the state administration.

When a significant proportion of voters feels endangered by the effects of such centrist governance, there is increasing support for radical alternatives on both sides of the political spectrum. When seen as providing the insecurity on the labour market, globalisation is one of the processes that contributed to the shift of political support among the general population. Rising unemployment, salaries that do not keep up with the inflation rate, economic as well as personal insecurity issues, lack of job prospects for younger generations—all of these contribute to a state of mind that is in search of an alternative to those who are perceived as creators, or as benefactors, often both, of the processes that have developed such a state of play: the elite. Some of the elite—and this perception often extends to the elite in general—are perceived as corrupt. Media reports certainly seem to bear out such views.

Dani Rodrik offers a "globalisation paradox" to explain the current issues that the state must deal with. The three elements of the paradox are deeply integrated

[29] Mudde (12 November 2019).

[30] Fukuyama (1989), p. 15.

globalization, national sovereignty, and democratic processes, but only two of the three can be achieved simultaneously.[31] This is where the problem is laid down for the elites. They have to sacrifice something. Liberal societies in the West have seemingly chosen to sacrifice national sovereignty in its more traditional form and preserve and support democracy and globalisation. Many societies in central Europe and especially further to the east have chosen to sacrifice democracy. Hence the rise of regimes that could be described as illiberal, authoritarian, autocratic or hybrid regimes. A specific form of these regimes is found in the Western Balkans and is described as "stabilitocracy".[32]

Ralf Dahrendorf considered the tensions within modern societies in the 1990s. "Addressing the same *problématique*, Dahrendorf's Quandary posits that, over time, maintaining global economic competitiveness requires countries either to adopt measures detrimental to the cohesion of civil society, or to restrict civil liberties and political participation,"[33] Anheier and Filip interpret. They conclude by offering examples of "the Brexit referendum and its arduous aftermath", the illiberal democracy of Orbán's Hungary, the autocratic developments in Russia or Turkey, populism in Italy and "the growing public indebtedness of many OECD economies, and imagining that Ralf "Dahrendorf would most likely have uttered despairingly: "Have I not told you so?"[34]

The reality is that many voters who previously supported the radical political left in liberal democracies have abandoned it in favour of the radical right. Their shift was not a long journey along the line of different ideologies across the central part of the spectrum. Instead, it was a short-distanced leap—the radical right and the radical left have a significant number of values in common. Animosity to open society is common to both sets of parties, as is support for the all-controlling state. Internationalism is almost non-existent among both sets of supporters during times of crisis. The current period is undoubtedly one of the focus points of the crisis. Charismatic leaders are offered devotion by followers on both the radical right and the radical left, the mobilisation of the masses at street level contributing to their perceived strength. At the same time they encourage, if not outright politically support, hostility to the media. The lines are thus becoming blurred. Instead of laying out the whole political spectrum between the two ideologies, the radical ideologies should be seen as existing in parallel and in proximity to each other.

The flight of voters towards radical choices reflects the rise of inequality, which voters of the centre have also felt. "The reduction of inequality," according to Thomas Piketty, was "above all a consequence of war and revolution and of policies adopted to cope with these shocks . . . in most developed countries between 1910 and 1950."[35] The resulting stability and security during the second half of the twentieth

---

[31] Rodrik (2011).

[32] Bieber (2018); Kmezić (2019), pp. 87–110; Pavlović (5 May 2017).

[33] Anheier and Filip (January 2020), Abstract.

[34] Anheier and Filip (January 2020), p. 19.

[35] Piketty (2015), p. 69.

century brought about a rise in inequality, which inevitably fed into voter dissatisfaction and rebellions.

"Disparity in wealth, especially when accompanied by disparity in values," argues Ray Dalio, "leads to increasing conflict and, in the government, that manifests itself in the form of populism of the left and populism of the right and often in revolutions of one sort or another."[36] This warning comes from a leading capitalist, a billionaire hedge fund manager with a perfect overview of global markets and societies. When political and economic shocks of the early twenty-first century are viewed in this context, it becomes clear that a new form of the centre-left, with aspirations to conquer a sizeable portion of the liberal centre, is needed in order to preserve the central values of the traditional left and thus stabilise society.

The centre-right is also facing a dilemma on how to solve the trilemma. They need to firmly develop a strong differentiation with far-right and radical movements if globalisation and democracy are to be preserved. If they are ambivalent in their decisions and consider partnering with radical, often nationalist, movements, the fundamental values of the centrist compromise are endangered, and societies become more closed. Sovereignty is strengthened, and globalisation is in place under such partnership, but democracy is under a severe challenge. Hungary and Poland are prime examples. The process could be named deliberalisation. It is pronounced in former communist countries of central and eastern Europe that have previously successfully and largely peacefully transitioned to democracy.

9.5 Mapping the Division

Ahmet Davutoglu, who intellectually developed new Turkish foreign policy, often named a "Neo-Ottoman", contends "four earthquakes" created a contemporary international system. The end of the Soviet Union and the Warsaw Pact provided for an "era of ceasefire" that was expected to be democratic but was not. The 9/11 attacks created a shift from freedom to security. Instead of institutionalising democracy, the issue was how to protect democracy, according to Davutoglu. The consequences of the global economic crisis of 2008 were widely discussed already. The fourth earthquake is a post-2011 set of events. He calls it a "structural earthquake that has destabilised national institutions in Middle East, Ukraine and some other places. Nation-states are not controlling all their sovereign territory."[37]

Discussion of Davutoglu's visions on crucial developments of the contemporary world is possible. However, it is inevitable that they reshaped relations between nations and changed burgeoning alternatives within the national spectrums. The West might attempt to re-establish a "rules based order", but even if successful, it will not be the same order. The rise of alternatives to the west-imposed order

[36] Dalio (4 April 2019).

[37] Davutoglu (6 June 2021).

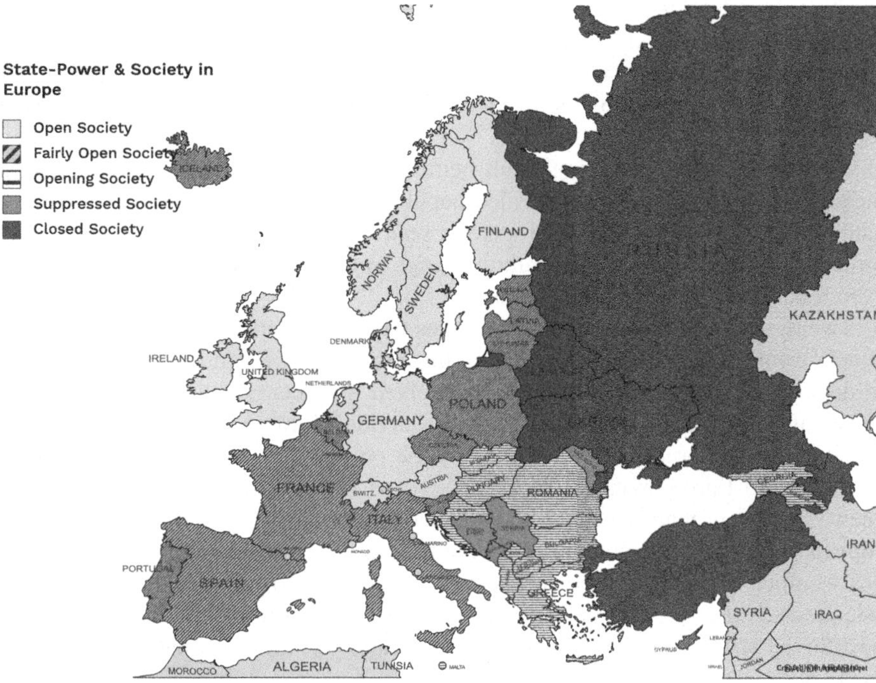

Map 9.2 State-power and society in Europe

provided for challenges to society's internal order. Liberal regimes are seriously challenged. Xenophobic identity politics attracts following, and some societies are shifting away from open.

Authoritarian regimes strongly influence, if not directly control the media whose independence and pluralism are in decline. The media freedom is thus degraded. The judiciary is politically influenced, and a heavily biased judicial system is thus created. Nepotism and rampant corruption mark public appointments in such societies where power is frequently abused. Although nationalist movements do not necessarily end up with such set of characteristics of the regime, the inspection of European regimes, personal, economic and media freedoms, human rights, corruption, and the rule of law has shown that usually the more nationalist regime in power, the less open society results from such conditions. Nationalist movements, argues Fukuyama, "may constitute a source of conflict for liberal societies, this conflict does not arise from liberalism itself so much as from the fact that the liberalism in question is incomplete."[38] This helps to further understand the resulting map of state-power and society in Europe (Map 9.2).

---

[38] Fukuyama (1989), p. 15.

The map reflects the state of play at the moment of the beginning of the pandemic. The project has offered a division of five different types of societies in Europe concerning state-power. The changes that have occurred since were not caused, but were instead accelerated, by the pandemic. Vital signs of changes had already been present. The retreat of the state was due to globalisation that primarily benefited elites, while masses increasingly felt betrayed by national leaders. The increased inequality within society has provided populist leaders with a powerful weapon in national debates. A strengthened state is seen by many as a tool to increase the protection of the masses. The resulting change might not necessarily be democratic, even if achieved by democratic means.

Twenty-four of forty-five European states with a population of over half a million people went through the transition from the communist system towards some form of democracy. Half of them were also involved in violent conflicts adding further layers of complexity. The perception of a divided Europe by different forms of societies and governance is confirmed by the project that consulted 20 indices. A western (old) Europe with an "open society" is added by a mixture of "old" and "new" Europe in mainly central and southern Europe with a "fairly open society", "opening society" in the countries on the fringes of central Europe, less-successful post-conflict societies of the Western Balkans and post-Soviet space with the "suppressed society", and states on the eastern edge of Europe that include several post-Soviet states with the "closed society". Naturally, there are several exceptions to the rule.

Gaps between these societies seem to be widening. They are caused by external factors like globalisation and attempts to establish a new international system, and internal factors reflected in increased support for nationalist movements and authoritarian models. In the minds of followers, such movements could stop global forces that undermine the position of "good people" in nation-states. Thus developed societies put minorities of any kind under pressure to conform with national values as interpreted by the perceived majority in a state. Charismatic leaders arise from such movements and, if successful, develop the strong autocratic rule, oppose international organisations, refuse some norms and undermine human rights. These processes are masked as preservation of national values, culture, tradition, sovereignty and independence. The process of developing and establishing irreversibly civil liberties and human rights, opening societies and accepting universal values of the open society has been put under pressure even in some still "open" or "fairly open" societies. The concept of the open society, firmly connected with the functioning democracy, is under nationalist scrutiny in countries with "opening society", stalled at least in countries with "suppressed societies", and even reversed in countries that developed "closed societies". A disunited Europe is a result and consequence of such developments.

References

Amnesty International (10 November 2020) EU: Inquiry into European complicity in Croatian border violence against migrants and refugees 'significant'. https://www.amnesty.org/en/latest/press-release/2020/11/eu-inquiry-into-european-complicity-in-croatian-border-violence-against-migrants-and-refugees-significant/. Accessed 5 Oct 2021

Anheier HK, Filip A (January 2020) The Rodrik Trilemma and the Dahrendorf quandary: an empirical assessment. Dahrendorf Forum IV Working Paper No. 1509

Bachelet M (26 February 2021a) 46th session of the Human Rights Council. Item 2 - High Commissioner's Oral Update. Statement by Michelle Bachelet, UN High Commissioner for Human Rights. https://www.ohchr.org/EN/NewsEvents/Pages/DisplayNews.aspx?NewsID=26806&LangID=E. Accessed 6 Oct 2021

Bachelet M (21 June 2021b) 47th session of the Human Rights Council. Item 2: Human rights update by the High Commissioner. https://www.ohchr.org/EN/NewsEvents/Pages/DisplayNews.aspx?NewsID=27178&LangID=E. Accessed 6 Oct 2021

Benedetto G, Hix S, Mastrorocco N. (1 July 2019) The rise and fall of social democracy, 1918–2017 [Working paper]. http://eprints.lse.ac.uk/104060/1/Rise_and_fall.pdf. Accessed 6 Oct 2021

Bieber F (2018) The rise (and fall) of Balkan Stabilitocracies. Horizons Winter 2018 (10). https://www.cirsd.org/en/horizons/horizons-winter-2018-issue-no-10/the-rise-and-fall-of-balkan-stabilitocracies. Accessed 6 Oct 2021

Dalio R (4 April 2019) Why and how capitalism needs to be reformed (Part 1). Linkedin. https://www.linkedin.com/pulse/why-how-capitalism-needs-reformed-ray-dalio/?published=t. Accessed 6 Oct 2021

Davutoglu A (6 June 2021) Turkish foreign policy and its approach to Southeast Europe. Talk at foreign policy forum, Zagreb (online)

Désir H (3 December 2019) OSCE Representative Désir concerned by enactment of law broadening "foreign agent" status to individuals in Russia. https://www.osce.org/representative-on-freedom-of-media/441002. Accessed 5 Oct 2021

Euronews (23 June 2021a) Sixteen EU countries denounce Hungary's new anti-LGBT law. https://www.euronews.com/2021/06/22/thirteen-eu-countries-denounce-hungary-s-new-anti-lgbt-law. Accessed 6 Oct 2021

Euronews (24 June 2021b) Macron, Merkel and 15 other EU leaders defend LGBT rights amid row over new Hungarian law. https://www.euronews.com/2021/06/24/macron-merkel-and-15-other-eu-leaders-defend-lgbt-rights-amid-row-over-new-hungarian-law. Accessed 6 Oct 2021

Fukuyama F (1989) The end of history? The National Interest, No. 16 (Summer 1989). pp 3–18

Gov.uk: Ethnicity facts and figures (7 August 2020) Regional ethnic diversity. https://www.ethnicity-facts-figures.service.gov.uk/uk-population-by-ethnicity/national-and-regional-populations/regional-ethnic-diversity/latest. Accessed 6 Oct 2021

Guterres A (2020) Secretary-general's Nelson Mandela Lecture: "Tackling the inequality pandemic: a new social contract for a new era" [as delivered]. Video Message for the International Nelson Mandela Day, 18 July 2020. https://www.un.org/sg/en/content/sg/statement/2020-07-18/secretary-generals-nelson-mandela-lecture-%E2%80%9Ctackling-the-inequality-pandemic-new-social-contract-for-new-era%E2%80%9D-delivered. Accessed 6 Oct 2021

Kmezić M (2019) EU rule of law conditionality: democracy or 'Stabilitocracy' promotion in the Western Balkans? In: Džankić J, Keil S, Kmezić M (eds) The Europeanisation of the Western Balkans: a failure of EU conditionality? Palgrave Macmillan, London, pp 87–110

Mijatović D (14 June 2021) Commissioner Mijatović urges Hungary's Parliamentarians to reject draft amendments banning discussion about sexual and gender identity and diversity. Consel de l'Europe: Commissaire aux droits de l'homme. Statement. https://www.coe.int/fr/web/commissioner/-/commissioner-mijatovic-urges-hungary-s-parliamentarians-to-reject-draft-amendments-banning-discussion-about-sexual-and-gender-identity-and-diversity. Accessed 6 Oct 2021

Mudde C (12 November 2019). Nativism is driving the far-right surge in Europe – and it is here to stay. The Guardian. https://www.theguardian.com/global/commentisfree/2019/nov/12/nativism-is-driving-the-far-right-surge-in-europe-and-it-is-here-to-stay. Accessed 6 Oct 2021

OSCEPA (13 April 2021) Troubled by recent developments in Turkey, OSCE PA human rights leaders stress importance of respect for democratic principles. https://www.oscepa.org/en/news-a-media/press-releases/press-2021/troubled-by-recent-developments-in-turkey-osce-pa-human-rights-leaders-stress-importance-of-respect-for-democratic-principles. Accessed 5 Oct 2021

Pavlović S (5 May 2017) West is best: how 'stabilitocracy' undermines democracy building in the Balkans. LSE blog. https://blogs.lse.ac.uk/europpblog/2017/05/05/west-is-best-how-stabilitocracy-undermines-democracy-building-in-the-balkans/. Accessed 6 Oct 2021

Piketty T (2015) Putting distribution back at the center of economics: reflections on capital in the twenty-first century. J Econ Perspect 29(1):67–88

Politico (23 June 2021a) It's Hungary vs. everyone after attacks on LGBTQ+ rights. https://www.politico.eu/article/its-hungary-vs-everyone-after-attacks-on-lgbtq-rights-euro-2020-viktor-orban/. Accessed 6 Oct 2021

Politico (24 June 2021b) 17 EU leaders sign LGBTQ+ rights letter in response to Hungary anti-gay law. https://www.politico.eu/article/16-eu-leaders-sign-lgbtq-rights-letter-in-response-to-hungary-anti-gay-law/. Accessed 6 Oct 2021

Politico (25 June 2021c) EU leaders confront Orbán over anti-LGBTQ+ bill. https://www.politico.eu/article/eu-leaders-confront-viktor-orban-over-anti-lgbt-bill-hungary-rights/. Accessed 6 Oct 2021

Reuters (24 June 2021) "Too much": EU leaders confront Hungary's Orban over new anti-LGBT law. https://www.reuters.com/world/europe/leaders-16-eu-states-call-block-fight-lgbti-discrimination-2021-06-24/. Accessed 6 Oct 2021

Rodrik D (2011) The globalization paradox: democracy and the future of the world economy. WW Norton, New York

The Guardian (15 June 2021a) Hungary passes law banning LGBT content in schools or kids' TV. https://www.theguardian.com/world/2021/jun/15/hungary-passes-law-banning-lbgt-content-in-schools. Accessed 6 Oct 2021

The Guardian (25 June 2021b) Fractious EU summit rejects Franco-German plan for Putin talks. https://www.theguardian.com/world/2021/jun/25/fractious-eu-summit-rejects-franco-german-plan-putin-talks. Accessed 6 Oct 2021

Timbro: Authoritarian Populism Index Report (February 2019) Timbro. https://populismindex.com/report/. Accessed 6 Oct 2021

Wilmès S (22 June 2021) Zeventien EU-lidstaten verenigen zich op initiatief van België om de rechten van LGBTIQ te verdedigen in Europa. https://wilmes.belgium.be/nl/dertien-eu-lidstaten-verenigen-zich-op-initiatief-van-belgie-om-de-rechten-van-lgbtiq-te-verdedigen. Accessed 6 Oct 2021

Index

A
Africa, 89
Albania, 10, 17, 19, 24, 26–28, 30, 32, 39, 41–45, 47–50, 52–55, 62, 66–68, 70, 72, 75, 80, 82–87, 90, 96, 99, 101–103, 105–113, 118, 119, 128–133, 142, 145, 146, 150, 153, 171
Albanian, 48–50, 53, 71, 108, 148, 149, 153, 154
Aliyev, I., 51
Alliance of Independent Social-Democrats SNSD, 48
Alternative für Deutschland, 172
America, 5, 46, 125
American, 9, 10, 47, 103, 129, 155
Amnesty International, 108–110, 113, 121, 129, 133, 138, 139, 141, 148
Anadolu News Agency, 124
AnorthotikoKommaErgazomenouLaou (AKEL), 173
Antifascist, 150
Armenia, 11, 17, 19, 25–28, 30, 32, 41, 47, 52, 61–63, 66, 80, 82, 96, 99, 118, 125, 128, 139, 140, 143, 146, 168
Article XIX, 95, 117, 118, 120, 122, 126
Ashkali, 110
Asian, 95, 172
Atlantic Council, 88
Austria, 17, 18, 24–26, 28, 30, 32, 40, 65, 81, 98, 127, 142, 145, 165, 166, 170
Austrian, 48, 172
Authoritarian, 3, 6, 7, 11, 20, 22, 31, 33, 41, 46, 48, 49, 52, 54, 87, 88, 104, 118, 121, 122, 139–141, 150, 157, 175
Authoritarianism, 2, 11, 12, 31, 43, 46, 50, 72
Autocracy, 31, 37, 39, 41–44, 46, 47, 49, 51, 118
Autocratic, 11, 12, 46, 48, 49, 126, 130, 144, 150, 175
Autocratization, 22, 31, 33, 42, 43
Azerbaijan, 11, 19, 20, 24, 26–30, 32, 38, 39, 41, 42, 61–63, 66, 78, 80, 82, 96, 99, 100, 102, 111, 118, 121, 126, 128, 130, 139, 140, 142–145, 168, 171
Azerbaijani, 51, 140

B
Bachelet, M., 148, 159, 168, 169
Balkan, 12, 21, 27, 46, 48–51, 53, 55, 70–72, 88–90, 109, 112, 140, 146, 148, 151–153, 155, 157, 158
Balkan-Egyptian, 109
Balkan in Europe Policy Advisory Group, 153
Baltic, 17, 63, 75, 78
Banja Luka, 90, 159
Bar, 90
Barnier, 1
BBC, 4, 123, 125, 155
BBC Türkçe, 125
Belarus, 11, 19, 20, 25, 27–30, 32, 39, 41, 61–63, 66, 75, 78, 80, 82, 96, 99, 108, 121, 122, 126, 128, 139–141, 143–145, 147, 169, 171
Belgium, 17, 18, 24, 26–28, 30, 32, 37, 39, 40, 44, 63, 65, 81, 98, 127, 142, 145, 165, 166
Belgrade, 70, 71, 90
Berlin, I., 61
Bertelsmann, 16, 43, 44

N. Andjelic, *Covid-19, State-Power and Society in Europe*, European Union and its Neighbours in a Globalized World 5, https://doi.org/10.1007/978-3-030-91073-0

Bieber, F., 12, 46, 50, 51, 54, 150, 153, 175
Bilbao, 138
Black, 138, 172
Blavatnik School of Government, 22, 24, 27, 137, 141, 142
Bloco de Esquerda, 173
Bloomberg, 7, 8
Boljare, 90
Bolsonaro, 2
Borisov, 2
Bosnia, 19–21, 24, 27, 38, 39, 41–44, 47–49, 51–54, 62, 67, 69–71, 78, 80, 83, 85–88, 90, 96, 100, 102–105, 107–113, 118, 129, 130, 133, 140, 142, 144, 146–149, 152, 153, 155, 157–159, 171
Bosnia-Herzegovina (B & H), 19–21, 24, 26–28, 30, 32, 38, 39, 41–45, 47, 49, 51–54, 62, 66–71, 78, 80, 82–86, 90, 96, 99–112, 118, 128–133, 142, 144–149, 152, 153, 155, 157–159, 171
Bosniak, 48, 50, 70, 72, 149, 157, 159
Bosnian, 48, 53, 54, 146, 149, 152–155, 157–159
Brexit, 1, 5, 9, 171, 172, 175
Brexiters, 2
British, 1, 6, 7, 171, 172
Brnabić, A., 70
Brussels, 1, 78, 90, 166
Budapest, 90
Bulgaria, 17, 19, 24, 26, 28, 30, 32, 41, 63, 66, 81, 95, 96, 99, 118, 125, 128, 138, 139, 141, 142, 145, 166
Bulgarian, 139
Burgess, J., 126

C

Canton 10, 156
Catalan, 9
Catholic
  Roman Catholic, 71
Caucasus, 11, 27, 39, 75
Ceausescu, E., 72
Center for Systemic Peace, 16, 19, 37–39, 41, 42, 47
Center for Women's Rights, 113
Central Asia, 95
Channel 4, 123
China, 8, 11, 88–90, 148, 152, 157
Chinese, 87–91, 104, 152, 153, 157, 158
Christian, 71
Ciudadanos, 172
Civicus, 16, 63, 64, 66–68
CNN Turk, 125
Cold War, 6, 8, 61, 87, 120, 170, 173
Communist, 15, 17, 20–22, 27, 39, 43, 44, 53, 63, 75, 78, 83, 85, 96, 100, 117, 118, 126, 129, 143, 150, 176, 178
Council of Europe, 117, 119, 121, 167
Čović, D., 2, 48, 158
COVID-19, 1–3, 7, 11, 15, 29, 121, 138–141, 148, 149, 151, 153–156, 167
Crimea, 118, 121
Croat, 48, 50, 158, 159
Croatia, 17, 19, 24, 26–28, 30, 32, 39, 41, 54, 63, 66, 82, 90, 96, 99, 118, 128, 142, 145, 154, 158, 166, 168, 169
Croatian, 6, 48, 158, 168
Croatian Democratic Union
  HDZ, 48
Cuba, 10
Cypriot, 173
Cyprus, 17–19, 24, 26, 28, 30, 32, 38–42, 65, 81, 98, 118, 126, 127, 138, 142, 145, 166
Czechia, 17, 18, 24, 26–28, 30, 32, 40, 63, 65, 75, 81, 96, 98, 127, 142, 145, 166

D

Dahrendorf, R., 175
Daily Telegraph, 8
Daly, T.G., 22, 33
Davutoglu, A., 176
Dayton Agreement
  Dayton, 42
De Croo, A., 166
Democracy, 1–5, 7, 8, 11, 12, 15–17, 22, 25, 29, 31, 33, 37, 39–44, 46–49, 51, 54, 55, 69, 77, 88, 93, 104, 119, 121, 124, 125, 134, 137–141, 148, 151, 166, 167, 170–172, 175, 176, 178
Democratic, 1–3, 5–8, 11, 12, 15, 21, 22, 27, 29, 31, 33, 39, 44, 46–49, 53, 54, 67, 87, 93, 104, 113, 121, 126, 137, 139–141, 150, 169, 172–176, 178
Democratic Front, 148
Democratic Party of Socialists (DPS), 50, 51, 150
Denmark, 17, 18, 24, 26, 28, 30, 32, 40, 61, 65, 80, 81, 98, 118, 127, 141, 142, 144, 145, 166, 170
Deutsche Welle (DW), 50, 71, 125
Deutsche Welle Türkçe, 125

Dodik, M., 2, 48, 149, 159
Đukanović, M., 2, 48–51, 54, 67, 70, 103, 150, 151
Duterte, R., 2, 51

E
Eastern Europe, 63, 95
Eastern European, 29, 95
East StratCom Task Force, 124
Eatwell, R., 2–4
Economic Policy Institute, 8
Economist, 16, 37–39, 41, 44, 49, 50
Economist Intelligence Unit (EIU), 16, 37–39, 41, 44
Egyptians, 110
England, 120, 146
English, 124, 171
Erdoğan, 2, 12, 125, 157, 171
Estonia, 17, 18, 24, 26, 28, 30, 32, 40, 65, 81, 96, 98, 118, 126, 127, 142, 145, 166
Eurasian, 21
Euronews, 123, 165
Europe, 2, 4, 7, 10–12, 15–17, 20–22, 25, 29, 33, 37, 39, 49–52, 61–63, 75, 89, 93–97, 103, 104, 108–112, 117–124, 126, 129, 130, 134, 137–139, 141, 144, 146–148, 151–154, 159, 165–171, 173, 175–178
European, 1–5, 7, 10, 15–33, 37–55, 61, 62, 69, 71, 75–80, 83, 88, 89, 95, 96, 111, 113, 117, 120, 124, 130, 137–140, 143, 144, 148, 150, 154, 156–158, 166–173, 177, 178
European Center for Not-For-Profit Law (ECNL), 137–140, 144
European Commission, 150, 154
European Convention on Human Rights, 138, 156
European Court of Human Rights, 7
European Court of Justice, 7
European Union (EU), 10, 44, 52, 78, 95, 96, 120, 124, 143, 148, 157, 158
Eurostat, 52

F
Facebook, 151–154, 156
Fidesz, 165
Financial Times, 6, 8, 90
Finland, 17, 18, 24, 26, 28, 30, 32, 40, 61, 65, 81, 98, 111, 118, 127, 141, 142, 144, 145, 166
First World War, 4
Foreign Policy, 10, 46, 49
Forsythe, D.P., 94
Foundation for the Advancement of Liberty, 16, 62, 64, 66, 68
France, 3, 7, 17, 18, 24, 26–28, 30, 32, 40, 65, 80, 82, 98, 118, 119, 122, 127, 138, 142, 145, 166, 170–172
Fraser Institute, 16, 75, 76, 79, 82–84, 90
Freedom House, 16, 43, 46, 61, 62, 64, 66–69, 117, 118, 125, 126, 128, 129, 132
Freeland, 9
FreiheitlicheParteiÖsterreichs Freedom Party, 172
French, 6, 7
Friedman, M., 76
Friedrich Naumann Foundation, 62, 94, 96, 97, 110–112, 129
Friedrich Naumann Stiftung, 62
Fruscione, G., 158
FTSE 100, 8
Fukuyama, F., 173, 174, 177

G
Gazeta Wyborcza, 122
Georgia, 11, 17, 19, 23, 24, 26–28, 30, 32, 38, 39, 41, 42, 47, 52, 61, 66, 78, 80, 81, 99, 118, 125, 128, 142, 144, 145
German, 6, 9, 48, 148, 149, 172
Germany, 3, 7, 10, 17, 18, 24–26, 28, 30, 32, 40, 65, 81, 98, 109, 122, 127, 138, 141, 142, 145, 166, 168, 172
Gilets Jaunes, 122
Glitnir, 4
Globalisation, 3, 5, 11, 170, 173, 174, 176, 178
Globe Post, 46
Gnjilane/Gjilan, 156
Goodwin, M., 2, 4
Google, 121
Greece, 17, 19, 24, 26–28, 30, 32, 39, 40, 44, 52, 63, 66, 75, 78, 80, 82, 89, 96, 99, 125, 126, 128, 138, 140, 142, 143, 145, 165, 166, 168, 172
Greek, 173
Grillo, B., 5
Gruevski, N., 49, 70, 90
The Guardian, 6, 9, 46, 48, 49, 72, 124, 165, 166
Gulf, 88
Guterres, A., 1, 9, 72, 169, 170

H
Haaretz, 6
Habony, A., 124
Havighurst, R., 61
Hayek, F., 60, 100

Heritage Foundation, 16, 75, 77–79, 82, 84, 89
Hobbes, T., 120
Hoxhaj, A., 55
Human Rights Watch (HRW), 109, 111–113, 137, 139–141, 148
Hungarian, 7, 51, 123, 124, 165, 167
Hungary, 6, 7, 17, 19, 24–28, 30, 32, 41–43, 61, 63, 66, 82, 88, 96, 99, 102, 118, 123, 128, 139–143, 145, 165, 166, 168–171, 175, 176
Hybrid, 6, 12, 41–44, 46, 51, 87, 139–141, 148, 171, 175

I

Iceland, 4, 17, 18, 24, 26, 28, 30, 32, 40, 65, 81, 98, 110, 111, 127, 139, 141, 142, 145
Independent, 48, 50, 51
India, 157
Institute for Democracy and Electoral Assistance (IDEA), 137–140, 149, 151, 154
International Centre for Not-for-Profit Law (ICNL), 23, 137
International Labour Organisation (ILO), 52, 53
International Monetary Fund (IMF), 23
International Republican Institute, 88
Iran, 11, 88
Ireland, 7, 17, 18, 20, 24–26, 28, 30, 32, 40, 61, 62, 65, 75, 80, 81, 98, 111, 127, 141, 142, 144–146, 166
Islamic, 70, 71, 85
Italian, 5, 7, 51, 53, 172
Italy, 3, 7, 10, 17, 19, 24, 26–28, 30, 32, 40, 44, 63, 65, 82, 98, 122, 127, 142, 145, 153, 165, 166, 168, 170–172, 175
Izetbegović, B., 2, 48, 72, 149

J

Janša, 124
Jeta Online, 154
Jobbik, 165
Johnson, B., 6, 7, 9, 119, 123, 172

K

Kaag, 166
Kaltwasser, C.R., 2
Kant, I., 61
Kapidžić, D., 43, 47, 48, 54
Kaupthing, 4
Khodorkovsky, 8
Kmezić, M., 46, 50, 175
Knežević, R., 150
Koalitionsfähig, 174
Komorane/Komoran, 155
Kosovo, 17, 19, 24, 26, 29, 31, 33, 38, 39, 41–46, 48–50, 52, 53, 55, 62, 66–69, 72, 82–86, 88, 99–108, 110–113, 125, 128–133, 140, 142–145, 147–150, 154, 156
Kosovo Polje/Fushe Kosove, 156
Kovács, 124
Krugman, P., 9

L

Landsbankinn, 4
Latvia, 17, 18, 24, 26, 28, 30, 32, 40, 65, 81, 98, 127, 141, 142, 145, 166
Lega, 172
Le Pen, 2, 172
Lindberg, 22, 31
Lithuania, 17, 18, 24, 26–30, 32, 40, 65, 78, 81, 98, 118, 126, 127, 142, 145, 165, 166
London, 1, 9, 124, 138, 171
Luce, E., 2
Lührmann, A., 22, 31
Luxembourg, 17, 18, 24, 26, 28, 30, 32, 40, 65, 81, 98, 111, 127, 142, 145, 165, 166

M

Macedonian, 53, 90, 154, 155, 158
Macron, E., 6, 54, 172
Maduro, N., 51
Malta, 17, 19, 24, 26, 29, 31, 33, 39, 41, 63, 65, 78, 81, 99, 118, 126, 128, 142, 145, 165, 166, 168
Mandela, 9
Mao Zedong, 104
Marković, M., 72
Mass line, 104
Medojević, N., 153
Merkel, A., 6, 9
Middle East, 176
Mijatović, D., 167
Milanović, B., 4, 8
Mitteleuropa, 39
Mlinište, 90
Modi, 2
Mogherini, F., 49
Moldova, 11, 19–21, 24, 26–28, 30, 32, 39, 41, 42, 47, 61, 66, 78, 80, 82, 99, 102, 118, 125, 126, 128, 140, 142, 143, 145
Montenegrin, 49–51, 54, 70, 103, 148, 150, 153

Montenegro, 6, 19–21, 25–27, 29, 31, 33, 39, 41–43, 45–54, 62, 66–68, 72, 82–86, 88, 90, 99, 101–103, 105, 106, 108–113, 128–133, 140, 143, 146, 148, 150, 151, 155, 156
Morrison, K., 102
Moscow, 88, 159
Mostar, 154, 159
Mounk, Y., 2
Movimento Cinque Stelle, 173
Movimento 5 Stelle (M5S), 172
    Five Star Movement, 172
Mudde, C., 2, 173, 174
Muslim, 70, 71, 88

N
N1, 129
Nagorno-Karabakh, 11
National, 7, 16, 46, 88, 93, 148, 172
National Front, 172
Nationalist, 2, 5, 9, 10, 12, 47, 48, 50, 54, 69, 70, 72, 78, 83, 86, 90, 133, 140, 148–150, 154, 158, 159, 171, 172, 176, 177
NATO, 69, 158
Nazis, 150
Neo-fascist, 122
Neoliberal capitalism, 3, 10, 11
Netherlands, 17, 18, 24, 26, 28, 30, 32, 40, 65, 81, 98, 111, 119, 127, 142, 144, 145, 166, 168, 172
New York Times (NYT), 33
Nicaragua, 148
9/11, 176
+90, 125
North African, 138
Northern Irish, 9
North Macedonia, 17, 19, 25–28, 30, 32, 41–43, 45, 47, 49, 52–54, 62, 66–72, 75, 81, 83–85, 87, 88, 90, 99, 101–103, 105, 107–113, 118, 128–133, 143, 146, 148, 150, 153–156, 158
Norway, 17, 18, 24–28, 30, 32, 40, 65, 80, 81, 98, 111, 118, 127, 142, 145, 172
Novi Pazar, 151, 153
Novi Sad, 151

O
Obrador, 2
OECD, 175
Orahovac/Rahovec, 156
Orbán, V., 2, 51, 118, 123, 124, 165, 166, 170, 175
Organised Crime and Corruption Reporting Project (OCCRP), 51
Orthodox, 51, 71, 85
OSCE, 23
Oxford University, 22, 24, 137, 141, 142

P
Pandemic, 1–3, 7–12, 15, 22, 23, 25, 29, 31, 33, 43, 49, 51, 72, 103, 108, 118, 121, 137–160, 169, 178
Pandemic Big Brother, 23, 137, 152
Pargendler, M., 9
Partijvoor de Vrijheid
    Party for Freedom, 172
Partisans, 150
Party of Democratic Action
    SDA, 48
Patos-Marinza, 90
Pavlović, S., 46, 50, 54, 175
Pekić, B., 12
Pelješac, 90
Perussuomalaiset
    Finns, 172
Petrova, T., 22
Philippine, 51
Piketty, T., 175
Podemos, 172, 173
Podgorica, 102
Poland, 6, 17, 19, 24, 26–30, 32, 40, 42, 63, 65, 82, 96, 98, 118, 122, 123, 128, 139, 140, 142, 143, 145, 166, 170, 171, 176
Pompeo, M., 87
Popper, K., 60
Populist, 2, 3, 5, 6, 12, 37, 39, 41, 42, 44, 47–49, 51, 100, 104, 120, 149, 170, 172–174, 178
Porčnik, T., 100
Portugal, 17, 18, 24, 26, 28, 30, 32, 40, 65, 82, 98, 108, 127, 142, 145, 165
Portuguese, 173
Post-communist, 22, 126, 143
Post-Ottoman, 124
Prague Security Studies Institute, 88
Prelec, T., 158
Prizren, 156
Pula, B., 54, 55
Putin, V., 2, 51, 121, 140, 171

R
Radeljić, B., 46, 53, 54
Radio Free Europe (RFE), 151
Rama, E., 2, 48, 49, 70, 148, 149, 171

Rassemblement National
National Rally, 172
Reagan, R., 76
Reporters sans frontières, 126
Reporters Without Borders, 16, 117, 128, 132
Republican Party, 153
Republika Srpska, 146, 149, 152, 155, 157
Reuters, 4, 7, 10, 70, 148, 166
Rodrik, D., 174, 175
Roma, 109, 110, 138, 169
Romani, 109
Rooney, B., 31
RT, 124
Russia, 6, 10–12, 19–21, 24, 26–30, 32, 41, 47, 61–63, 66, 75, 78, 80, 82, 88, 96, 99, 100, 102, 108, 111, 118–121, 123, 124, 126, 128, 139–143, 145, 157, 158, 168, 169, 171, 175
Russian, 8, 11, 78, 87, 88, 118, 121, 124, 125, 148, 158, 159, 169

S
Salvini, 2, 122
Sarajevo, 50, 51, 70–72, 148, 150, 157
Saudi Arabia, 11, 157
Scandinavian
Scandinavia, 21, 37, 61, 75, 118, 144, 172
Schengen, 10
Schenker, H., 158
Scotland, 146
Scottish, 9
Sebija, 72
Second World War, 4, 150, 173
Seine-Saint-Denis, 138
Serb, 48, 50, 51, 71, 85, 103, 108, 159
Serbia, 6, 7, 19–21, 23, 24, 26–30, 32, 39, 41–49, 52, 53, 62, 66–68, 70, 72, 80, 82–88, 90, 95, 96, 99, 101, 103–113, 118, 126, 128–133, 138–140, 142–146, 148, 150–153, 157, 158, 171
Serbian, 7, 12, 46, 50, 51, 53, 54, 85, 88, 104, 123, 139, 149, 150, 152–154, 156–158
Skopje, 70, 71, 154, 158
Slavs, 154
Slovakia, 17, 19, 24, 26–28, 30, 32, 40, 63, 66, 81, 99, 125–127, 138, 139, 142, 145, 166
Slovenia, 17, 18, 24, 26–28, 30, 32, 39, 40, 65, 80, 82, 96, 98, 108, 124, 127, 139, 142, 145, 166
Social Democratic Party, 154
Soros, G., 7, 8
South Asia, 89
Soviet, 8, 11, 12, 15, 20, 21, 29, 39, 61, 63, 100, 111, 140, 141, 158, 176, 178
Spain, 3, 9, 17, 18, 24, 26–28, 30, 32, 40, 52, 65, 81, 98, 119, 122, 127, 142, 145, 166, 168, 172
Sputnik, 124, 125
Srebrenica, 129
Stabilitocracy, 46, 49, 54, 175
Stainaker, G., 148, 149
Stiftung, B., 126, 133
Sverigedemokraterna
Sweden Democrats, 172
Sweden, 17, 18, 25–28, 30, 32, 40, 65, 80, 81, 98, 111, 118, 124, 127, 139, 141, 143, 145, 166, 172
Switzerland, 17, 18, 20, 24–28, 30, 32, 40, 61, 62, 65, 75, 80, 81, 98, 118, 123, 127, 141, 142, 145, 172
Syriza, 78, 172, 173

T
Thaçi, H., 70
Thatcher, M., 76
Timbro, 173
Tirana, 70, 71, 148
Totalitarian, 8, 100, 140, 150
Transparency International, 16, 95–97, 99–103
Trotsky, L., 100
TRT, 124, 125
TRT World, 125
Trump, 2, 6, 10, 157
Turkey, 6, 11, 19–22, 24–30, 32, 39, 41, 42, 47, 52, 61–63, 66, 75, 78, 80, 82, 83, 88, 96, 99, 100, 110, 111, 118–122, 124–126, 128, 139–143, 145, 168, 169, 171, 175
Turkish, 12, 21, 124, 125, 157, 176
Turkmenistan, 95
Turković, 157
Tuzla, 153
Twitter, 153, 154
Tzifakis, N., 158

U
Ukraine, 11, 19, 20, 24–28, 30, 32, 38, 41, 42, 47, 61, 63, 66, 75, 78, 82, 89, 96, 99, 100, 102, 118, 126, 128, 139, 141–143, 145, 169, 171, 176
United Kingdom (UK), 7, 8, 17, 18, 24–28, 30, 32, 40, 65, 71, 80, 81, 96, 98, 122, 123, 127, 138, 141, 142, 144–146, 171, 172

United Nations (UN), 1, 9, 10, 42, 72, 113, 148, 159, 168–170
United States (US), 8, 10, 87, 88, 153
Universal Declaration of Human Rights, 93–95
University of Gothenburg, 16, 23, 25, 29, 31, 33, 96, 97

V

Vachudova, M.A., 46, 53, 54
Vásquez, I., 100
V-Dem Institute, 16, 23, 25, 29, 31, 33, 37, 38, 41–43, 49, 76, 96, 97, 99, 101, 117, 126, 128, 132
Venezuela, 51
Vetevendosje, 69, 149, 150
Visegrád Four News Agency, 124
V4NA, 124
VOA Turkish, 125
Voice of America (VOA), 125
Vučić, A., 2, 46, 48, 49, 54, 67, 70, 89, 104, 118, 123, 149, 152, 157, 171

W

Wales, 146
Warsaw Pact, 176
WB6, 21
Welsh, 9
West, 2, 11, 33, 39, 49, 61, 69, 88, 95, 104, 124, 126, 157, 158, 175, 176
Western Balkans
    Balkans, 3, 12, 17, 20, 21, 25, 29, 37–55, 61–63, 67–72, 75, 80–91, 96–105, 108–113, 126, 129–134, 141, 146–159, 175, 178
Western Europe, 29, 63, 95, 166
Wilders, 2
World Bank, 16, 52, 75, 78–80, 82–84, 109
World Economic Forum, 16, 76, 79, 80, 82–84

X

Xi, 2, 157

Y

Yerevan, 12
YouTube, 120, 125, 154
Yugoslav, 15, 83
Yugoslavia, 83

Z

Zaev, Z., 71
Zielonka, J., 2

The manufacturer's authorised representative in the EU is Springer Nature Customer Service Centre GmbH, Europaplatz 3, 69115 Heidelberg, Germany. If you have any concerns regarding our products, please contact ProductSafety@springernature.com

Printed and bound by CPI Group (UK) Ltd, Croydon, CR0 4YY
28/09/2026
02224088-0006